SOUNDINGS IN CULTURAL CRITICISM

SOUNDINGS IN CULTURAL CRITICISM

Perspectives and Methods in Culture, Power, and Identity

in the New Testament

Francisco Lozada Jr. and Greg Carey

Fortress Press

Minneapolis

SOUNDINGS IN CULTURAL CRITICISM

Perspectives and Methods in Culture, Power, and Identity in the New Testament

Cover image: Giacomo Balla, *Mercurio Passa Davanti al Sole (Mercury Passes Before the Sun)*, 1914, © 2012 Artists Rights Society (ARS), New York/SIAE, Rome; Photo credit: Erich Lessing / Art Resource, NY.

Cover design: Tory Herman

Library of Congress Cataloging-in-Publication Data

ISBN: 978-0-8006-9800-3

CONTENTS

PREFACE

The authors and editors dedicate this volume to Professor Fernando F. Segovia, Oberlin Graduate Professor of New Testament and Early Christianity in the Divinity School and Graduate Department of Religion at Vanderbilt University, in anticipation of his sixty-fifth birthday. We also express our admiration and appreciation to Dr. Elena Olazagasti-Segovia, Senior Lecturer in Spanish at Vanderbilt. All of us have worked with Fernando as students or as professional colleagues. All of us find our careers—many of us, our lives—shaped by his influence.

We have chosen to diverge from a common academic tradition. On the occasion of milestone birthdays a prominent scholar often receives a Festschrift, a collection of essays produced in his or her honor. Because such volumes typically address only other scholars, and because they often lack conceptual coherence, few of them reach a broad audience or influence the field of biblical studies. We deem it particularly fitting that a volume dedicated to Fernando Segovia should prove useful to teachers and students as well as to professional scholars and that such a volume should represent a significant and coherent—though not necessarily unified—intervention in our field.

Fernando himself provides the model for such an endeavor. His collaboration with Mary Ann Tolbert, the two-volume anthology *Reading from This Place* (1995) and the anthology *Teaching the Bible* (1998), represents a milestone development in biblical studies.[1] *Reading from This Place* emerged at a moment when many professional biblical scholars were beginning to attend to the role of real readers, including their variegated relations to culture, power, and identity, in the process of interpretation.[2] The *Reading from This Place* project was unique in that for the first time remarkably diverse groups of interpreters gathered in one space to explore the intersection of social location and biblical interpretation. The published volumes that resulted from those conferences included programmatic essays by Segovia and Tolbert that still inform both interpretive work and classroom teaching almost twenty years later. The current volume honors Fernando's work in several ways: it features collaborative scholarship from a diverse international team of scholars, it represents up-to-date critical engagement with culture, power, and identity in the work of interpretation, and it aims to reach both classrooms and professional libraries.

Fernando Segovia's career both reflects and has influenced the larger shape of contemporary biblical studies. We will rehearse only the broad outlines. His revised doctoral dissertation, *Love Relationships in the Johannine Tradition* (1982), employs both philological research and redaction criticism to explore the sectarian history of the Johannine community and the theological significance of love in that context.[3] Fernando's work on John's Gospel takes a literary turn in his study of the Farewell Discourse, *The Farewell of the Word* (1991). As other scholars noted at the time, Fernando's concerns with the redaction history and social circumstances of the Fourth Gospel continued, but they now reflected stronger literary and rhetorical sensitivities, reading the text "as an artistic and strategic whole."[4] These literary, or narrative, approaches further developed in essays concerning the Fourth Gospel's plot and in Fernando's collaboration with other scholars on a variety of literary and social studies of that Gospel. These studies frequently combine narrative approaches with social-scientific insights.[5]

Reading from This Place, then, marks a major turn in Fernando Segovia's work and in contemporary New Testament interpretation. As Fernando's scholarship progressed from historical criticism (including redactional analysis) to literary and social scientific interpretation, so did New Testament studies. Throughout his career, Fernando has combined such concerns with theological matters, particularly liberation theology.[6] Around 1995 and 1996, however, we begin to see a concern with what Fernando and others call "cultural studies." Whereas historical criticism locates meaning in the *ancient* contexts from which biblical texts emerge, as do social-scientific approaches, while literary criticism finds meaning *within* the text itself, cultural studies opens biblical interpretation not simply to the past and to the text but to all the contexts in which the text has been interpreted and deployed. A great deal of Fernando's scholarship describes the emergence of diverse practices in such cultural interpretation. Would Fernando admit that some of his most compelling work also *prescribes* how it may move forward?[7]

Fernando Segovia's interventions in cultural studies demonstrate his commitment to intellectual work that engages people's lives and fosters liberation. In this respect, he works as public theologian as well as biblical scholar. Indeed, Fernando has served as president of the Academy of Catholic Hispanic Theologians in the United States and will serve as president of the Society of Biblical Literature in 2013–2014. Space prohibits a full bibliographic account, but Segovia's work includes the Johannine literature, Latino/a theology,[8] postcolonial and diaspora studies,[9] and minority criticism.[10] Collaboration represents a distinctive commitment of Fernando's work, and many of the contributors to this book have coedited volumes with Fernando, contributed essays to volumes Fernando has edited, and/or included Fernando's contributions in their own edited work.

Today biblical scholarship includes an astonishing array of methodological approaches. The scholars who contribute to the field represent its global reach and ethnic/racial diversity. No longer is it the case that a woman's gender provides the primary definition of her scholarship or status—though gender certainly remains a powerful factor in the profession. For that matter, gender studies now take account of men as well as women. Diversity in terms of gender identification (beyond the male/female dichotomy) and sexual orientation has won explicit attention. Fernando Segovia has participated in and contributed significantly to the proliferation of voices and approaches in contemporary biblical studies, notably to matters of culture, power, and identity. One cannot deny the progress that has occurred.

At the same time, it is fair to say that only a minority of biblical scholars pay explicit attention to the real people who read the Bible, whom Segovia identifies as "flesh and blood readers," or to their role in the process of interpretation.[11] Especially rare is the introductory textbook that attends to such matters. Meanwhile, conversations regarding culture, power, and identity in interpretation have continued over the past decades. Not only does this volume express these developments through up-to-date contributions from an outstanding team of scholars, we intend it to serve classroom settings as a supplemental reading. The essays cover a wide range of New Testament texts and a broad range of interpretive questions. By advancing the conversation concerning the role of culture, power, and identity in interpretation, and by providing an accessible format for students and general readers to explore these ideas, we build upon the work of many predecessors, including Professor Fernando F. Segovia. We extend our thanks to each of our contributing authors, as well as to Andrew Benko for work on the bibliography.

In gratitude,

Francisco Lozada Jr. and Greg Carey

Notes

1. Fernando F. Segovia and Mary Ann Tolbert, ed., *Reading from This Place*, vol. 1: *Social Location and Biblical Interpretation in the United States* (Minneapolis: Fortress Press, 1995); *Reading from This Place*, vol. 2: *Social Location and Biblical Interpretation in Global Perspective* (Minneapolis: Fortress Press, 1995); and *Teaching the Bible: The Discourses and Practices of Biblical Pedagogy* (Maryknoll: Orbis, 1998). The current volume includes a contribution by Professor Tolbert, while the editors worked as research assistants for the *Reading from This Place/Teaching the Bible* project.

2. See the introduction to this volume by Greg Carey.

3. *Love Relationships in the Johannine Tradition: Agapē/Agapan in 1 John and the Fourth Gospel*, SBLDS 58 (Chico: Scholars, 1982); cf. Segovia, "The Love and Hatred of Jesus and Johannine Sectarianism," *CBQ* 43 (1981): 258–72; Segovia, "The Theology and Provenance of John 15:1–17," *JBL* 101 (1982): 115–28; Segovia, "The Structure, *Tendenz*, and *Sitz im Leben* of John 13:31–14:31," *JBL* 104 (1985): 471–93; Segovia, "The Tradition History of the Fourth Gospel," in *Exploring the Gospel of John: Essays in Honor of D. Moody Smith*, ed. R. Alan Culpepper and C. Clifton Black (Louisville: Westminster John Knox, 1996), 179–89.

4. *The Farewell of the Word: The Johannine Call to Abide* (Minneapolis: Fortress Press, 1991), viii; see R. Alan Culpepper's review (*JBL* 112 [1993]: 721-22).

5. "The Journey(s) of the Word: A Reading of the Plot of the Fourth Gospel," in *The Fourth Gospel from a Literary Perspective*, ed. R. Alan Culpepper and Fernando F. Segovia, *Semeia* 53 (Atlanta: Scholars, 1991), 23–54; Segovia, ed., *What Is John?*, vol. 1: *Readers and Readings of the Fourth Gospel*, SBLSymS 3 (Atlanta: Scholars, 1996); Segovia, ed., *What Is John?*, vol. 2: *Literary and Social Readings of the Fourth Gospel*, SBLSym 7 (Atlanta: Scholars, 1998); and John Painter, R. Alan Culpepper, and Fernando F. Segovia, ed., *Word, Theology, and Community in John* (Saint Louis: Chalice, 2002).

6. As evidenced in Segovia, ed., *Discipleship in the New Testament* (Philadelphia: Fortress Press, 1985).

7. Apart from his essays in *Reading from This Place* ("And They Began to Speak in Other Tongues: Competing Modes of Discourse in Contemporary Biblical Criticism" [vol. 1, 1–32]; "Toward a Hermeneutics of the Diaspora: A Hermeneutics of Otherness and Engagement [vol. 1, 57–73]; "Cultural Studies and Contemporary Biblical Criticism: Ideological Criticism as Mode of Discourse" [vol. 2, 1–17]; and "Toward Intercultural Criticism: A Reading Strategy from the Diaspora" [vol. 2, 303-30]); see his "My Personal Voice: The Making of a Postcolonial Critic," in *The Personal Voice in Biblical Interpretation*, ed. Ingrid Rose Kitzberger (London: Routledge, 1999), 25–37.

8. Ada-María Isasi-Díaz and Fernando F. Segovia, ed., *Hispanic/Latino Theology: Challenge and Promise* (Minneapolis: Fortress Press, 1996); Eleazar S. Fernandez and Fernando F. Segovia, ed., *A Dream Unfinished: Theological Reflections on America from the Margins* (Maryknoll: Orbis, 2001); Segovia, ed., *Toward a New Heaven and a New Earth: Essays in Honor of Elisabeth Schüssler Fiorenza* (Maryknoll: Orbis, 2003); Segovia, "Toward Latino/a American Biblical Criticism: Latin(o/a)ness as Problematic," in *They Were All Together in One Place? Toward Minority Biblical Criticism*, ed. Randall C. Bailey, Tat-siong Benny Liew, and Fernando F. Segovia, SBLSS 57 (Atlanta: Society of Biblical Literature, 2009); and Segovia, "Mujerista Theology: Biblical Interpretation and Political Theology," *Feminist Theology* 20 (2011): 21–27.

9. Segovia, ed., *Interpreting Beyond Borders*, Bible and Postcolonialism (Sheffield: Sheffield Academic, 2000); Segovia, *Decolonizing Biblical Studies: A View from the Margins* (Maryknoll: Orbis, 2000); Stephen D. Moore and Fernando F. Segovia, ed., *Postcolonial Biblical Criticism: Interdisciplinary Intersections*, Bible and Postcolonialism (New York: T. and T. Clark, 2007); Fernando F. Segovia and R. S. Sugirtharajah, ed., *A Postcolonial Commentary on the New Testament Writings*, The Bible and Postcolonialism 13 (New York: T. and T. Clark, 2007).

10. "Theological Education and Scholarship as Struggle: The Life of Racial/Ethnic Minorities in the Profession," *Journal of Hispanic/Latino Theology* 2 (1994): 5–25; Segovia, "Poetics of Minority Biblical Criticism: Identification and Theorization," in *Prejudice and Christian Beginnings: Investigating Race, Gender, and Ethnicity in Early Christian Studies* (Minneapolis: Fortress Press, 2009), 279–311; and "Racial and Ethnic Minorities in Biblical Studies," in *Ethnicity and the Bible*, ed. Mark G. Brett (Leiden: Brill, 1996), 469–92; and Randall C. Bailey, Tat-siong Benny Liew, and Fernando F. Segovia, ed., *They Were All Together in One Place? Toward Minority Biblical Criticism*, SBLSS 57 (Atlanta: Society of Biblical Literature, 2009), including Bailey, Liew, and Segovia, "Toward Minority Biblical Criticism: Framework, Contours, Dynamics," 3-43, and "Segovia, "Toward Minority Biblical Criticism: A Reflection on Achievements and Lacunae," 365–94.

11. See Francisco Lozada Jr., "Teaching the New Testament: Toward an Expanded Contextual Approach," in this volume.

Contributors

Eric D. Barreto is Assistant Professor of New Testament at Luther Seminary in Saint Paul. He is the author of *Ethnic Negotiations: The Function of Race and Ethnicity in Acts 16* (2010).

Jennifer G. Bird is Associate Professor of Religion and Director of the Women's and Gender Studies Program at Greensboro College in Greensboro, North Carolina. She is the author of *Abuse, Power, and Fearful Obedience: Reconsidering 1 Peter's Commands to Wives* (2011).

Greg Carey is Professor of New Testament at Lancaster Theological Seminary and Resident Scholar at the Evangelical Lutheran Church of the Holy Trinity in Lancaster, Pennsylvania. He is the author of *Elusive Apocalypse: Reading Authority in the Revelation to John* (1999); *Ultimate Things: An Introduction to Jewish and Christian Apocalyptic Literature* (2005); *Sinners: Jesus and His Earliest Followers* (2009); and *The Gospel according to Luke: All Flesh Shall See God's Salvation* (2012).

Stephanie Buckhanon Crowder teaches in the School of Religion at Belmont University in Nashville, Tennessee. The author of *Simon of Cyrene: A Case of Roman Conscription* (2002), she has also published in *The African American Pulpit, Women at the Well*, vol. 2; *The People's Bible*; and *The Chalice Introduction to the New Testament*. Her work on the Gospel of Luke can be found in *True to Our Native Land: An African American New Testament Commentary* (2007).

Musa W. Dube is Professor of New Testament at the University of Botswana. She is the author of *Postcolonial Feminist Interpretation of the Bible* (2000), coeditor of *Postcolonial Perspectives in African Biblical Interpretation* (2012), and author of several chapters and journal articles.

Eleazar S. Fernandez is Professor of Constructive Theology at United Theological Seminary in New Brighton, Minnesota. He is author or editor of *Burning Center, Porous Borders: The Church in a Globalized World* (2011);

New Overtures: Asian North American Theology in the Twenty-First Century (editor, 2011); *Reimagining the Human: Theological Anthropology in Response to Systemic Evil* (2004); *Realizing the America of our Hearts: Theological Voices of Asian Americans* (coedited with Fumitaka Matsuoka, 2003); *A Dream Unfinished: Theological Reflections on America from the Margins* (coedited with Fernando Segovia, 2000); and *Toward a Theology of Struggle* (1994).

Kwok Pui-lan is William F. Cole Professor of Christian Theology and Spirituality at Episcopal Divinity School in Cambridge, Massachusetts. She is the author of *Discovering the Bible in the Non-Biblical World* (1995); *Introducing Asian Feminist Theology* (2000); and *Postcolonial Imagination and Feminist Theology* (2005); and coauthor of *Occupy Religion: Theology of the Multitude* (2012).

Tat-siong Benny Liew is Professor of New Testament at the Pacific School of Religion, where he is also serving as Vice President for Academic Affairs and Dean. He is the author of *Politics of Parousia: Reading Mark Inter(con)textually* (1999); and *What Is Asian American Biblical Hermeneutics? Reading the New Testament* (2008).

Francisco Lozada Jr. is the Charles Fischer Catholic Associate Professor of New Testament and Latina/o Studies at Brite Divinity School in Fort Worth, Texas. He is the author of *A Literary Reading of John 5: Text as Construction* (2000) and *New Currents through John: A Global Perspective* (2006).

Stephen D. Moore is Professor of New Testament at Drew Theological School. He is the author of *Literary Criticism and the Gospels* (1989); *Mark and Luke in Poststructuralist Perspectives* (1992); *Poststructuralism and the New Testament* (1994); *God's Gym* (1996); *God's Beauty Parlor* (2001); *Empire and Apocalypse* (2006); *The Bible in Theory* (2010); *The Invention of the Biblical Scholar* (with Yvonne Sherwood, 2011); and *The Bodybuilder, the Sex Worker, and the Sheep.*

Jeremy Punt is Professor of New Testament in the Theology Faculty at Stellenbosch University, South Africa. He is the author of several articles and chapters on New Testament hermeneutics, past and present, as well as in the intersection of New Testament and cultural studies.

Abraham Smith is Professor of New Testament at Perkins School of Theology, Southern Methodist University in Dallas, Texas. He is the author of *Comfort One Another* (1995); coeditor of a *Semeia* volume (1998); one of the New Testament editors for the *New Interpreter's Study Bible* (2003); and author of several articles and chapters on Mark, Acts, and Paul.

Yak-Hwee Tan is Program Secretary for Reflection and Research at the Council for World Mission in Singapore. Prior to her current position, she taught New Testament Studies and Theology at Taiwan Theological College and Seminary in Taipei, Taiwan. She is the author of *Re-presenting the Johannine Community: A Postcolonial Perspective* (2008). Her research interests are Johannine literature, biblical theology, feminist criticism, postcolonial criticism, and ecological hermeneutics.

Mary A. Tolbert is the George H. Atkinson Professor of Biblical Studies at the Pacific School of Religion. Her publications include *Sowing the Gospel: Mark's World in Literary-Historical Perspective* (1989) and *Perspectives on the Parables: An Approach to Multiple Interpretations* (1978). With Fernando F. Segovia she coedited *Teaching the Bible: The Discourses and Politics of Biblical Pedagogy* (1998); *Reading from This Place: Social Location and Biblical Interpretation in Global Perspective* (Fortress, 1995), and *Reading from This Place: Social Location and Biblical Interpretation in the United States* (Fortress, 1995).

Introduction and a Proposal

Culture, Power, and Identity in White New Testament Studies

Greg Carey

As the Great Depression set in, labor unrest ignited throughout the southern United States.[1] Earning two dollars for a sixteen-hour shift, coal miners in East Tennessee paid for their own picks, shovels, and blasting powder. The coal with which they heated their homes cost three times as much as they received for extracting it. Miners grimly joked that they paid the company for the privilege of working. The mine workers organized with the United Mine Workers of America and went on strike. In short order the mining company evicted them from company-owned homes and hired professional killers. Eventually the Tennessee National Guard came out to protect the mines from the workers who had resorted to violence themselves. Sharecroppers in Arkansas likewise began to organize, as planters still used both black and white workers to provide cheap labor in the absence of slavery.[2] The same pattern emerged: farmers applied force and intimidation to break their strike, labor organizers were beaten and killed, and the National Guard mobilized to establish order as violence erupted on all sides. The Arkansas conflict saw white and black workers banding together, with law enforcement officers monitoring the churches where laborers gathered. Similar scenes featured millworkers and other labor groups who found themselves dependent upon exploitative employers. The forces of law and order sided with the employers in every case.

Christian activists, especially clergy and theology students, played important roles on both sides of the conflict. Prominent theological institutions such as Union Theological Seminary in New York and Vanderbilt University's School of Religion supplied white pro-labor leaders such as Myles Horton, Howard Kester (whose wife Alice did not attend seminary but was highly active in the movement), Claude Williams, and James Dombrowski. These radicals had studied with and continued to rely upon support from teachers at both institutions, notably Union's Reinhold Neibuhr, the great theologian whose fundraising clout energized movements and individuals throughout the South, and Vanderbilt's Harry Ward and Alva Wilmot Taylor. Black ministers, often without advanced theological degrees, also emerged locally and as national organizers. On the other hand, prominent local clergy like J. Abner Sage of Marked Tree, Arkansas, supported the industrialists and plantation owners. For his part, Sage publicly accused the labor organizers as communists while organizing support for white sharecroppers who abandoned the labor movement. White churches rejected the ministries of people like Kester and Williams, indicating that few churchgoing whites shared their views.

In significant ways the Southern labor movement provided a foundation for the Civil Rights Movement. Popular imagination identifies the Civil Rights Movement with the 1950s and 1960s, marked by crucial moments such as *Brown v. Board of Education* (1954) and the leadership of Rosa Parks and Martin Luther King Jr. in the Montgomery Bus Boycotts (1955–1956). However, African Americans had been mobilizing toward racial justice for decades, and the labor conflicts provided crucial opportunities for white and black organizers to collaborate. As one dramatic example, the white Presbyterian pastor and Vanderbilt alumnus Claude Williams found it difficult to swallow food during his first common meals with black colleagues (a common motif in the recollections of white radicals of that era) but later woke up to find the black YMCA organizer Ned Pope sleeping beside him in the same bed. The experience of shared hospitality, shared facilities, and a common struggle led to relationships and institutions that would nourish the Civil Rights Movement for decades. Myles Horton's Highlander Folk School (now Highlander Research and Education Center) hosted training sessions attended by Rosa Parks and Martin Luther King Jr. while the Baptist preacher Clarence Jordan established the racially integrated Koinonia Farm (now Koinonia Partners) in Americus, Georgia in 1942.

A white native Alabamian, I elect the white folks involved in those labor struggles as "my people," fictional ancestors in the faith and predecessors in my work as a biblical interpreter. Myles Horton grew up an hour's drive from my hometown, while Clarence Jordan graduated from my alma mater, the Southern Baptist Theological Seminary. However, I flatter myself by identifying with Horton, Jordan, and the like, as "my people" also include the preachers who sided with exploitative employers and defended segregation. "My people" certainly include poor laborers and segregationists, categories that are far from mutually exclusive. Most of "my people" cared about the Bible and how it is interpreted, and most applied the Bible to the struggles of their day. I remember my grandmother admonishing me to avoid law school since Jesus had pronounced, "Woe to the lawyers" (Luke 11:52, KJV). How does such a heritage of culture, power, and identity bear upon the work of biblical interpretation?

CULTURE, POWER, AND IDENTITY IN NEW TESTAMENT INTERPRETATION

The question of real readers pushed its way into biblical studies in the early 1990s with a splash of significant publications, collectively bearing the promise—or threat—of transforming the field in profound ways. Several major multi-author works appeared in a brief span of time, each of them introducing fresh perspectives on biblical interpretation. Today we might say that these works raised the question of how biblical interpretation relates to culture, power, and identity. How do culture, power, and identity—the things that constitute real, "flesh-and-blood" readers—shape and nourish the process of interpretation?[3]

In 1991 R. S. Sugirtharajah's edited volume *Voices from the Margin: Interpreting the Bible in the Third World* presented to public view interpreters who could name how their *identity* influenced how they interpreted the Bible. Introducing a volume that included Caribbean, South and Central American, African, East and South Asian, and Palestinian authors—as well as African American and Native American scholars—Sugirtharajah challenged what he called "the ahistorical, objective, abstract, universal reading discourse" that dominated professional biblical interpretation.[4] More simply, Sugirtharajah intended to undermine the then-conventional goal of "objectivity" in interpretation, the idea that an interpreter's relationship to culture and power—her or his identity—should not shape interpretation.

Sugirtharajah presented his anthology as the result of about two decades of global biblical scholarship from locations previously excluded from academic biblical studies; however, for many readers in Europe and North America, *Voices from the Margin* represented a revolutionary introduction to new questions in biblical interpretation. How do the identities of interpreters and interpretive communities shape and nourish the process of interpretation?[5]

Voices from the Margin represented just one key example among many works devoted to the question of identity (or social location) and biblical interpretation. That same year *Stony the Road We Trod: African American Biblical Interpretation* presented the work of African American interpreters who had met together over a five-year period in the 1980s.[6] Feminist biblical scholarship had already produced similar projects,[7] but two major anthologies shared feminist interpretation with a much broader audience, the *Women's Bible Commentary* (ed. Carol A. Newsom and Sharon H. Ringe) and the two-volume project,

Searching the Scriptures (ed. Elisabeth Schüssler Fiorenza).[8] *Searching the Scriptures* intentionally foregrounded feminist interpretation as a global project. With an emphasis upon socio-political liberation, *The Bible and Liberation: Political and Social Hermeneutics* (ed. Norman K. Gottwald and Richard A. Horsley) in 1993 likewise represented a global perspective. Justo L. González introduced Hispanic American interpretation to a broad audience in 1996.[9]

The conversation moved ahead significantly with Fernando F. Segovia and Mary Ann Tolbert's 1995 publication of a two-volume anthology, *Reading from This Place*.[10] These volumes stood apart for two reasons. First, funding from the Lilly Foundation allowed authors who represented truly global constituencies to share their work in face-to-face contexts—a format somewhat similar to the *Stony the Road We Trod* project. And second, the conversations and essays all focused upon a common theme: attention to social location as a factor in biblical interpretation. This programmatic level of reflection set the path for an outburst of publications related to global, liberationist, postcolonial, minority, feminist, womanist, and queer interpretation that has continued for decades.

These major projects not only introduced broad popular audiences to culture, power, and identity as factors in interpretation, they continue to influence scholars as well. Significantly, almost all of these publications are multiauthor works. That is, no single author is qualified to represent the diverse possibilities that present themselves when interpreters consider how real, flesh-and-blood readers (and groups of readers) interact with the Bible.

In 1995 it looked as if the discipline of biblical studies was about to experience a seismic shift both in the composition of its practitioners and in the modes of interpretation that would reach the public. At that time a certain triumphalist tone insinuated itself into Fernando Segovia's writing, as he employed the past tense to trace a trajectory from "objectivist" historical criticism through literary criticism and into the sort of cultural analysis to which he pointed.[11] Indeed, since 1995 the public has enjoyed access to an emerging and diverse array of resources devoted to interpretation from particular social locations and ideological commitments, including commentary resources and major collaborative research projects.

HOW THINGS STAND

Unfortunately, the promise of 1995 remains substantially unfulfilled. Thankfully, some scholars still pursue how culture, power, and identity inform interpretation in specific contexts. These studies range from technical works with scholarly audiences to resources that support general readers and religious communities. Specialized journals, notably *Biblical Interpretation* and *The Bible and Critical Theory*, host emerging conversations. Professional organizations such as the Society of Biblical Literature now include over a dozen program units that could not have existed just a few decades ago: African Biblical Hermeneutics, African-American Biblical Hermeneutics, Asian and Asian-American Hermeneutics, Bible and American Popular Culture, Bible and Film, Contextual Biblical Interpretation, and the like. And certainly the raw number of scholars from underrepresented populations has exploded.

But in significant ways nothing has changed. Culture, power, and identity scarcely surface in the major introductory textbooks assigned to undergraduate and theology students—as if these questions have no place in the conversation.[12] New Testament scholars occasionally author non-fiction bestsellers. Almost every author of such books is white, and though these books usually debunk popular misconceptions of the Bible, they almost never address real readers in terms of race, ethnicity, class, or sexual identity. Major works in the field continue to ignore such questions. Large meetings of scholars, such as the five thousand or so who attend Society of Biblical Literature Annual Meetings, confirm this impression. It is as if some special sessions feature culture, power, and identity, while the rest of the discipline moves along as if nothing has changed.[13] Major sessions include a few women but scarcely any persons of color. One might interpret these developments in terms of whiteness: the field has managed to assimilate new voices and perspectives, but without divesting its white center of its privilege. Today Sugirtharajah could reproduce a title like *Voices from the Margin*, and the title would remain as appropriate as ever.

One factor counters the field's apparent segregation: in their attempt to foster diversity, many educational and religious institutions go out of their way to foreground the voices of racial and ethnic minorities. (This is not yet the case with sexual minorities, and feminist interpretation often receives little discussion as if its accomplishments could be taken for granted.) However, few resources (a) speak to culture, power, and identity in biblical interpretation (b) from diverse global contexts (c) for introductory and general audiences (d) in a format that covers a representative range of New Testament books and "traditional" interpretive questions. This volume aims to address that deficit.

While the past few decades have witnessed the proliferation of voices previously excluded from public biblical interpretation, the discipline's center remains largely intact and in some ways unexamined. Whiteness constitutes one fundamental constituent of that center among others. While persons of color have reflected upon whiteness, few white people have proposed strategies for acknowledging how whiteness shapes biblical interpretation or what whiteness-sensitive interpretation might look like.[14] Thus we find the remarkable situation in which "minority" criticism is performed almost exclusively by minorities, while the analysis of white interpreters is performed, well, almost exclusively by minorities.[15] Contributions from persons of color are absolutely necessary, but the discipline cannot move far unless white interpreters also invest themselves in the conversation. Here I will venture one proposal as part of what I hope to contribute to a broader conversation.[16]

What exactly do we mean by whiteness? Aside from the observation that some people identify themselves as "white"—or do not self-identify as persons of color—can we name critical factors that constitute whiteness, particularly in the context of the United States? Shall we turn to pop culture, which often examines whiteness as a point of humor? *White Men Can't Jump*, proclaimed the title of a 1992 movie, the comedian Dave Chappelle remarks that white people do weird things when they get high, and stuffwhitepeoplelike.com features essays on TED Conferences and "Being the Only White Person Around." Do we want to add that white people can't dance, can't integrate their minds with their bodies and emotions, display peculiar affinities for the products of "minority" and "global" cultures, and so forth? In a word, no.

Speaking confessionally, I raise the question of whiteness because I have often found myself frustrated by accounts of "white" biblical interpretation, "white" pedagogy, and so forth, in which the adjective "white" lacks content. All too briefly, let us survey some of the ways in which people analyze whiteness, using these as resources for a particularly focused account of white biblical interpretation.

Many identify whiteness with an unspoken privilege. Gale A. Yee, an Asian American scholar, recalls job interviews in which she was asked to identify how her race and ethnicity "made any difference" in her scholarly work. White colleagues could regard her identity as an Asian American, specifically Chinese American, as "different"—but different from what? Presumably, an unspoken white norm.[17] In part, then, whiteness entails the privilege of being "normal"—of needing no reflection, definition, or analysis. But Yee refuses to stop there. She also calls Asian American scholars to "make whiteness transparent as a culturally constructed and racialized category," to tease out what a difference *whiteness* makes.[18]

We must not too quickly move beyond that unspoken privilege, for it stands as one basic component of whiteness—a characteristic confirmed by its own negation. That is to say, whiteness often comes with a measure of denial and minimization. Denise Kimber Buell remarks that white liberal Christians in the United States avoid thinking of Christian identity in racial or ethnic terms despite the racial logic that we encounter within the New Testament itself (see Rom. 9:25; 1 Pet. 2:9-10).[19] Often the last thing white people want to do is acknowledge race as a factor in our own experience.[20]

The privilege that accompanies whiteness relates intimately with the traditional norm of biblical scholarship: "exegesis." In my first undergraduate biblical studies course, our textbook (widely adopted at the time) advanced the distinction between "exegesis" and "eisegesis," the error of allowing one's own theological tradition to determine interpretation without "letting the text speak afresh and on its own."[21] The authors recognized the legitimacy of reading the Bible in conversation with one's own heritage, they affirmed that responsible interpretations might be diverse, but they also encouraged reading "out of" the text rather than "into" it. The classic notion of exegesis assumes a fixed, rational, and universal process of interpretation. It also promotes a certain kind of detachment, as if the interpreter were a disembodied mind, free from the constraints of context and daily life.

Privilege shapes knowledge. At least, it shapes our perceptions and values, even in academic contexts. In my own reflections on Matthew's story of the Canaanite woman (15:21-28), I found myself wondering whether to assess the woman as a victim or a hero. Is she a victim because she declines from an assertive voice to accepting Jesus' designation of her as a dog? Or is she a hero for persuading Jesus to free her daughter from demonic possession? Encounters with womanist ethics, a theological movement largely among African American women, has called to my attention the degree to which my privilege limits my own range of vision. A privileged person thinks in terms of free moral choices. Women of color, writes Katie Geneva Cannon, necessarily make their choices in contexts defined by multiple systems of oppression. "Black women live out a moral wisdom in their real-lived context that does not appeal to the fixed rules or absolute principles of the white-oriented, male-structured society. Black women's analysis and appraisal of what is right or wrong and good or bad develops out of the various coping mechanisms related to the conditions of their own cultural circumstances. Black women have justly regarded survival against tyrannical systems of triple oppression as a true sphere of moral life."[22] Informed by womanist ethics, we may move beyond reductionist assessments of the Canaanite as simply a hero or a victim to a more nuanced appreciation for how she endures humiliation in order to win her daughter's liberation.

If whiteness relates not only to privilege but also to how one interprets the world and establishes values, then whiteness also involves the ability to define not only content, what *counts* as biblical interpretation, but also the questions and interpretive strategies that form legitimate interpretation. With whiteness as an unspoken norm, white interpreters cannot recognize that their questions and categories are limited. The integration of public schools led to black students studying with white students—but without the pedagogical strategies that had been effective in the segregated black schools.[23] Likewise, a color-blind biblical scholarship invites non-white interpreters into a conversation that does not acknowledge—or benefit from—sources of wisdom with which the discipline's white center is unfamiliar.

Fundamentally, whiteness is at once a creation of white culture and its closely guarded secret. If I understand J. Kameron Carter's highly sophisticated account, the invention of whiteness has roots in an ancient Christian theological project, the attempt by Christian theology to transcend its Jewish roots and to claim a universal identity.[24] Ironically, Christians created race as a functional category when they circumscribed Judaism in racial terms. According to Carter, white theology fails to work "pentecostally"; that is, rather than overcoming nationalism as the (Jewish) church did on Pentecost, white theology seeks to establish a stable, non-Jewish, identity.[25] When Christian "mission" accompanied Western imperialism, it applied racialized discourse to other societies, thus legitimating their subjugation and conversion. Thus, "race" applied to non-European and non-Christian peoples but not to European Christians themselves. White theology emerged from the Christian invention of race, but without investigating or defining what it means to be white. "White" comes to mean "human," while other racial groups are both distinctive and inferior.

For the purposes of this essay, then, "whiteness" functions as the attempt to define *other* groups as non-white without subjecting white identity itself to critical reflection.[26] But what about whiteness in biblical interpretation? Biblical scholarship in its modern configuration came to the United States, largely from Germany, not long before the Civil War.[27] That same period witnessed the emergence of the distinctively American tradition of common sense biblicism.[28] Largely ignoring critical biblical scholarship, and without regard to church tradition or to the passages' historical and literary contexts, common sense biblicism seeks to resolve theological and ethical questions by lining up biblical passages for and against certain propositions.

Could it be that this biblicist mode of interpretation coalesced in the United States during the antebellum debates concerning slavery? During roughly the same period, "no creed but the Bible" biblicism shaped sectarian movements eventuating in the Disciples of Christ, Christian Church, and the Churches of Christ.[29] As for slavery debates, the three largest streams of white American Protantism—the Baptists, Methodists, and Presbyterians—all split over the issue prior to the Civil War, with white Methodists and Presbyterians reuniting only after the heyday of the civil rights movement. Biblical arguments for and against slavery in the antebellum period, like those regarding segregation well into the twentieth century, often pitted the favored passages of one side aligned against those of the other.[30] Even highly educated clergy, educated in biblical interpretation and the history of doctrine, resorted to biblicist arguments during the period. New Orleans' Benjamin Palmer, "father" of the Southern Presbyterian church, (in)famously defended slavery on the basis of the so-called "curse of Ham" from Gen. 9:25-27. This common interpretation predates Palmer perhaps by a century. In this framework, Noah's curse that Ham's son Canaan and his descendants would fall into servitude applied to the people of Africa. Thus, the slavery of Africans amounted to God's will. Palmer's interpretation relied upon rich elements of continental philosophy and other intellectual resources, but his basic argument for slavery—and later, for segregation—turned upon this widely accepted reading of Genesis.[31]

Whites used the Bible to defend slavery to one another, having already employed biblicist arguments to audiences of their own slaves. African American cultural historians and biblical scholars have uncovered diverse and sophisticated strategies by which slaves resisted the dehumanizing interpretations imposed by their masters' appointed preachers.[32] The direct application of biblical passages to the work of social control marks both the beginnings of African American hermeneutics and American biblicism.

Similar arguments, often grounded in Ezra's condemnation of foreign wives among the holy people, have been applied to defend segregation and to oppose interracial marriage. With respect to the curse of Ham, slavery advocates saw European whites as the descendants of Shem and Africans as Canaan's descendants. Reading Ezra, segregationists identified whites with Israel and blacks with the people of the land. One still encounters this argument in racist circles. (As a point of reference, Alabama did not remove a constitutional prohibition of interracial marriages until 2000, while a 2011 poll finds that 46 percent of Mississippi Republicans believe interracial marriage should be illegal.)[33] Remarkably, however, prominent white advocates of racial reconciliation—like many antebellum abolitionists—have also adopted biblicist approaches to the Bible. In other words, biblicist interpretation can serve either oppressive or liberating ends.

Clarence Jordan, a white Georgia Baptist with a college degree in agriculture and a Ph.D. in Greek New Testament, founded the Koinonia Farm as a racially integrated community in Americus, Georgia in 1942. While Koinonia Partners exists today as his legacy, Jordan is better known for two other associations. Habitat for Humanity emerged from persons associated with Koinonia, and Jordan's translation of much of the New Testament into "Southern" provided the script for the popular musical, *Cotton Patch Gospel*.[34] Though radically progressive on race and other social issues, Jordan often employed biblicist interpretation despite his advanced theological training. One biographer describes Jordan's approach to the Bible as "literal."[35] Jordan's translation of the parable of the Good Samaritan (Luke 10:25-37) has charmed audiences of the musical: Jordan translates the Samaritan, traditional enemy to Jews in Jesus' day, as "a black man." Where Jesus' parable has a Samaritan assisting a victim where Jewish figures did not, Jordan has a black man assisting a victim where white religious leaders likewise did not extend assistance.

This translation does not represent Jordan's original insight. Black and white preachers alike had suggested the Good Samaritan as a model for overcoming racial animosity for decades; Jordan merely incorporated this tradition into his translation. Moreover, Jordan basically copies the structure of pro-slavery and segregationist arguments—but he turns that biblicist model to dramatically different purposes. If Shem (Genesis) and the Israelites (Ezra) relate to white people, so does the victim in Jesus' parable. And if Ham/Canaan and the people of the land indicate African Americans, so does the Samaritan. It just so happens that the Samaritan is a hero, rather than a victim, of the story.

Biblicism's real significance does not lie in the interpretations it authorizes, as a biblicist approach does not control the results of interpretation. Instead, biblicism proposes boundaries for significant conversations: arguments must ground themselves in plausible interpretations of biblical texts, but certain kinds of interpretation are ruled out. One may not acknowledge diverse points of view in Scripture, appeal to the process of editing and selection that has created the canon as we now have it, consult the history of interpretation, or emphasize the cultural gaps between the biblical worlds and contemporary interpretation. As "common sense" interpretation that establishes apparently clear boundaries for interpretation, biblicism fails to transform the conversation. Benjamin Palmer and Clarence Jordan alike turned to the Bible to articulate their views of race. Palmer and Jordan found what they were looking for as well: white people and black people in stories that do not name characters in that way. Informed by white anxiety to define identity in terms of the Bible and practicing a biblicist hermeneutic, Palmer and Jordan could not escape the categories they inherited from America's race history.

Common sense biblicism blossomed at the same time that Americans debated the Bible's teaching on slavery—and at the same time that European biblical scholarship emerged in North American colleges and seminaries.

Biblicism met the perceived white need to locate ideas, and persons, within neatly constructed categories. When people today invoke the Bible to resolve pressing questions, asking "What does the Bible say?" about thorny issues like sexuality, finance, and war, they follow the biblicist framework. This is no less true when the resources of academic biblical scholarship lend sophistication to their discussions. Major church bodies have enlisted biblical scholars to assess "what the Bible says" about sexual minorities, but scholarly "expertise" has failed to generate consensus. Greater analysis is required, including the consideration of how culture, power, and identity—the forces that shape individuals and communities—empower and constrain, shape and bind the work of interpretation.

Notes

1. The following narrative largely follows from Anthony P. Dunbar's classic study, *Against the Grain: Southern Radicals and Prophets 1929–1959* (Charlottesville: University Press of Virginia, 1981).

2. Douglas A. Blackmon, *Slavery by Another Name: The Re-Enslavement of Black Americans from the Civil War to World War II* (New York: Anchor, 2008).

3. Fernando F. Segovia emphasized the "flesh-and-blood reader" in "Toward a Hermeneutics of the Diaspora: A Hermeneutics of Otherness and Engagement," in *Reading from This Place*, vol. 1: *Social Location and Biblical Interpretation in the United States*, edited by Fernando F. Segovia and Mary Ann Tolbert (Minneapolis: Fortress Press, 1995), 57–59.

4. "Introduction: The Margin as a Site of Creative Re-visioning," in *Voices from the Margin: Interpreting the Bible in the Third World*, edited by R. S. Sugirtharajah (Maryknoll: Orbis, 1991), 4.

5. I apologize that space does not allow a fuller discussion of the work that prepared the way for the volumes discussed here, nor does it allow engagement with similar volumes that I have chosen to omit.

6. Cain Hope Felder, ed., *Stony the Road We Trod: African American Biblical Interpretation* (Minneapolis: Fortress Press, 1991).

7. See Adela Yarbro Collins, ed., *Feminist Perspectives on Biblical Scholarship*, SBLBSNA 10 (Chico: Society of Biblical Literature, 1985).

8. Carol A. Newsom and Sharon H. Ringe, ed., *Women's Bible Commentary* (Louisville: Westminster John Knox Press, 1992); Elisabeth Schüssler Fiorenza, ed., *Searching the Scriptures*, vol. 1: *A Feminist Introduction* (New York: Crossroad, 1993); and Elisabeth Schüssler Fiorenza, ed., *Searching the Scriptures*, vol. 2: *A Feminist Commentary* (New York: Crossroad, 1994).

9. *Santa Biblia: The Bible through Hispanic Eyes* (Nashville: Abingdon, 1996).

10. *Reading from This Place*, vol. 1: *Social Location and Biblical Interpretation in the United States* (Minneapolis: Fortress Press, 1995); and *Reading from This Place*, vol. 2: *Social Location and Biblical Interpretation in Global Perspective* (Minneapolis: Fortress Press, 1995). A third volume emphasized the implications of emerging discourses in biblical interpretation for pedagogy in biblical studies: Fernando F. Segovia and Mary Ann Tolbert, eds., *Teaching the Bible: The Discourses and Politics of Biblical Pedagogy* (Maryknoll: Orbis, 1998).

11. See "And They Began to Speak in Other Tongues": Competing Modes of Discourse in Contemporary Biblical Criticism," in *Reading from This Place*, vol. 1, 1–32.

12. See the essay by Francisco Lozada Jr., "Teaching the New Testament: Toward an Expanded Contextual Approach," in this volume.

13. For a technically sophisticated account of this phenomenon, but with a different focus, see the essay by Stephen D. Moore and Yvonne Sherwood, "Biblical Studies 'after' Theory: Onward toward the Past," in three parts: "Part One: After 'after Theory', and Other Apocalyptic Conceits," *BibInt* 18 (2010): 1–27; "Part Two: The Secret Vices of the Biblical God," *BibInt* 18 (2010): 87–113; and "Part Three: Theory in the First and Second Waves," *BibInt* 18 (2010): 191–225.

14. Notable exceptions include Shawn Kelley, *Racializing Jesus: Race, Ideology, and the Formation of Modern Biblical Scholarship* (London: Routledge, 2006); and Jeffrey S. Siker, "Historicizing a Racialized Jesus: Case Studies in the 'Black Christ,' the 'Mestizo Christ,' and White Critique," *Biblical Interpretation* 15:1 (2007): 26–53.

15. The term "minority" criticism, as employed by "minority" scholars (see Randall C. Bailey, Tat-siong Benny Liew, and Fernando F. Segovia, eds., *They Were All Together in One Place? Toward Minority Biblical Criticism*, SBLSS 57 (Atlanta: Society of Biblical Literature, 2009), emerges from a specific location in the United States.

16. Thanks to Fernando F. Segovia, who challenged me to take on this project in a personal conversation several years ago. This strategic exploration of white interpretation corresponds to several strategies articulated by Segovia in "Poetics of Minority Biblical Criticism: Identification and Theorization," in *Prejudice and Christian Beginnings: Investigating Race, Gender, and Ethnicity in Early Christian Studies*, edited by Laura Nasrallah and Elisabeth Schüssler Fiorenza; Minneapolis: Fortress Press, 2009), 279–311.

17. "Yin/Yang Is Not Me: An Exploration into Asian American Biblical Hermeneutics," in *Ways of Being, Ways of Reading: Asian American Biblical Interpretation*, edited by Mary Foskett and Jeffrey Kah-Jin Kuan (Saint Louis: Chalice, 2006), 152–53.

18. "Ying/Yang Is Not Me," 162.

19. "God's Own People: Specters of Race, Ethnicity, and Gender in Early Christian Studies," in *Prejudice and Christian Beginnings*, edited by Laura Nasrallah and Schüssler Fiorenza, 160.

20. Eduardo Bonilla-Silva, *Racism without Racists: Color-Blind Racism and the Persistence of Racial Equality in the United States* (Lanham: Rowman and Littlefield, 2006); Alice McIntyre, *Making Meaning of Whiteness: Exploring Racial Identity with White Teachers* (Albany: SUNY Press, 1997), 45–47; Zeus Leonardo, "The Souls of White Folk: Critical Pedagogy, Whiteness Studies, and Globalization Discourse," *Race Ethnicity and Education* 5 (2002): 32.

21. John H. Hayes and Carl R. Holladay, *Biblical Exegesis: A Beginner's Handbook*, rev. ed. (Atlanta: John Knox Press, 1987), 17.

22. *Black Womanist Ethics*, AAR Academy Series 60 (Atlanta: Scholars, 1988), 4.

23. Kate Willink, *Bringing Desegregation Home: Memories of the Struggle toward School Integration in Rural North Carolina*, Palgrave Studies in Oral History (New York: Macmillan, 2009), 30–31.

24. *Race: A Theological Account* (New York: Oxford University Press, 2008). Gay L. Byron points out that early Christians, like many of their pagan counterparts, associated blackness (along with Egyptian or Ethiopian identity) with various forms of wickedness and whiteness with purity and penitence (*Symbolic Blackness and Ethnic Difference in Early Christian Literature* (New York: Routledge, 2002), and Denise Kimber Buell surveys the importance of racialized discourse in the emergence of modern religious and theological studies, particularly by identifying Christianity as "universal" in opposition to "particularistic" Judaism, see *Why This New Race? Ethnic Reasoning in Early Christianity* (New York: Columbia University Press, 2005), esp. 21–29.

25. *Race*, 311.

26. Cheryl B. Anderson, "Reflections in an Interethnic/racial Era on Interethnic/racial Marriage in Ezra," in *They Were All Together in One Place? Toward Minority Biblical Criticism*, edited

by Randall C. Bailey, Tat-siong Benny Liew, and Fernando F. Segovia, SBLSS 57 (Atlanta: SBL, 2009), 52.

27. Others have traced the influence of racialized discourse in Germany, as represented in the historiography of Johann Herder. Herder argued that the characteristics of a human people (*Volk*) emerged organically from their material climate—Kelley, *Racializing Jesus*, 35–37; Jonathan M. Hall, *Ethnic Identity in Greek Antiquity* (New York: Cambridge University Press, 1997, 7–8). This legacy surfaces at key moments in the history of biblical scholarship, as in Albert Schweitzer's notorious claim that only the "German temperament" could produce excellent scholarship on the life of Jesus (*The Quest of the Historical Jesus* [ed. John Bowden; Fortress Classics in Biblical Studies; Minneapolis: Fortress Press, 2001], 3–4).

28. I use "American" here as an adjective to describe phenomena characteristic of the United States. While "American" is inaccurate, this usage is far more concise than available alternatives.

29. On white biblicism in the antebellum period, see Randall Balmer, "Casting Aside the Ballast of History and Tradition: White Protestants and the Bible in the Antebellum Period," in *African Americans and the Bible: Sacred Texts and Social Textures*, edited by Vincent L. Wimbush (New York: Continuum, 2001), 193–200.

30. Baptist historian Bill J. Leonard characterizes antebellum pro-slavery arguments as "literalist," in contrast to abolitionist arguments that generalized from broad spiritual principles ("Biblicists, but not Always Biblical? Revisiting Baptist Hermeneutics," in *The Challenge of Being Baptist: Owning a Scandalous Past and an Uncertain Future* (Waco: Baylor University Press, 2010), 53–74. I would argue for a biblicist streak in abolitionist hermeneutics as well.

31. For an intellectual biography of Palmer, see Christopher M. Duncan, *Benjamin Morgan Palmer: Southern Presbyterian Divine* (Ph.D. diss., Auburn University, 2008). On the curse of Ham and Palmer's appropriation of it, see Stephen R. Haynes, *Noah's Curse: The Biblical Justification of American Slavery* (New York: Oxford University Press, 2002), esp. 125–74.

32. For example, John Saillant, "Origins of African American Biblical Hermeneutics in Eighteenth-Century Black Opposition to the Slave Trade and Slavery," in *African Americans and the Bible: Sacred Texts and Social Textures*, edited by Vincent L. Wimbush (New York: Continuum, 2001), 236–50; Sterling Stuckey, "'My Burden Lightened': Frederick Douglass, the Bible, and Slave Culture," in *African Americans and the Bible: Sacred Texts and Social Textures*, edited by Vincent L. Wimbush (New York: Continuum, 2001), 251–65; Vincent L. Wimbush, *The Bible and African Americans*, Facets (Minneapolis: Fortress Press, 2003); Clarice J. Martin, "'Somebody Done Hoodoo'd the Hoodoo Man': Language, Power, Resistance, and the Effective History of Pauline Texts in American Slavery," *Semeia* 83/84 (1998): 203–33; Allen Dwight Callahan, "'Brother Saul': An Ambivalent Witness to Freedom," *Semeia* 83/84 (1998): 235–50; Abraham Smith, "Putting 'Paul' Back Together Again: William Wells Brown's *Clotel* and Black Abolitionist Approaches to Paul," *Semeia* 83/84 (1998): 251–62; Allen Dwight Callahan, *The Talking Book: African Americans and the Bible* (New Haven: Yale University Press, 2006).

33. On Ezra, interracial marriage, and Alabama, see Cheryl B. Anderson, "Reflections in an Interethnic/racial Era on Interethnic/racial Marriage in Ezra", 50. The Mississippi poll was conducted by Public Policy Polling and reported on April 7, 2011. Online: http://publicpolicypolling.blogspot.com/2011/04/barbour-bryant-lead-in-mississippi.html, accessed June 21, 2011.

34. Jordan's translations: *The Cotton Patch Version of Luke and Acts: Jesus' Doings and the Happenings* (New York: Association, 1969); *The Cotton Patch Version of Matthew and John* (New York: Association, 1970); *The Cotton Patch Version of Paul's Epistles* (New York: Association, 1968); *The Cotton Patch Version of Hebrews and the General Epistles* (New York: Association, 1973). The musical: Tom Key, Russell Treyz, and Harry Chapin, *Cotton Patch Gospel: A Toe-Tapping Full-Length Musical* (Woodstock: Dramatic, 1983).

35. Ann Louis Coble, *Cotton Patch for the Kingdom: Clarence Jordan's Demonstration Plot at Koinonia Farm* (Scottdale: Herald, 2001), 39–41.

PART I

Historical Reconstruction

1

Writing History, Writing Culture, Writing Ourselves

Issues in Contemporary Biblical Interpretation

Mary Ann Tolbert

Writing history is a disciplined form of writing fiction.[1] Like fiction writers, historians must select and organize disparate elements into an arguable, persuasive, interesting, and constructive plot. This historical plot is not forced on the writer by the events or elements themselves, which he or she is trying to describe or explain, but instead is chosen by the writer on the basis of a variety of factors, including, at least, current historical theories, other contemporary explanatory models, social group perspectives, and personal preferences. In the case of the latter, for example, I might find that demographics and statistics make historical accounts more convincing than would someone like Mark Twain, who in his "Chapters from my Autobiography" quotes British Prime Minister Disraeli as saying, "There are three kinds of lies: lies, damned lies, and statistics."[2]

Historical fashions change over time as well. For most of the nineteenth and twentieth centuries, histories focused on wars, royal courts, and mass events. By the end of the twentieth century that focus was shifting to look more at the everyday life of common people, using when possible both the material culture uncovered by archeology and the written and oral narratives of individuals (diaries, papers, letters, and so on). In addition, those elements, theories, and forms of explanation, which each group of historians finds to be more persuasive, are the ones that group will use to select material and to write the historical work. If I think that psychological factors best explain behavior and events (for example, family dynamics molded the charismatic but disturbed personality of Hitler) instead of, say, sociological or economic ones (for example, German society set up by the poverty, defeat, and social dynamics arising from World War I eagerly accepted the high nationalism Hitler proclaimed), I would be inclined to write my historical plot with more emphasis on family history than on social circumstances and select material from the vast sources available that supported my particular perspective. None of these explanatory theories is necessarily better or worse than others, none produces a more accurate history, but they do provide different angles on the same events and emphasize some data and sources from that period over others. While some writers of history certainly combine in their works more than one perspective, attempting to provide a "thick" description and analysis of events, almost all must limit their investigations in some way to provide an intelligible plot for their readers to follow.

While the selection and organization of material (the plotting of the historical narrative) and the use of various external explanatory models demonstrates the profound connection of history writing to the writing of any other kind of fiction, history writing differs from other fiction writing in a very important manner: its disciplined use of sources. While most fiction can come almost wholly from the author's imagination, historical writing must be based upon publicly shared evidence, written sources, and the careful adjudication of eyewitness reports[3] and secondary literature. It is this dependence on critically evaluated public sources that allows historical writing to make epistemological claims that other forms of fiction cannot make. So, history is "true" in a way that other fiction may not be, and furthermore, its "truth" is publicly verifiable by others studying the same sources. Using the word "true" in relation to history writing here may be a bit misleading. Since history depends on sources, which may be more or less reliable, and the historian's act of filling the gaps between and among those sources, historical reconstructions are actually better evaluated on a probability scale: some reconstructions of past events are more or less probable than others. The availability of sources and quality of those sources are often at the heart of such judgments. This reliance on sources also explains why *prehistory* is defined as that period in any culture before writing; important events certainly happened, but without a written record of some kind, no history can be written about those events.

Writing History as Biblical Interpretation

These basic points about writing history are important to keep in mind when exploring the last three centuries of biblical scholarship. For most of that period, interpreting biblical texts was synonymous with writing history. Indeed, historical criticism, in its various modes, has been the dominant form of scholarly biblical study practically since the origin of modern biblical scholarship during the European Enlightenment of the seventeenth and eighteenth centuries.[4] That use of history writing makes sense when you realize that all the texts of the Bible come from ancient Mediterranean cultures, separated from contemporary life by vast material, cultural, and linguistic differences. In addition, the use of history as the primary method of interpretation has also been driven by the peculiarly Protestant notion concerning the purity and power of origins. The early Protestant call for *sola scriptura* ("scripture alone") to be the basis of all dogma and practice was based on the reformers' belief that scripture related the purest revelation of God, which much of the church's practice and teaching had fallen away from during the first millennium and a half of church life. Returning to that original revelation, according to many early and even present day Protestants, is the path to purging the church of bad practices and returning it to purer forms of worship and belief. Yet, even for early Protestants like Martin Luther, each book within the biblical canon had to be carefully tested to prove its theological value and authority, and some were found lacking.[5] If even *sola scriptura* cannot be relied upon to provide the earliest, most authentic moment of revelation, then where is it to be found?

The search for that elusive moment of purest revelation has certainly formed the ideological[6] motivation, whether consciously admitted or not, for many of the various "quests of the historical Jesus" that have dominated New Testament scholarship for the past three centuries. Most often, like the early Protestant reformers, the desired result of such a difficult scholarly quest is not merely a widely praised project of writing history but more crucially the uncovering of that special time of purity and power, which can now bring strength, passion, and correct action back to Christianity itself. It is important to realize that even the historical efforts of nineteenth and twentieth century biblical scholars, which for the most part followed the objective, scientific paradigm of historical positivism,[7] were nevertheless profoundly undergirded by the ideology of origins that arose during the Christian Reformation.

Even in its heyday, historical positivism was a troubled approach to interpreting the Bible. Its scientific grounding argued that using the available sources objectively and publicly should lead to repeatable results and consensus on the origins of early Christianity and Israel/Judah, but instead, one biblical scholar after another presented historical studies that differed widely from the results of other scholars. Under a positivist view, only one of these studies could be correct and the others must be in error. Indeed, many books on biblical interpretation from the nineteenth and early twentieth centuries opened with a section showing how all the other works on its topic were wrong or lacking in some crucial way. However, no consensus seemed to emerge from all of these many studies.

One problem that all historical studies of early Christianity encounter is the scarcity and ambiguous nature of the sources available; at least for Hebrew Bible studies, material culture as uncovered through centuries of archeological research can provide some limited assistance in establishing or discrediting claims made in the texts about cities and cultural practices. Ancient Christianity had few, if any, material markers of its existence; Christian households seemed to be mostly similar to all other households in their area. In addition, however important Christianity may seem today, in the first century C. E., it was an obscure sect from the eastern Mediterranean, like many other such groups, and unworthy of comment by writers outside of its loyal adherents. Since extra-biblical sources for the beginnings of Christianity are so scarce (and problematic), scholars are left with the writings of committed adherents, all of whom write after the time of Jesus and most of whom (perhaps all) believe fervently in his resurrection from the dead. That strong belief that Jesus was still alive within the church through visions, inspired speaking, and dreams, while perfectly understandable from the standpoint of faith, make the historical boundary lines between the words of Jesus and those of his later inspired followers far more permeable and blurred than most modern historians would desire. Moreover, scholars are divided on the purposes motivating the writing of many of the New Testament texts, especially the gospels. Because true literacy was rare in Greco-Roman antiquity with only perhaps 10% to 15% of people able to write and read (and most of those in the wealthier classes of society), why were these texts written at all, and by whom and for whom, and for what purpose and in what genre? These crucial issues are all still open questions.

In a set of two groundbreaking essays written in the mid-1990's, Professor Fernando Segovia set out to plot the history of twentieth century biblical studies by positing an increasing theoretical and practical challenge to positivistic historical criticism by a number of competing paradigms of analysis.[8] Segovia demonstrated that while the paradigm of historical criticism dominated the first half of the twentieth century, by the 1960s and 70s it was being disrupted by three other critical contenders in biblical scholarship: what Segovia called "cultural criticism," meaning those approaches to interpreting the texts that employed sociological and anthropological perspectives and theories;[9] "literary criticism," which viewed the biblical texts first and foremost as *texts*, with plots, characters, narrative sequencing, and rhetorical effects;[10] and "cultural studies or ideological criticism." This third challenge to historical criticism came from a variety of studies investigating the ideological perspectives of the texts and the interpreters of those texts from a diversity of social factors such as race, ethnicity, gender, sexuality, national and religious identity, etc. This diverse group, Segovia called "cultural studies or ideological criticism" and devoted his second essay to characterizing its methods, motives, and modes.[11]

Most important for this last group, though the insight could also be found in some studies using literary criticism, was the postmodern position that "texts" themselves are actually created in the interpretative process. Texts have no meaning in isolation from human readers; they are simply marks on a page. The active work of interpreting those marks constructs them into meaningful "texts," but a significant part of that construction project is the experience, understanding, assumptions, and educational conditioning brought to the process by the interpreter. Indeed, throughout this essay, I have tried to underscore the crucial active, creative nature of interpretation by referring to *writers* of interpretations instead of the more passive-sounding *readers* of texts. The process of interpreting the Bible (or actually any other script) is an dynamic process of writing a new "text" into existence, whether oral (for example, a sermon) or physically written. My own inclinations, education, social location, cultural conditioning, philosophical assumptions, and religious views are integral parts of this new writing project, whether I am conscious of them or not. In fact, if I am not conscious of them, they are likely to have even greater impact on the new text I create through my interpretation than if I were conscious of them from the beginning.

In the almost twenty years since Segovia wrote these remarkable essays, the challenges to more traditional, positivistic historical criticism have broken both its theoretical and practical hold on biblical interpretation. In addition, the three paradigms, which Segovia recognized as disrupting and overturning the older positivist agenda of writing biblical histories, have in the intervening years in part morphed and merged with each other and in part rigidified into new "dominant" discourses. Although concerns with history are still fundamental to many interpretations of biblical texts, those concerns have been newly defined through the lens of culture.

Writing Culture as Biblical Interpretation

Segovia's two paradigms of "cultural criticism" and "cultural studies" both foregrounded "culture" as central to understanding and interpreting biblical texts, whether the subject of exploration was the culturally conditioned nature of the texts or of the interpreter or, better still, of both. For writing history as biblical interpretation, once the undergirding principles of historical positivism began to collapse, anthropology and especially sociology arrived to provide new theoretical and methodological foundations. Particularly in the early years of "cultural criticism," the scientific aura of sociological and anthropological theories appealed to many biblical historians used to the objective, quasi-scientific claims of older positivistic methods. The shift to writing "socio-history" was not as threatening to older patterns of research as the shift required for literary criticism or for cultural studies. Indeed, in my view of the contemporary state of biblical scholarship, socio-history is now the dominant paradigm of analysis and the dominant mode of scholarly discourse about the Bible.

Socio-history has much to recommend it. As we have seen, the sources for historical writing about early Christianity[12] are scarce and difficult to use for a variety of reasons. In fact, the written sources from all of Mediterranean antiquity are limited and fragmentary. Trying to write a history based on such partial data is like trying to put together a jigsaw puzzle with two-thirds of the pieces missing and the picture on the box top gone. The pieces that are available can be put together in a variety of possible ways, but how are we to judge one configuration to be more probable than another? Using social theories and cultural models drawn from other cultures, for which more information, more evidence might be available, would be one sensible way to fill the gaps among the fragmentary sources we have and to provide a fuller picture than the sources themselves alone would allow. Contemporary New Testament scholars have an array of social and cultural theories drawn from modern studies of agrarian and peasant societies, sectarian communities, non-literate cultures, and colonized countries to employ in studying the texts and early communities of first-century Christianity.[13] Although these studies must be used with care because they come from other, sometimes quite recent cultures, they provide a wealth of possible material for establishing more probable historical fictions.

Like the current fashion in the wider arena of historical studies, home, family, and village life has priority in many recent biblical socio-histories.[14] That emphasis is also appropriate since in its earliest years Christianity was not a religion of royal or imperial interest nor did it generate wars and rebellions, all events that came later in its history. Moreover, socio-historical research is able to talk about ancient family life not simply by noting the places in the New Testament where such issues are raised but even more vitally by engaging as source material other Greek and Roman writings on those issues available from an array of classical sources from this period. Indeed, one of the lasting benefits of the development of sociological and anthropological approaches to New Testament history writing has been the opening up of the wider world of Greco-Roman sources and studies for use in understanding New Testament texts. From the importance of ancient rhetorical theories to the legal status of slaves, from the use of taxation farming to views of medical texts to the structures of Hellenistic cultic associations, socio-history has demonstrated conclusively how firmly and fully early Christianity was constituted by the social, cultural, and religious world of its origins. Writing New Testament history now must always be a project in writing that larger culture as a central part of the interpretative process.

Socio-history as the new dominant paradigm for historical studies still struggles with the other two "challengers" identified by Segovia in his essays. Of the two, literary criticism seems to be the least visible at present. Literary criticism entered biblical studies in the 1960s and 70s primarily in its more "formalist" guise; those perspectives were already disappearing in the wider world of literary studies at the moment they were just entering biblical scholarship, as Segovia noted in his study.[15] As literary criticism developed in biblical studies through the 1990s, its emphases moved from focusing mainly on the configurations of the text itself to analyzing the relationship of the reader to the text, a movement paralleled in the wider literary world. The lack of many solely literary studies of the New Testament in contemporary scholarly writings may reflect the merging of its concerns about the reader's role in interpretation with the explicitly ideological investigations generated by the diverse group working under the "cultural studies" umbrella. In addition, the best of the biblical socio-historians merge literary concerns into their historical work, recognizing that the biblical texts are still *texts* and need to be evaluated as such before social data can be extracted or social theories applied. One of the clearest ways to see the effect of literary criticism on socio-historical research is by noting the importance of rhetoric in current studies. Speaking and writing in first-century Mediterranean antiquity was shaped by a centuries long tradition of rhetoric, the art of speaking well and persuasively. No one learned to write Greek or later Latin without studying large parts of this tradition. Under those circumstances, finding evidences of a variety of rhetorical patterns in Paul's letters or the gospels is not at all surprising. Recognizing these patterns for what they are and then analyzing them has generated very perceptive insights in recent sociohistorical work.[16]

While many of the issues raised by the more formalist studies of literary criticism have been incorporated into the cultural and social analyses of socio-history, the boundary between what Segovia called "cultural studies" and current work in socio-history, with one major exception, is still surprisingly strong. The "cultural studies" paradigm, as Segovia outlined it, focused on the realization that the "text" itself is constructed by the reader in the process of reading. The reader, or as I term it, the writer of biblical interpretation is as essential to the "text" as any historical, social, theoretical, or narrative data might be. Moreover, that writer is shaped profoundly by the social and cultural matrix in which he or she lives and writes. The often-unexamined assumptions of that matrix are fused into the "text" being interpreted. Thus, women, ethnic and racial minority groups, sexual minorities, and other socially marginalized groups have recognized the worth of investigating the power dynamics found both in ancient texts/contexts and in the past "traditional" interpretations that have created those texts in ways that have served to support the continued marginalization of so many. For example, do the New Testament texts really provide no evidence for the leadership of women in early Christianity or did the generations of male interpreters reading those texts overlook, minimize, and omit that evidence because of their own views concerning the role of contemporary women?[17] Not surprisingly, the latter has been thoroughly shown to be the case.

Only by raising to full consciousness the effects social location, national and religious commitments, and educational practices may have on what any writer sees, deems important, and fashions into his/her writing of biblical culture or history can the underlying assumptions of class, gender, race, ethnicity, sexuality, religion, and national origin, which are invariably implicated in the interpretative process, become clear and transparent to audiences. The mask of omniscience, which most writers hide behind in creating their interpretations, has to be dropped so that the ideological issues behind these interpretations can be examined. For this process, it is not sufficient simply to add an early footnote or paragraph to an interpretation that lists socio-demographic data about the writer, as many now do. Thus, to know that I am a white Christian woman, born and living in the United States, educated in North American universities in the 1960s and 70s, and a member of a sexual minority group does not in itself help those who read my writing understand the ways that social data situates my experience and shapes my views, although it might be suggestive. To make the process more transparent, less hidden, I need to reflect on the manner in which those factors about me have formed what I see and believe about the New Testament. I know, for example, that my many, often painful experiences as a woman trying to break into a profession that was practically all male when I began teaching thirty-five years ago has conditioned me to be more open to a hermeneutics of suspicion than to one of agreement; calls for "consensus," "the common good," and "supporting the company line," were all things I was often asked to do, even when doing so was clearly not in my best interests. As new voices are raised in the interpretative process, new discourses about the politics and power of biblical interpretation may come to the forefront of discussion.

WRITING OURSELVES AS BIBLICAL INTERPRETATION

You might wonder why I and many others think it is important for the process of New Testament interpretation to be open and transparent. The answer to that question has to do with the social and religious authority many people, even those who are not Christian, bestow on the Bible. Whether it is valued as the root of faith or only as an iconic Western text, interpretations of the Bible have social and religious power. Writing an interpretation of the New Testament is, thus, not only an act of scholarly research, but also an act of political power because the interpretations scholars create have the potential to affect the actual lived existence of millions of people around the world. This power is the "elephant in the room" that very few biblical scholars will ever discuss openly. The stakes of writing biblical interpretations can be very high, and that makes knowing as much as possible about the assumptions and beliefs of those wielding that power crucial. However, even with the demise of historical positivism with its objective, quasi-scientific claims, it is still very unusual for contemporary socio-historians to register even a minimum of their socio-demographic data in their writings. Reflecting on one's social location, which is *de rigueur* for ideological critics, still seems to apply mainly to those writers whose marginalized status cannot really be denied or avoided.[18] How biblical interpreters write *ourselves* as part of the interpretative process appears to be one of the major divisions in contemporary twenty-first-century scholarship.

By finding reflections on the writer's social location in some biblical scholarship but not in others, one might infer that some scholars have "agendas" or at least some lens that makes their vision partial rather than total, while other scholars do not suffer these impediments. That inference is not in the least correct: we have seen how even the positivist historical critics of the nineteenth and twentieth centuries were often deeply motivated by the desire to reform contemporary faith and practice by revealing the pure moment of revelation in the historical Jesus. All critics have ideological commitments, and many New Testament scholars have deeply held religious views that strongly affect how they write their biblical interpretations, how they shape their historical fictions. Yet for many, these commitments are well hidden in their writings. One recent example of how these commitments can affect sociohistorical interpretations can be found in some current New Testament "Empire Studies."

Earlier I alluded to the fact that there was one major exception to the closed boundary between socio-history and "cultural studies." That crossover is postcolonial criticism. Postcolonial criticism entered biblical studies in the 1990s as more scholars from the two-thirds world began to write biblical interpretations.[19] Many from formerly or currently colonized countries pointed to the fact that early Christianity itself was a colonial religion, beginning as it did under the dominance of the Roman Empire. Moreover, the Bible has a history of use as a tool of European or Western colonial expansion, overwhelming native religions and supplying some of the justifications for the colonization process itself. Many scholars from around the world have investigated both the anti-colonial polemics and the colonial accommodations that live together in hybrid configurations in most colonial texts, like those found in the New Testament.[20] Over the last decade, postcolonial perspectives and reading strategies have been combined with socio-historical interpretations in a variety of ways. One group now works under the banner of "Empire Studies."[21] While these studies have added greatly to our understanding of the Roman Empire, some of them emphasize only the presence of what they argue to be anti-colonial polemics in the New Testament, regardless of the well-documented earlier use of the same writings in supporting Western colonization. Indeed, it is often *because* of their earlier role in Western colonization that their anti-colonial polemics need now to be emphasized. Yet, this clearly ideological drive to cleanse Jesus and the New Testament of their earlier use as supports for imperialism (perspectives that are still important for many within more mission-oriented, evangelical Christian circles) and reclaim them for liberal theology with its current postmodern, postcolonial concerns is often hidden behind the mask of impersonal sociohistorical writing. It is certainly not wrong for writers of biblical histories to be motivated by passionately and personally held ideological views; my argument in fact is that it is unavoidable for any writer. What is problematic is that these ideological commitments are too often covered by the scientific, objective-sounding style of socio-historical writing, and no effort is made on the part of the writer to offset that style or even trouble its surface.

Why would some writers want to avoid mentioning the commitments and passions that they, for the most part, know motivates their writing of biblical interpretations? Why is having an "agenda," which we all have, or partial vision, which is simply part of our human condition, seen as a detriment to the acceptance of our writings as biblical scholars? One effect of admitting to one's agenda has plagued many of the perspectives under the "cultural studies" umbrella for years: if you say you are writing from a certain standpoint, many will assume that the only people who could be interested in what you have to say will be others from the same standpoint. So feminist scholars must be speaking only to women or scholars of color only to people of color. This effect of admitting one's agenda has had a tendency to "silo," to use a current business term, various perspectives in cultural studies in ways that, in my view, have limited their potential for change and challenge by limiting their audience and dialogue partners.

I suspect that one factor standing behind this phenomenon of preferring an impersonal, objective writing style in biblical interpretation is the way in which we all learned to read the Bible initially. Reading and writing are learned skills that each person must develop within the educational and cultural settings in which they live. For most Christians, learning how to understand the Bible required learning a particular kind of reading, especially if that reading was to be done in one of the more antiquated Bible translations. This practice of Bible reading is taught within the context of faith communities or churches.[22] Through worship practices, lectionary readings,[23] and other formal occasions in Christian communities, many Christians learn to read the Bible as God's Word for all people and all cultures. This idealizing and totalizing reading process, I believe, is what many Christians then expect to find in any "true" biblical interpretation. To be acceptable writers of biblical interpretations for these audiences, it follows that writers need to sound as if they, too, are omniscient or can replicate that god-like totalizing vision. The way we have learned to read the Bible deeply influences the way we hear writers of biblical interpretation. When those writers admit to their necessarily partial views, they violate the reading expectations most Christians, especially, have learned to expect from the Bible, making their interpretations sound less authoritative and powerful. This situation becomes a major ethical dilemma when the writers who omit any indication of their assumptions, ideologies, and agendas are largely white males of dominant Western cultures, while those acknowledging their concerns are overwhelmingly minority and two-thirds world writers. Yet, that dilemma is still the situation in which writers of biblical interpretations find ourselves well into the beginning of the third millennium of Christianity. I do not know how this situation will resolve, or even if it will resolve, but I do know that all writers of biblical interpretations deserve to have their creations evaluated both intellectually and ethically for the power they wield and the ends they hope to accomplish. Such evaluations ought to apply equally to socio-historians as well as to the many, more explicitly ideological writers under the cultural studies umbrella.

Notes

1. This essay is written in honor of my inspiring colleague and dear friend, Fernando F. Segovia, who, it must be said, writes essays of this type far better than I do.

2. Published in the *North American Review*, 1906. Most scholars doubt the accuracy of Twain's attribution, since the quotation cannot be found in any of Benjamin Disraeli's papers or writings.

3. Eyewitness reports are notoriously problematic for historians. Both ancient and modern historians recognize the critical value of such reports for writing history, but they also recognize the need to evaluate each report carefully to authenticate its account. The ability of eyewitnesses to the same event to relate strikingly different reports about what happened is a favorite theme of literature; see, for example, the famous 1950's Japanese movie "Rashomon," directed by Arkira Kurosawa.

4. For an older but still excellent, brief discussion of the principles, issues, and figures of that early period, see Hendrikus Boers, *What is New Testament Theology? The Rise of Criticism and the Problem of a Theology of the New Testament*, (Philadelphia: Fortress Press, 1979).

5. In the Prefaces Luther wrote for many of the books of the New Testament, he makes his famous assessment of the Letter of James as a "right strawy epistle," meaning that it was a letter of straw, not authoritative for the church because it omitted any mention of the importance of the life, death and resurrection of Christ and what for Luther was the center of Christian faith, the belief in justification by grace through faith. For further discussion of Luther's readings of scripture, see Oswald Bayer, "Luther as an Interpreter of Holy Scripture," in *The Cambridge Companion to Martin Luther*, edited by Donald McKim (Cambridge: Cambridge University Press, 2003), 73–85.

6. I am using the concept of "ideology" here and throughout this essay in its general sense of a set of ideas, symbols, and opinions, whether conscious or not, that affect actions. The more particular Marxist view of "ideology" as a false consciousness brought about by the material interests of upper classes is not the meaning intended in this essay.

7. Historical positivism has its roots in the work of the French sociologist Auguste Comte (1798 to 1857), who argued that history, like all other sciences, could generate generalized "laws" controlling human and social development by the objective analysis of empirical data from the past.

8. "'And They Began to Speak in Other Tongues': Competing Modes of Discourse in Contemporary Biblical Criticism," in *Reading from This Place*, vol. 1: *Social Location and Biblical Interpretation in the United States*, edited by Fernando Segovia and Mary Ann Tolbert (Minneapolis: Fortress Press, 1995), 1–32; and "Cultural Studies and Contemporary Biblical Criticism: Ideological Criticism as Mode of Discourse," in *Reading from This Place*, vol. 2: *Social Location and Biblical Interpretation in Global Perspective*, edited by Fernando Segovia and Mary Ann Tolbert (Minneapolis: Fortress Press, 1995), 1–17.

9. "And They Began to Speak in Other Tongues," 20–28.

10. Ibid., 15–20.

11. Ibid., 28–32; and "Cultural Studies and Contemporary Biblical Criticism," 7–17.

12. The issues of sources and the use of social theories are somewhat distinct for historians who work primarily in the Hebrew Bible period from those who work on the origins of early Christianity. From this point on in this essay, I will focus my comments on the latter only.

13. One of the first excellent studies of early Christianity using these perspectives can be found in Wayne A. Meeks, *The First Urban Christians: The Social World of the Apostle Paul* (New

Haven: Yale University Press, 1983). More recently, see also L. Michael White and O. Larry Yarbrough, eds., *The Social World of the First Christians: Essays in Honor of Wayne A. Meeks* (Minneapolis: Fortress Press, 1995); Anselm C. Hagedorn, Zeba A. Crook, and Eric Steward, eds., *In Other Words: Essays on Social Science Methods and the New Testament in Honor of Jerome H. Neyrey* (Sheffield: Sheffield Phoenix, 2007); Deitmar Neufeld and Richard E. DeMaris, eds., *Understanding the Social World of the New Testament* (London: Routledge, 2010).

14. For example, see Halvor Moxnes, ed., *Constructing Early Christian Families: Family as Social Reality and Metaphor* (New York: Routledge, 1997); Trevor J. Burke, *Family Matters: A Socio-Historical Study of Kinship Metaphors in 1 Thessalonians* (London: T & T Clark, 2003).

15. "And They Began to Speak in Other Tongues," 15–16.

16. A recent example of the difference recognizing rhetoric at work in the text can make to interpretation can be found in the concern with "eyewitness" reports in the New Testament gospels. Looking at the understanding of "eyewitnesses" in mainly only one Hellenistic historian, Polybius, who actually praises his own perspective as unique, and reading that view in a rather positivist fashion into the mention of eyewitnesses in John, Richard Bauckham finds new evidence for the early, eyewitness authorship of the Gospels of John and Mark (from his study of the sayings of Papias); see *Jesus and the Eyewitnesses: The Gospels as Eyewitness Testimony* (Grand Rapids: Eerdmans, 2006). On the other hand, by looking at a large collection of Greek and Roman historians' views concerning eyewitnesses and comparing their views with other Greek writings, Clare Rothschild develops a convincing analysis of the rhetorical uses of "eyewitness reports" for establishing the credentials of the author of Luke and Acts; see, *Luke-Acts and the Rhetoric of History: An Investigation of Early Christian Historiography* (Tübingen: Mohr Siebeck, 2004).

17. Feminist biblical criticism has provided copious examples of what earlier male interpreters simply refused to see in biblical texts; for a sampling, see, Elisabeth Schüssler Fiorenza, ed., *Searching the Scriptures,* vol. 1: *A Feminist Introduction* (New York: Crossroad, 1993) and *Searching the Scriptures*, vol. 2: *A Feminist Commentary* (New York: Crossroad, 1994).

18. Although I believe this statement to be generally true, it is a little harsh, since there are many white male scholars who work hard to understand and acknowledge their social locations and the effects of those locations on their scholarly research.

19. Postcolonial criticism was the direction that Fernando Segovia's later scholarship took in a variety of works; see, for example, Fernando Segovia and R. S. Sugirtharajah, *A Postcolonial Commentary on the New Testament Writings* (London: T & T Clark, 2009).

20. As an example, see these two recent studies from an Australian context: Mark G. Brett, *Decolonizing God: The Bible in the Tides of Empire* (Sheffield: Sheffield Phoenix, 2008), and Michele A. Connolly, *Disorderly Women and the Order of God: An Australian Feminist Reading of the Gospel of Mark,* Ph.D. diss., Graduate Theological Union, 2008.

21. See, for example, Richard A. Horsley, ed., *In the Shadow of Empire: Reclaiming the Bible as a History of Faithful Resistance* (Louisville: Westminster John Knox, 2008); and Warren Carter, *The Roman Empire and the New Testament: An Essential Guide* (Nashville: Abingdon, 2006).

22. In a fascinating study of Bible reading practices in Latin American Catholic base communities by the Instituto de Estudos da Religião in the early 1990's in Brazil, Paulo Fernando Carneiro de Andrade demonstrated that social location was of less importance for biblical interpretation than the practice of Bible reading congregants were taught within their church communities. Within small rural communities, Roman Catholics who lived in the same social circumstances, side by side with Evangelical Protestants developed radically different biblical interpretations because of the practices they learned from their religious leaders; see, "Reading the Bible in the Ecclesial Base Communities of Latin America: The Meaning of Social Location," in *Reading From This Place*, vol. 2: *Social Location and Biblical Interpretation in Global Perspective* (ed. Fernando F. Segovia and Mary Ann Tolbert; Minneapolis: Fortress Press, 1995), 237–49.

23. I believe that learning to hear the Bible through brief lectionary readings, as is quite common in many forms of Christianity, has pre-disposed many Christians to accept brief "prooftexts" as the ultimate biblical evidence for any situation. Proof-texts, those small fragments

of biblical narratives that are pulled out of context and mixed together with other small fragments from all over the Bible, are similar enough in length and shape to lectionary readings to seem a "normal" way to read the Bible.

2

Decolonizing the Darkness

Bible Readers and the Colonial Cultural Archive

Musa W. Dube

The shadow of empire in the production of modern readings should also be underlined.[1]

INTRODUCTION: PLAYING IN THE DARK!

Thinking about decolonizing the darkness takes me down the memory lane to the days when I used to play hide and seek with my brothers and sisters in our parents' farm. Having moved from Zimbabwe to Botswana after land dispossession, our parents chose not to live in the city or village, but on the farm. I grew up on this farm. It is a place which I still call home and where my father still lives, my mother having passed on. Growing up on the farm, we used to play hide and seek way into the early hours of the night. There are many versions of this game. In our version, the seeker takes her or his place by the base, where there is a drum. S/he closes her/his eyes and calls out "Black Mampatile. *A lo iphithile?*" (Black hider, have you hidden yourself?) *Banyana baiphithile? Basimane baiphithile?* (Have the girls and boys hidden themselves?) The hiders respond, "No! No!" as they run out to different directions to find their best hiding place. This could be behind the house, a tree, a drum, a ban, a planter, a plough, a tractor, or under a wheel barrow . . . wherever! One needs to hide and not be found. The seeker continues calling, "Black Mampatile *A lo iphithile?*" and the hiders continue answering, "No! No!" until they all have securely hidden themselves. The seeker gets the hint that the hiders have all found their secure places when there is no answer to the question, *A lo iphithile?* At this point, the seeker opens his/her eyes and starts looking for each of the

31

hiders. Each time the seeker finds a hider, the seeker tries to touch the hider, while the hider races towards the middle point to touch the base before the seeker touches her or him. The winner of the game is the one who hides the most, the one who cannot be found regardless of the seeker's thorough search.[2] The person who gets touched first, before reaching the base, becomes the next seeker. Then the game starts all over again.

My siblings and I used to play this game way into the early hours of the night while adults were sleeping. The game never lost its magic as we seemed to play it over and over and over and over again. Each time we tried to play hide and seek during the day, our parents objected. Just as the storytelling was forbidden during the day, we were also forbidden to play hide and seek during the day. So we played during the night, in the darkness. I was thinking of how we used to play in the dark; how we used to hide in the dark; how we would seek in the dark and run for the base in the dark. I wondered why we were never afraid of the darkness or any danger. I wondered why our parents never worried about their children playing in the dark. All we thought of at the time was the thrill of the game: the challenge to hide, to seek, to run, to win, to lose and to start all over again, never getting discouraged by losing, nor searching for people who are hiding in the dark, never giving up on trying to be the best hider and never giving up when you were found out and became the seeker.

It has been a long time since I played the beloved game of hide and seek with my brothers and sisters. But we still return to the farm for family and national holidays with scores of our children and their children, who have taken over the game of hide and seek. While I do not play hide and seek anymore, I have noticed that whenever I am back home, I am amazed by the capacity of the dark night to bring on some of the most breathtaking scenery I have ever seen. I get to watch the moon and the stars rise, marching in slowly, taking their rightful place and populating the sky like a billion diamonds, all the while silently. No clutter. No noise. Hush, this could be heaven happening. When the moon finally sets the Milky Way takes on a greater intensity, with breathtaking beauty. It often makes me feel like I am in this big black igloo, roofed with a billion stars. Yes, a billion stars, twinkling in the darkness. Several times I have said to myself, "I am convinced that this is certainly one of the Seven Wonders of the World." I am totally captured by the beauty of the dark night. Being back home, at the farm, has made me realize that in the city I do not see the stars at all. In fact, I often forget that they exist for they are hidden by city lights.

Living in the city, a place of street lights, has made me realize that those who live in their particular lights are not capable of seeing a whole lot—they miss the beauty of a billion stars shining up above the sky. What they see is just a blank sky—"blinded by their own lights." Indeed those outside the darkness fear the darkness and name the darkness as evil, backward, dangerous and without light. They are often unsettled by the darkness, by the unknown, feeling that something is going to come out of the darkness and grab them. The fear of the darkness is thus the fear of the Other. It is the fear of another power, unknown power. Consequently, modern cities have street lights. The art of carrying a lamp or torch[3] or the use of any form of light is the desire to suppress this different power. In short, most contemporary cities are built around fear of the darkness, which unfortunately leads to more "blindness" than seeing. It is the same fear perspective that makes us take a torch outside to light our way out. When we pick a torch or lamp, it seems better, but in fact it becomes worse since we become further limited. We get to see only within the narrow route of our light/s, while all that is outside our lights becomes even darker, un-seeable, unknowable, scary. If you switch your light off and wait some minutes, however, you will soon realize that, in fact, you can see better in the dark—you can see that there is in fact light in the darkness.

These experiences have made me think deeply about the obvious—the long and persistent image of the African continent as "the dark continent." The image often carries all that we know way too well in the colonial characterization of the Other—savagery, barbarism, backwardness, illness, evil force, uncivilized, unknown, death, failure, infancy. The print world, the TV and writers, from all walks of disciplines– educational, political, cultural and economic structures—are ever so faithful and consistent in projecting the African Continent as the "Dark Continent." It is a stereotype that in fact sanctions and maintains the exclusion of the continent academically, politically, culturally, and economically. In this essay, I seek to highlight how the modern colonial cultural archive constructed the Others and their spatial places—focusing on the construction of Africa and its people. In his book, *Decolonizing Biblical Studies: A View From the Margins,* Fernando Segovia writes that the "tradition of Western empire-building was accompanied by a very prominent socioreligious dimension as well. . . . The Western missionary movement."[4] Following on Segovia's observation, this chapter seeks to highlight how biblical readers of the modern colonial times (that is missionaries) were central to constructing the Other negatively and how their constructions were adopted by many celebrated academic thinkers and writers, such as Georg Hegel, Joseph Conrad, and Sigmund Freud. While several missionaries will be commented upon, I will use the case of John Mackenzie to highlight that Western bible readers of modern times were integral participants in the construction of the colonial cultural archive. In conclusion, I will return to my introduction to highlight the art of playing in the dark,[5] as an integral part of decolonizing biblical studies, and, indeed, several other academic disciplines that were informed by modern colonial cultural archive.

CHAMPIONS OF THE COLONIAL CULTURAL ARCHIVE

Now Back to Africa as the "dark continent." First, a brief history about the concept is in order. Africa received its appellation, the "dark continent," from Henry Stanley, a naturalized American who was commissioned to find the missionary David Livingstone. Stanley returned to explore the rivers and lakes of central Africa, recording his adventures in the book *Through the Dark Continent* in 1877.[6] He published another volume in 1890 entitled *In Darkest Africa: Quest, Rescue and Retreat of Emin Governor of Equitima*, where he opens his book by saying "thick shadows fall upon the distant land and over the silent sea and oppress our heads as we glide away through the dying light towards the *dark continent*."[7] Stanley gave detailed descriptions of his journey each day—describing the events, the land, the people and his encounters so much so that seemingly nothing remains outside his documentary pen. Indeed his pen is the colonizing instrument, for African people and their lands seemingly come to exist only within his documentary framework. In his journey, Stanley encounters an impressive King Mtesa in the region of Uganda. He writes that King "Mtesa has impressed me as being an intelligent and distinguished prince. . . . I think I see in him light that *shall lighten darkness in this region*."[8] But for Mtesa to achieve this task, Stanley does not only insist that he needs the "hearty sympathies that Europe can give him," he also vows that "I shall destroy his belief in Islam and teach him the doctrines of Jesus of Nazareth."[9] Stanley's journeys into the African continent were inspired by the missionary David Livingstone, who made it his calling to mobilize the colonization of the Continent through Christianity, Commerce and Civilization. Stanley peddles the ideology of his mentor.

The writings of Stanley inspired another colonizing pen to continue spinning the myth of the so-called "dark continent." In 1908, Joseph Conrad wrote his novel, *Heart of Darkness*.[10] To read Joseph Conrad's novel after reading Stanley's books, is to be unwittingly thrown into the synoptic gospels of colonialism. Redactional Criticism is in order. Conrad's language, plot, tone, setting, description and events are closely modeled on Stanley's travel narratives. It is the description of the land, its people, rivers, sailing, hostile encounters, friendly support, disease, death, barbarism, savagery, and suffering with an unstoppable determination to get into Africa. Both writers evoke impending and increasingly foreboding dangers and darkness. *Heart of Darkness* features Marlow, who is sent to find and bring Kurtz, an agent in charge of an ivory trading post in the interior of central Africa. Kurtz is sick but unwilling to leave. While Conrad is somewhat critical towards colonialism, he nevertheless subscribes to it. Describing the violence of colonialism, Conrad holds, "it was just robbery with violence, aggravated murder on great scale, and men going at it blind . . . as it is proper for those who tackle the *darkness*."[11] He goes on to say, "the conquest of the earth which mostly means the taking it away from those who have a different complexion or slightly flatter nose than ourselves is not a pretty thing when you look into it too much."[12] Nevertheless, Conrad's *Heart of Darkness* does not grant the colonized Africans any agency or humanity, for his narrative depiction stands among the most memorable colonial art of mute, infantilized savages in the darkness and the beginning of time—not yet fully formed mature people. Indeed at times in Conrad's novel African people are characterized as inseparable from trees. Although Kurtz finally gets into the ship, he dies on the way. Kurtz leaves a report about Africa, summarily recommending: "Exterminate all the brutes."[13] *Heart of Darkness* thus weaves and extends the blanket of fear and subjugation, the ideology of subjecting those who are supposedly in the dark, by inviting Eurocentric lights of salvation—a role that it assigns to Western women characters of colonizing countries. While Stanley and Conrad's travel narratives were written more than a century ago, the image of Africa as the "dark continent" has not gone away, as attested, for example, the numerous movies and safari videos posted on YouTube. Similarly, the recently produced and massively popular novels of the Scottish writer Alexander McCall Smith flirt with the same.[14] In so doing, these contemporary works of art tap into the psychology of millions of Western readers, who subscribe to this image. What I found even more weird—to say the least—is that as I was writing this paper, my computer kept underlining the phrase "dark continent" in green, because in its memory it is a name which must be written in capital letters!

With these two writers, Stanley and Conrad, we have some of the earliest and most consistent construction of Africa as the "dark continent." In Stanley's massive volumes in particular we also have some of the earliest attestation of how African people and the continent come under the modern European gaze and textual description, so much so that, nothing of it must be left outside the surveillance and documenting eye of the white explorer—plants, rivers, mountains, people, cultures, dress, food, behavior, houses. Travel narratives, diary entries, letters, reports, official documents and books were central to this project. Colonial devotees of sorts, missionaries, traders, soldiers, wives, and explorers of all sorts wrote the Bible of colonialism and contributed with dedication to the chapter on the "dark continent." This becomes the Eurocentric textualization of Africa and its people in the framework of the "dark continent." It becomes a self-referencing and self-sustaining archive that continues to proclaim the Continent as "the dark continent," ideologically and structurally.

This ambi-dexterous spinning of the rhetoric of dark Africa was crucial for legitimating the so-called three Cs—Christianity, Commerce and Civilization—championed by David Livingstone. There was determination that nothing must escape the documentary eye of the colonial traveler. In this new invention of Africa,[15] Stanley and Conrad were but two individuals in a huge gang of colonizers, all dedicated to writing Africa and its people as the "dark continent." To focus on Stanley and Conrad, while leaving out some venerated academic thinkers, such as Georg Hegel (1770–1831) and Sigmund Freud (1856–1939), might be tantamount to casting a net that catches small fish while big fish get away. Freud and Hegel, the celebrated academic icons, generously indulged in this discourse. Freud spoke of an adult women's sexuality as the "dark continent,"[16] thus demonstrating that his theoretical framework fully draws from the colonial cultural archive and highlighting its gendered character as well. Hegel, an imminent German philosopher whose ideas supposedly revolutionized European philosophy, was elaborate. In his 1830–1831 lectures, Hegel made some of his most damning philosophical statements about the Continent and its people. I quote Hegel at length:

> The peculiarly African character is difficult to comprehend, for the very reason that in reference to it we must give up the principle which naturally accompanies all our ideas—the category of Universality. In Negro life the characteristic point is the fact that consciousness has not yet attained to the realization of any substantial objective existence—as for example, God, or Law—in which the interest of man's volition is involved and in which he realizes his own being. The distinction between himself as an individual and the universality of his universal being, the African, in uniform, underdeveloped oneness of his existence has not yet attained; so the Knowledge of an absolute Being, an Other and a Higher than himself, is entirely wanting. The Negro, as already observed, exhibits the natural man in his completely wild and untamed state . . . there is nothing harmonious with humanity to be found in this character. . . .

> The copious and circumstantial accounts of Missionaries completely confirm this.[17]

If one reads Stanley and Conrad's narrative constructions of the "dark continent" together with Hegel's perspective, it is easy to see that theirs was an elaboration of the famed philosopher's standpoint. Of note here is that Hegel is consistent with other colonial gangsters in characterising Africa and its people as lacking divine knowledge, inhuman and immature. But above all, it is notable that Hegel refers to the missionary writings to substantiate his stance about Africa and its people. It was a whole symphony of Western writers operating within and constructing the colonial cultural discourse. These writings were not meant for or addressed to Africans. Rather it was Europeans writing to each other about Africa—substantiating why they need and should colonize the Continent for their own ends. To read these narratives as an African is to walk in a nightmare of racism and eurocentricism. It is, to use Phyllis Trible's words, to read "texts of terror."[18] It requires a skill of reading through Rahab's prism—a concept I developed in my earlier writing that involves sensitivity to both patriarchal and imperialist discourses at the same time.[19]

The Case of John Mackenzie

In what follows I want to highlight the construction of darkness in the *Papers of John Mackenzie*, who was a missionary from 1854–1899 among Batswana, but who also served several places in Southern Africa such as present day South Africa, Zambia and Zimbabwe. Of course, he was not the first missionary in Southern Africa since he stood in the whole line of the likes of Dr. J. T. van der Kemp (arrived in Africa, 1799), John Campbell (1812), Robert Moffat (1817), and David Livingstone (1841), among others. Moffat translated the Setswana Bible during the years 1817–1857, making it the first complete Bible translation in Southern Africa. The translation indicated that African languages, and cultures, were being moved from orality to textuality—and not in their own terms. Accordingly, in 1840 when Robert Moffat went to print his translations of the New Testament, he preached a sermon that highlighted his full embrace of the rhetoric of the darkness. The title of the sermon was "Africa, or the Gospel of Light Shining in the Midst of Heathen Darkness."[20] The title itself speaks volumes, for the gospel and Africa are posed as stark opposites. In an earlier paper, I have analyzed the contents of Moffat's Bible translation, highlighting how it was informed by the colonial rhetoric of darkness, as attested by its translation of indigenous divine figures as demons.[21]

For now, it is important to sketch and examine how the rhetoric of darkness was narrativized by the Scottish missionary, John Mackenzie. The analysis will be based on the *Papers of John Mackenzie*, selected and edited by Anthony Dachs in 1975. Having had a collection of more than three thousand written items, Mackenzie is noted for having been a voluminous writer/documenter of all things African, which is another way of saying he was an active contributor to the colonial cultural archive.[22]

In his application for the position of a missionary, dated 16 June 1854, John Mackenzie wrote that: "After consideration I was led to the conviction that my path of duty lay in becoming a Minister or Missionary of the Gospel. My mind has recently been more particularly directed to the condition of our fellow-men *in heathen lands*; and it seems to me that a Christian can engage in no more glorious work than in efforts '*to illuminate the dark places of the earth*' with the light of the Gospel of peace."[23] Unfortunately, Mackenzie's application was turned down. On the 16th of August 1854, Mackenzie diarized his disappointment and determination by writing directly to God: "O Lord Jesus, when I turn to *those lands of heathen darkness* where thou art not known, where Thy wondrous love has not been told, and *find people lying in idolatry*, I desire more earnestly to cry to Thee that Thou wouldst rise and reign in the hearts of men in all lands and may the messengers of the gospel be prosperous in their blessed mission."[24]

Mackenzie resubmitted his application a year later (19 July 1855) stating that, "I feel more deeply than ever that duty calls on me, not only to preach the Gospel but to publish it to a certain class of *my fellow-men viz., the heathen*."[25] Mackenzie's application was approved and he went into training. In his ordination speech of 1858, Mackenzie maintained the same rhetoric. He held that "As to *civilization* and to temporal interests of the people, I conceive that I am *furthering both* when I preach *the gospel*, for if a man becomes a Christian he cannot continue to live in the *habits of a heathen*."[26] In these quotes, which are characteristic of his future writing, it is notable that Mackenzie casts his targets and their lands in a consistent web of heathenism and darkness. He perceives his targets as stupefied "people lying in idolatry." He proposes to "illuminate" the dark places of the earth using a particular torch—the gospel and civilization, which, as he says, he does not differentiate but sees them as a continuum. The twinning of the gospel and his version of civilization is consistent with his predecessors, Livingstone and Stanley.

But what was darkness and what was heathenism? It is when one reads his letters from Southern Africa, his "mission station," that his idea of darkness becomes outlined. Moreover, it is notable that Mackenzie reported the words of other speakers from his own perspective. Mackenzie's language allows us to further understand the construction of darkness, which he sharply contrasts with the gospel, and its impact on the Batswana that he served—and to some extent the resistance he encountered. Thus in a letter that he wrote to Rev. Moffat on the 27 June 1862, he writes:

> It is now more than a year since Montsioe the chief assumed an attitude of open hostility towards the Christian subjects. Matters were hastened by the usually large number of young people who under religious impression, ceased to take an interest in those subjects which may engage the attention of the young in heathen town. When these enquiries were about to be enrolled in classes and thus take position as "*bathu ba bhuku*" (that is people of the book), the chief resolved to prevent their doing so. His decision was that they must first observe *the usual customs* of their forefathers and especially that they must join the *reed dance*, and afterwards might "join the words of God." Moleme and the disciples were opposed to this course, as one which virtually obliged them to serve two masters—a thing which, they said, God's word told them no one could do. . . . This was followed by another "crime," their refusal to join digging the "*garden of rain*" (*tsimo ya pula*). This is, as you are aware, a *heathen* ceremony, and those who take part in it are of course abettors of rain making."[27]

Two of these young people were sons of King Montsioe. They are documented by Mackenzie as pleading with their father, saying, "You are still our father and in all things belonging to your kingdom we are still your most willing subjects; only concerning *our old customs and the Word of God*, we have believed the latter—we have 'entered into the Word—and therefore may not join in the *dark deeds* of our forefathers, who did not have the knowledge which we possess."[28] Notably here these sons speak the missionary language of darkness and heathenism. (And notably, too, Mackenzie's description is thoroughly male, marking, the structural marginalisation of women in modern colonial economy.) Similarly, King (Chief) Mahura, who supposedly was begging to have a missionary posted to his people, spoke in the language of Mackenzie saying, "My people are still in *darkness*; my children are living like *wild beasts of the field*. Other chiefs make me ashamed when they tell me their sons can read and write both in Setswana and Dutch."[29] In these quotes it becomes clear that darkness and heathenism are equated to the usual indigenous customs of the people. Among these are the reed dance (Bojale/Bogwera initiation schools for teenagers), rituals of rainmaking and hunting. The light that shines in this darkness in this context is the book (Bible), the word of God, the capacity to read and write. Mackenzie proposed to light this darkness with the gospel and European civilization, for as he underlined, "if a man becomes a Christian, he cannot continue to live in the habits of a heathen."[30] The saving light and the darkness are posited as two opposites that have no meeting point, for one cannot serve two masters. In the letters of Batswana to the Newspaper *Mahoko a Becwana* that ran between 1883–1896, the Batswana constantly challenge the negative characterization of their traditions.[31] Similarly, Kgosi (chief) Montsioe does not see the biblical faith and Setswana traditions as two irreconcilable opposites. He does not even prioritize biblical teachings over Setswana ones. Rather, he insists that his sons "must first observe *the usual customs* . . . they must join the *reed dance*, and *afterward* might "join the words of God."

The continuum of the gospel with western civilization as magnificent lights in the darkness meant that western clothes, books, wagons, cheap beads, four corner houses, mirrors, sunken wells, schools, churches, Bibles, and food would become important ingredients of illuminating the dark and heathen people and their lands.[32] They would be the transactions for taking the land from those whose nose are flatter and whose skin color is darker, to use Conrad's words. In his book, *Stitches on Time,* Sauraby Dube analyses these colonial entanglements in India (Chhattisgarh) pointing out that "The master language of reason and race contracted lasting links between civilization and the Savior."[33] He points out that "an integral part of the evangelical project of the missionary was also committed to civilizing converts through the initiation of a set of practices revolving around building, clothes, writing and the printed word."[34] These practices such as food, eating ice cream, crispy white table clothes were, what Sauraby Dube calls, "a wider creation of home-cooked hegemonies" that constituted what he entitled the "travelling light"—marching on in the hands of its bearers to illuminate the dark heathen places and people. Jean and John Comaroff, who have dedicated their careers to analyzing the colonial encounter in Southern Africa, argue that it was not always political and military power that made the most deepening impact, but rather these travelling lights of gospel and Western civilization. They hold that "what distinguished the reports of missionaries from the self-effacing travel narratives was their personalized, heroic form, for as soldiers of the spiritual empire, their biographies—their battles with forces of the darkness—linked individual achievement to the conquests of civilization . . . here a naturalizing language presented the African landscape as virgin and devoid of society and history, waiting to be watered and tilled by the evangelical efforts."[35]

As one whose gaze, documentation and narrativization of Batswana lands and its people was a construction of heathen and in darkness—thereby inviting a certain illumination—Mackenzie became mesmerized by his own prophecy. Teaching the gospel/bible was not enough. He became restless. He wanted the European civilization component, in the form of colonization, to be realized to complete this circle. The political context of numerous conflicts that characterized Southern Africa at the time (the tussles between black people and the Dutch Boers in the interior) came handy to John Mackenzie. He began to persistently call for formal British colonization of Batswana. I must point out that this had very little to do with the context on the ground, for it was consistent with Mackenzie's ordination speech. It was a position he held even before departure. Indeed, Mackenzie was not alone in propounding a continuum of the gospel with European civilization, for in his letters to John Kirk, Livingstone admittedly said that he brings professionals of all sorts with him, in his quest to open Africa for commerce, Christianity and civilization for, as he said, "That you may have a clear idea of my objects, I may state from the start that they are more than meets the eye. They are not merely exploratory... . I hope it may result in an English colony."[36]

Consequently Mackenzie's papers eloquently and repeatedly testify that the gospel and Eurocentric civilization were two faces of the same coin. John Mackenzie, accordingly, did not hesitate to take the political office in March 1884, openly saying, "I am willing to give the Imperial Government my hearty and earnest service."[37] Operating within the continuum of gospel and Western civilization, Mackenzie explained that political "Commissionership means the social establishment of people in civilized life; the Tutorship means their moral and spiritual development and elevation. . . . I do not know which the greater work is. I aspire to honour doing both."[38] In his schema of things he had elaborate suggestions about the lands of those he held to be heathens in the dark. In a letter written to Colonel Lanyon, Mackenzie summarized his recommendations as follows: "In a word, then, my suggestion is proscribe the leaders and such as are disaffected to Government, but offer to all farmers under Jantye to become tenant-farmers under the Queen as owner of the country. Give them a lease for ten years, reserve the power then to renew the lease, or sell the farm to the tenant; or if he has proved incapable, eject him and let him sink to his own level among the inferior laboring class."[39]

Here with ease Mackenzie has no difficulty in making a recommendation that would dispossess indigenous people of their lands—which in his vision must now belong to the queen. When he lost his political post to Cecil John Rhodes, Mackenzie did not abandon his position. "Once more Mackenzie resorted to public action in Britain, returning to London in November 1885 to present his case personally. He called for crown Colony as far as Zambezi and for the establishment of a separate High Commissioner, freed from the influence of the Cape Government."[40] Indeed Botswana was finally declared a British Protectorate for other reasons (protection of the trade route to the north against Germans from the west, Portuguese from the east and Boers from the Cape Colony), but whatever, the end satisfied Mackenzie's deepest desire.

In the above sections, I have sought to highlight how the narrative of darkness was weaved in modern colonial times as a rhetorical device of legitimizing the domination of Africa and its people.[41] The rhetoric of darkness and heathenism sought to invite a certain illumination with the medicine of gospel and western civilization. The two became two faces of the same coin. The discourse of darkness is an ideology of alienating all that does not correspond with the west and to domination by creating "Western imitators." Above all, I have highlighted that Bible readers have been central to the construction of the colonizing cultural archive, which informed other academic disciplines, such as literature, philosophy and psychology. Concerning this modern historical context, Segovia underlines that: "From the point of view of biblical criticism, therefore, it is clear that the academic study of the texts of ancient Judaism and early Christianity, given the formation and consolidation of the discipline in the course of the nineteenth century, parallels the second major wave of Western missionary movement as well as the transition period to the second, high phase of Western imperialism and colonialism. . . . Consequently, the shadow of empire in the production of modern readings should also be underlined."[42]

Acknowledging the shadow of the empire in biblical studies calls for the art of being able to play in the dark, to seek in the dark, and to see the breath-taking million stars shining in the dark. It is the art of decolonizing the darkness.[43]

Notes

1. Fernando F. Segovia, *Decolonizing Biblical Studies: A View From the Margins* (Maryknoll: Orbis, 2000), 128.

2. Vincent Wimbush, "Interpreters—Enslaving/Enslaved/Runagate," *JBL* 130 (2011): 5–24.

3. "Torch" indicates what is known in the United States as a flashlight.

4. Segovia, *Decolonizing Biblical Studies*, 127. This paper is written in honor of Fernando F. Segovia.

5. Toni Morrison, *Playing in the Dark: Whiteness and the Literary Imagination* (New York: Vintage, 1993).

6. H. M. Stanley, *Through the Dark Continent*, vol. 1 (New York: Dove, 1975 [1877]).

7. H. M. Stanley, *In Darkest Africa: Quest, Rescue and Retreat of Emin Governor of Equitima* (Toronto: Scribner, 1890), 32. Current and all subsequent emphases are added.

8. Stanley, *Through the Dark*, 152.

9. Ibid.

10. Joseph Conrad, *Heart of Darkness* (New York: Bantam, 1981).

11. Ibid., 9.

12. Ibid.

13. Ibid., 76.

14. Alexander McCall Smith, *The No. 1 Lady Detective Agency* (New York: Anchor, 2002), 91, 223, 230, 234.

15. V. Y. Mudimbe, *The Invention of Africa: Gnosis, Philosophy, and the Order of Knowledge* (Bloomington: Indiana University Press, 1988).

16. Sigmund Freud, *The Question of Lay Analysis (The Standard Edition)* (New York: Norton, 1926).

17. G. W. F. Hegel, *The Philosphy of History*, trans. J. Jibree (New York: Dover, 1956), 93.

18. Phyllis Trible, *Texts of Terror: Literary-Feminist Readings of Biblical Narratives*, Overtures to Biblical Theology (Philadelphia: Fortress Press, 1984).

19. Musa Dube, *Postcolonial Feminist Interpretation of the Bible* (Saint Louis: Chalice, 2000).

20. Robert Moffat, "Africa, or the Gospel of Light Shining in the Midst of Heathen Darkness" (London: John Snox, 1840).

21. Dube, *Postcolonial Feminist Interpretation*, 213–19.

22. A. J. Dachs, ed., *Papers of John Mackenzie* (Johannesburg: Witwatersrand University Press, 1975), xiii.

23. Ibid., 68.

24. Ibid.

25. Ibid., 70.

26. Ibid., 72.

27. Ibid., 100–101.

28. Ibid., 100.

29. Ibid., 99.

30. Ibid., 72.

31. Part Themba Mgadla and Stephen C. Volz, ed., *Words of Batswana: Letters to Mahoka a Becwana 1883–1896*, trans. P. Mgadla and S. C. Volz (Vlaeberg: van Riebeeck Society, 2006), 122–231.

32. Jean Comaroff and John Comaroff, *Of Revelation and Revolution*, vol. 2: *The Dialetics of Modernity on South African Frontier* (Chicago: University of Chicago Press, 1997).

33. Sauraby Dube, *Stitches on Time: Colonial Textures and Postcolonial Tangles* (Durham: Duke University Press, 2004), 32.

34. Ibid., 41.

35. Jean Comaroff and John Camaroff, "Through the Looking Glass: Colonial Encounters of the First Kind," *Journal of Historical Sociology* 1 (1988): 6–30.

36. Reginald Foskett, ed., *The Zambezi Journal and Letters of Dr. John Kirk, 1858–1863*, vol. 1 (Edinburgh: Oliver & Boyd, 1965), 309.

37. Dachs, *Papers of John Mackenzie*, 125.

38. Ibid., 133.

39. Ibid., 112.

40. Ibid., 153.

41. Musa Dube, "Savior of the World But Not of This World: A Post-colonial Reading of Spatial Construction in John," in *The Post-colonial Bible* (ed. R. S. Sugirtharajah; Sheffield: Sheffield Academic Press, 1998), 118–135.

42. Segovia, *Decolonizing Biblical Studies*, 128.

43. As reflected in Segovia's title, *Decolonizing Biblical Studies*.

3

"The Others" in Galatians

Texts and the Negotiation of Identity

Jeremy Punt

Fernando Segovia's concern with the Other has seen him develop a hermeneutical stance that is at once alert to otherness in biblical texts, yet also capable of exploring it in multifaceted ways.[1] He has gone beyond description of characteristics of postcolonial biblical criticism to develop a set of constructive proposals which he relates to other hermeneutical programmes. Central to his argument has been the promotion of a hermeneutical model of otherness and engagement, which views texts, readings of texts and their readers as others—not to be bypassed, overwhelmed or manipulated but to be acknowledged, respected and engaged.[2] This he supplements by a reading strategy of intercultural criticism, which approaches the same threefold of texts, readings of texts, and their readers as literary or aesthetic, rhetorical or strategic, and ideological or political products, which have to be analyzed as well as critiqued in dialogue.[3] The textual posture of intercultural criticism he later defines as a strategy of "reading across," attempting to break with the scientific reading strategies' characterized by competitiveness, hierarchy, empiricism, and objectivism.[4] Inspired and stimulated by Segovia's work, and in furthering the critical dialogue that he encourages, this contribution focuses on Paul's engagement with Otherhood or Otherness in his use of the Scriptures of Israel, particularly in Galatians.

Both self-consciousness as well as a certain portrayal of the Others and their Otherness informs the identity claimed and negotiated by people and groups. This framing of identity renders interesting results when applied to ancient times and to the New Testament texts such as the Pauline letters. When Paul concluded that he together with the Galatian addressees were like Isaac children

45

of the promise (*kata Isaak epaggelias tekna este*; Gal. 4:28), he claimed Abraham as his ancestor, and as ancestor of all followers of Jesus.[5] With Abraham as husband of both Sarah and Hagar, and father of both Isaac and Ishmael, Paul had to resort to qualified distinctions. Through a constructive appeal to Sarah as well as by distancing the Jesus followers from Hagar's lineage, Paul laid claim to an identity reliant upon the construction of the self as much as of the Other. But Paul's claim does not reside only in his and his fellow believers' alignment with Abraham through the free woman, but also in an attempt to establish their identity as contrary to that of "children of the slave" (*ouk esmen paidiskēs tekna*; 4:31). Examples of self-definition and constructing the identity of others can be multiplied in Galatians, as processes in which memory and texts are situated in a context(s) marked by unequal relations of power.[6]

Constructions of Ancient Identity through Memory and Texts

Social identity and social memory studies have enormous implications for the nature of New Testament hermeneutics, as well as for the manner in which research in the discipline is conducted. Such studies also fit in well with and complement Segovia's notion of "intercultural criticism." Social identity theory calls attention to the formation of group mind-sets and accompanying insider-outsider group relationships. It was developed to address issues of group prejudice, where groups' reasoning and behavior are influenced and distorted at a larger scale and through complex mechanisms, including the construction of shared social values. Dealing with the intricate relationship between human psychological functioning at individual levels and large-scale social processes and events which affect and are affected by such functioning, social identity theory wants to understand the conditions within which individuals choose a certain (group) identity and act accordingly as members of a group. Such group identity is not dependent upon group cohesion or physical and direct interaction with other people, and may involve individuals who do not even associate with the same group.[7]

Both social identity and social memory theories are valuable in tracking both how and why traditions formed and changed, as well as how they were maintained and abolished. Identity, including ethnic identity, is a social construct, construed according to mutable descriptions of and expectations for groups.[8] The collective memory of a group and its sense of identity are reciprocally related, memory and identity feeding off one another, and therefore those who belong to the same group share (or at least ascribe to) the same past.[9] Borne out by how group characteristics can be dropped or added over time, the differences connected to an ethnic identity are real and observable, but granting power to such differences is synthetic and can be regulated.[10]

An appeal to memory in the accompaniment of texts as devices invoked to argue for a certain identity was neither unique to Paul nor foreign in the New Testament world. Yet, the Scriptures of Israel were primary, even if not the sole, constituent artifacts in Pauline cultural memory. The Scriptures were both indispensable for thinking about group identity and cohesion as well as instrumental for Paul in construing and reconstructing identity.[11] Paul's negotiation of the identity of the early Jesus-follower communities through the Scriptures did not depend upon what today would be called meticulous exegesis. Paul's use of these texts comes closer to invoking them as significant handles or parameters of memory, memory about God, the faithful and events of the past, than historical source documents.[12] A primary value in treating texts as memory is the emphasis on remembering as being not so much about the restoration of some original self, but rather *re*-membering, of putting past and present selves together, moment by moment, in a process of provisional (re)construction.[13] The notion of cultural memory which attempts to link the three elements, memory (the contemporized past), culture, and the group (or community) to each other[14] puts Paul's use of the Scriptures of Israel in perspective, particularly in their use to negotiate the identity of the early communities of Jesus followers.

Additionally, recent studies are favoring a more nuanced approach to the ancients' notion of identity, suggesting that an identity politics construed by and large in opposition to real or imagined Others is too one-sided and simplistic. "[A]ncient societies, while certainly acknowledging differences among peoples (indeed occasionally emphasizing them) could also visualize themselves as part of a broader cultural heritage, could discover or invent links with other societies, and could couch their own historical memories in terms of a borrowed or appropriated past. When ancients reconstructed their roots or fashioned their history, they often did so by associating themselves with the legends and traditions of others."[15]

This does not imply, of course, that the Other was unimportant to ancient identity constructions and negotiations, as the Other remained an important if not always explicit or direct reference point. It does mean, though, that the way in which the Other was appropriated was not simply through creating or using existing contrasts, as Others and their traditions were not only challenged, vilified, or denied but also taken up and retooled.

Paul's appropriation of "his" and "his people's" Abraham narrative for the new communities of Jesus followers would not have been out of the ordinary. While Paul's language about the Others was less than favorable—among other things, he refers to them as "slave children"—and his rhetorical strategy sharply pointed, challenging and maybe even decrying their tradition *and* position, his position was not based on a simple binary contrast.[16] Kirk's depiction of the constant interplay between narrative and communal identity is appropriate for understanding the role of the Abraham narrative in Galatians and the Pauline letters generally.[17] "Through narration of its master narrative a group continually reconstitutes itself as a coherent community, and as it moves forward through its history it aligns its fresh experiences with this master narrative, as well as vice versa."[18] In Galatians, appeals to the Other play a substantial role in Paul's definition of the community's identity.

OTHERING IN GALATIANS AND IMPERIAL INFLUENCES

The largely oral world of the early followers of Jesus was replete with various traditions and cultures, in many instances including those from the Jewish context. The concern with identity in the light of Jesus Christ, or at least for negotiating such an identity, is prominent in the Pauline letters.[19] Groups such as Paul and the Galatian Jesus-followers increasingly carved out a language and an ethos which incorporated beliefs about Jesus Christ, while these beliefs also structured their language and ethos. In this way they formatted a social world part of which was the construction of a particular identity. It was an on-going dynamic and non-monolithic process, but not unlike those of other groups during the same period.

GALATIANS AMID POWERFUL INFLUENCES

Paul's striving to articulate a new identity, built in part upon the vestiges of his own history and that of the Jewish people, took place within the Roman imperial context and its contemporary scripts of power. Those who resisted the contemporary dominance through visions of future utopia nonetheless were obliged to use the language and images of the current social system to formulate and construct a new world that could be considered attainable and conceivable.[20] Similarly, Paul's re-descriptions of his communities' identity took up the scripts of the religiously influential (Jewish), the politically dominant (Roman), and the socio-culturally normative (Greek/Hellenistic).

In line with ancient practices and an imperial context that negotiated identity through appropriating the identity formulations or frameworks of other groups, and then reinterpreting and tailoring an identity for the new group, Paul often relied on the biblical Abraham narratives (see Rom. 4, 9, 11; 2 Cor. 11; and Gal. 3–4). However, in Paul's formulations the Abraham narratives no longer authorize a specific and special relationship between God and Israel and their election in particular. Paul reinterprets Abraham as more than an exemplary figure of faith for Jesus followers, with the Abraham narrative re-appropriated as sanctioning discourse for the new communities with which Paul is involved. Such is also the nature of Paul's argument in Galatians and in Gal 4:21—5:1 in particular, which is briefly illustrated here.

CONJURING UP OTHERNESS

Otherness is present and constructed in various ways in Galatians. First, Paul's own identity is characterized by otherness at different levels. On the one hand Paul's status as self-proclaimed apostle to the Gentiles (for example, 2:2, 7) did not mean relinquishing his Jewish identity (2:15). On the other hand Paul's mission brought about his presence in alien territory. "[Paul] came to understand what it means to be an 'other,' so much so that he partly became an 'other.'"[21] Regardless of Paul's implicit (for example, Gal. 3:6-9) and explicit (Gal. 4:28) claims of sharing in Abraham's legacy, his letter to the Galatians indicates his concern against being sidelined from that legacy and its accompanying traditions and identity: his concern to remain within the "Israel of God" (Gal. 6:12-16).

Paul's own realization of sliding toward the boundary of otherness notwithstanding, he engaged such strategies in his own arguments as well. Apart from his self-implication in othering, Paul's strategy in negotiating identity by way of emphasizing otherness resembles imperial othering in a number of respects. Assuming the letter is directed to the southern Roman province of Galatia, the imperial context provides an important setting for understanding its othering-discourse.

Paul, in the second place, and with little-concealed irritation if not agitation towards them, referred to the letter recipients as "foolish Galatians" (Ō anoetai Galatai; Gal. 3:1). If the letter indeed was directed to a community located in the Roman province of Galatia[22] this may have served as an ethnic slur. For the citizens of the Roman province to be addressed as "Galatians," and "foolish" on top of that, would be a grave insult, an ethnic insult invoking connotations of being equated with the descendants of the rather infamous Celtic people of the North. More than ethnicity was involved, however, as at the time an accusation of foolishness was a gendered insult incurring downward slippage,[23] with Galatian men aligned with one of the stock traits ascribed to women. Further still, used in a social setting where the Roman concept of "idiotic" or "foolish" dominated, Paul's remark framed his relationship with the Galatian congregation in terms reminiscent of empire.

Third, Paul othered another group whose identity is unknown but caused him much anguish and even anger (see Gal. 5:12; possibly also Gal. 1:8-9).[24] It is probably the close proximity of Paul and his distracters, in many respects the similarity between them,[25] that contributed to Paul's agitated over-reaction in Galatians. Opinions differ about the origin and identity of those Paul identified as his opponents in Galatia.[26] It has been suggested that they were emissaries from Antioch or Jerusalem who were tracking Paul since he left Antioch,[27] raising the question whether they were the same group elsewhere referred to, as in Phil. 3:2 (dogs, doers of evil deeds); 2 Cor. 11:5 and 12:11 (super-apostles); or 2 Cor. 11:15 (ministers of Satan)? With the question as to their own identity wide open, those Paul identified as his distracters appear to have held a different opinion from his own regarding the criteria and nature of the identity of Jesus-followers.

EMPIRE, SCRIPTURES, AND THE RECYCLING OF IDENTITY

An important, constant element in Paul's identity claims was the Scriptures of Israel, whether concerning self-identity (Gal. 2:15-21); the identity of community members (Gal. 3:6-9) or of the distracters (Gal. 5:12; 6:12-13), and notwithstanding the correlation with imperial, imposed identity. However, in the end, the Scriptures of Israel also become the Other in Galatians, in an intricate and complex way.[28] The Scriptures serve on the one hand a legitimating function while they on the other hand and at the same time were used against themselves. Very little if any of Paul's argument is not supported by claims from the Scriptures, as is particularly evident in Gal. 2:15-5:1. On the other hand, Paul used Scripture against itself too, as probably best seen in his deliberate (Gal. 4:24) allegorizing of the Abraham narrative (Gal. 4:21-5:1), and also in invoking law (Lev. 19:18 in Gal. 5:14) in a letter aimed against Law (Gal. 3:24-25).

Paul's recycling of the past through memory and scripture provides insight into his and his environment's cultural, political and social structure. Mendels relates different ways in which memory functions or is forced to function to the nature of the prevailing context in a nuanced way.[29] In this regard, a totalitarian state's enforcement of a specific memory amidst abundant pluralism of past memories in the religious sphere may help to explain Paul's invocation of Abraham memories in groups of Jesus followers in a geo-political context of recycled imperial Roman memories.

What does this say about Paul's negotiation of identity in Galatians? The link between the formation and evolution of biblical texts and the constantly changing constructions of identity are self-evident.[30] However, if Stimpson[31] is correct in arguing that "[a] mark of otherness is one's inability to shape one's psychological, social and cultural identity," the sharp side of negotiating identity and Otherness especially has to be acknowledged. In fact, as "[a]cts of identity formation are themselves acts of violence,"[32] similarity in terms of identity already implies difference in the sense that the constructing of self always invokes and construes the others, the outsiders.[33] Paul's letters and the other New Testament documents were constructed in many social locations, and perceptions of identity, of who or what constituted "self" and "Other," were foundational during such constructive energies.

Notes

1. Paper prepared for a volume honouring Fernando F. Segovia on his sixtieth-fifth birthday.

2. Fernando F. Segovia, "Toward a Hermeneutics of the Diaspora: A Hermeneutics of Otherness and Engagement," in *Reading from this Place*, vol. 1: *Social Location and Biblical Interpretation in the United States*, ed. Fernando F. Segovia and Mary Ann Tolbert (Minneapolis: Fortress Press, 1995), 57–73. An example of othering the social setting of texts is when it is used as mere background or illustration in literary representation. See Davina C. Lopez's argument on first-century visual culture informing the interpretation of Paul's letters: "Visualizing Significant Otherness: Reimagining Paul(ine Studies) through Hybrid Lenses," in *The Colonized Apostle: Paul through Postcolonial Eyes*, ed., Christopher D. Stanley, Paul in Critical Contexts (Minneapolis: Fortress Press, 2011), 74–94.

3. Fernando F. Segovia, "Toward Intercultural Criticism: A Reading Strategy from the Diaspora," in *Reading from This Place*, vol. 2: *Social Location and Biblical Interpretation in Global Perspective*, ed. Fernando F. Segovia and Mary Ann Tolbert (Minneapolis: Fortress Press, 1995), 303–30.

4. Fernando F. Segovia, "Reading-across: Intercultural Criticism and Textual Posture," in *Interpreting Beyond Borders*, ed., Fernando F. Segovia, The Bible and Postcolonialism 3 (Sheffield: Sheffield Academic, 2000), 59–83.

5. While Paul's own claim upon Abrahamic lineage would not have raised eyebrows given his association with Jewish tradition (e. g., Gal 1:13-14 *emēn anastrophēn pote en tō Ioudaismō*; cf. Phil. 3:4-6), the inclusion of the Galatian community was another matter. Even scholars who argued for a sizable Jewish presence in Galatia do not see the makeup of the Jesus follower community as devoid of Gentiles by any means.

6. This, therefore, is not a study of Paul's "opponents" as such in Galatians or in general, but an investigation of the interplay between texts and identity, in Galatians in particular.

7. Henri Tajfel, "Introduction," in *Social Identity and Intergroup Relations*, ed. Henri Tajfel, European Studies in Social Psychology (New York: Cambridge University Press, 1982), 4; John C. Turner, "Toward a Cognitive Redefinition of the Social Group," in Tajfel, ed., *Social Identity and Intergroup Relations*, 15–40.

8. See Jan Assmann, "Collective Memory and Cultural Identity," *New German Critique* 65 (1995): 125–33; Jan Assman, *Religion and Cultural Memory: Ten Studies*, trans. R. Livingstone, Cultural Memory in the Present (Palo Alto: Stanford University Press, 2006); Doron Mendels, *Identity, Religion, and Historiography: Studies in Hellenistic History*, JSPSup 24 (Sheffield: Sheffield Academic), 1998; Doron Mendels, *Memory in Jewish, Pagan, and Christian Societies of the Graeco-Roman World*, Library of Second Temple Studies 45 (London: T&T Clark, 2004).

9. See Jan Assmann, "Cultural Memory: Script, Recollection, and Political Identity in Early Civilizations," *Historiography East and West* 1 (2003): 162–69; Santiago Guijarro, "Cultural Memory and Group Identity in Q," *BTB* 37 (2007): 92. Although Assmann can agree with Martin Walser that memories arise from within the individual, Assmann insists that memories that connect with society "make their way into the interstices of communication and, if only they are significant enough, they end up in the visible *outer* world of symbols, texts, rituals, and monuments, and form the basis of a cultural memory that can last hundreds or thousands of years," see *Religion and Cultural Memory*, 178.

10. In contrast, an essentialist position of identity such as found in attempts at an "ontology of Judaism" reduces ethnicity to irreducible qualities, appealing to bloodline and kinship, insisting upon demonstrable links to land, history, language, culture, religion or myth of origins. Lines between insider and outsiders are conceived as rigid and unbroken, with the boundaries themselves taking on a inviolable status. See Sze-kar Wan, "The Letter to the Galatians," in *A Postcolonial Commentary on the New Testament Writings*, ed., Fernando F. Segovia and R. S. Sugirtharajah, The Bible and Postcolonialism (New York: T&T Clark, 2007), 246–47.

11. J. Punt, "Identity, Memory, and Scriptural Warrant: Arguing Paul's Case," *JECH*, forthcoming.

12. Recent studies in memory stress that memory is susceptible to modification, since the interests driving it are generally closer connected to sense-making than factual accuracy. See Bernard C. Lategan, "History and Reality in the Interpretation of Biblical Texts," in *Konstruktion von Wirklichkeit: Beiträge aus geschichtstheoretischer, philosophischer und theologischer Perspektive*, ed. J. Schröter and A. Eddelbüttel, Theologische Bibliothek Töpelmann, 127 (Berlin: de Gruyter, 2004), 136.

13. On the one hand "Christian thought, behavior, attitudes, values, and self-understanding were forged textually," but on the other hand "the multiple self-representations we encounter in the texts are themselves constructs," Averil Cameron, *Christianity and the Rhetoric of Empire: The Development of Christian Discourse*, Sather Classical Lectures 57 (Berkeley: University of California Press, 1991), 21, 32. So too, "the Scriptures of Israel are themselves the expression of, and the consequence of, a process by which a coherent remembering of a common past and a shared experience of divine presence has been forged out of the inchoate multiple pasts, largely lost to us, of disparate peoples," see Judith M. Lieu, *Christian Identity in the Jewish and Graeco-Roman World* (Oxford: Oxford University Press, 2004), 67.

14. Assman, *Collective Memory and Cultural Identity*, 129.

15. Erich S. Gruen, *Rethinking the Other in Antiquity* (Princeton: Princeton University Press, 2011), 3–4.

16. However, it can be debated whether Paul's affirmation of Abraham as ancestor from the ranks of the Other and criticism of the contemporary Other does not imply Pauline criticism of the Other's interpretation and use of Abraham in "their" traditions and claims. Other questions remain, though, including: how, in what way, and by which mechanisms were existing identities appropriated and retooled for further use in (often) another context? Is it possible to adjudicate the success of such identity appropriation and dissemination strategies, and if so, by which measures?

17. Alan Kirk, "Social and Cultural Memory," in *Memory, Tradition, and Text: Uses of the Past in Early Christianity*, ed. Alan Kirk and Tom Thatcher, Semeia Studies 52 (Atlanta: SBL, 2005). The power of narrative allows communities to establish profound links that go beyond temporal or spatial limitations. Invoking and preserving narratives are often then means for communities to rise above unfamiliarity in time, space and experience, enticing people into a hitherto unknown

world. See Herbert Anderson and Edward Foley, *Mighty Stories, Dangerous Rituals: Weaving Together the Human and the Divine* (San Francisco: Jossey-Bass, 1998), 4. See Mary E. Hess, "The Bible and Popular Culture: Engaging Sacred Text in a World of Others," in *New Paradigms for Bible Study: The Bible in the Third Millennium*, ed., Robert M. Fowler, Edith Vogvogel Blumhofer, and Fernando F. Segovia (London: T&T Clark, 2004), 209. When narratives are claimed by a group with vested interests, the importance of the narratives increase vastly, along with the tension created regarding the agency of reauthoring the materials.

18. Kirk, "Social and Cultural Memory," 5.

19. Identity concerns were and are not peripheral to people's social and personal lives, and should not in the New Testament documents be portrayed as being in contrast to theological concerns such as the love command. "The search for and the preoccupation with defining the self are symptoms of our condition, both Jewish and Christian—especially, it would seem, when we are confronted with the experience of a God who seeks to destroy such deep-seated longings within us," (Sean Freyne, "Vilifying the Other and Defining the Self: Matthew's and John's Anti-Jewish Polemic in Focus," in *"To See Ourselves as Others See Us": Christians, Jews, "Others" in Late Antiquity*, ed. Jacob Neusner and Ernest S. Frerichs, Scholars Press Studies in the Humanities (Chico: Scholars, 1985), 141 n2.

20. Judith Perkins, *Roman Imperial Identities in the Early Christian Era*, Routledge Monographs in Classical Studies (London: Routledge, 2008), 172–76, refers to Tertullian who in the later second and early third centuries ascribed harsh punishments to the Roman overlords and relished his own joyous reaction in anticipation of their brutal suffering (see *De Spectaculis* 16.6) yet condemned the cruelty of the games (see *De Spectaculis* 19.1).

21. Paula Eisenbaum, "Paul as the New Abraham," in *Paul and Politics: Ekklesia, Israel, Imperium, Interpretation*, ed. Richard A. Horsley (Harrisville: Trinity International, 2000), 145. See also Benjamin H. Dunning, *Aliens and Sojourners: Self as Other in Early Christianity*, Divinations: Rereading Late Ancient Religion (Philadelphia: University of Pennsylvania Press, 2008). Taking up an outsider identity in Paul is complex, since the Otherness that he proclaims for believers resides in difference from this world as well as difference in certain customs and traditions (some of which even he shared) among the faithful.

22. In the south of Asia Minor rather than in the northern territory on the subcontinent. See David A. Fiensy, "The Roman Empire and Asia Minor," in *The Face of New Testament Studies: A Survey of Recent Research*, ed. Scot McKnight and Grant R. Osborne (Grand Rapids: Baker, 2004), 48–50.

23. Jouette M. Bassler, *Navigating Paul: An Introduction to Key Theological Concepts* (Louisville: Westminster John Knox, 2007), 45.

24. The other is often constructed in situations of conflict, which can be described by a number of criteria ("laws"): conflict with external opponents strengthens boundaries; conflict with external opponents reinforces group structures; conflict intensifies in relation to the proximity of opponents; conflict binds opponents together; and conflict contributes to a unitary view of opponents. See Lawrence M. Willis, *Not God's People: Insiders and Outsiders in the Biblical World*, Religion in the Modern World (Lanham: Rowman & Littlefield, 2008), 9–10.

25. Jonathan Z. Smith, "What a Difference a Difference Makes," in *"To See Ourselves as Others See Us": Christians, Jews, "Others" in Late Antiquity*, ed. J. Neusner and E. S. Frerichs, Scholars Press Studies in the Humanities (Chico: Scholars, 1985), 46–47.

26. The identity and even the form of referring to Paul's direct opposition in Galatia is unresolved, with some referring to "judaizers," "opponents," "agitators," or "troublemakers," and so on. Others reject such terms for semantic, ideological and historical reasons; for example, Mark D. Nanos prefers "influencers" ("The Inter- and Intra-Jewish Contexts of Paul and the Galatians," in *Paul and Politics: Ekklesia, Israel, Imperium, Interpretation*, ed. Richard A. Horsley (Harrisburg: Trinity International, 2000), 151. Evidently the portrait of these people depends largely on the canvas used for the social setting of the Galatian letter.

27. Wan, "The Letter to the Galatians," 257–58.

28. For a more contemporary setting for the Bible as Other, see also F. F. Segovia, "The Text as Other: Toward a Hispanic American Hermeneutic," in *Text and Experience: Toward a Cultural Exegesis of the Bible*, ed. Daniel Smith-Christopher, Biblical Seminar 35 (Sheffield: Sheffield Academic, 1995), 276–98.

29. Mendels, *Identity, Religion, and Historiography*, xvi.

30. Wills, *Not God's People*, 3.

31. Catherine R. Stimpson, "Feminist Criticism," in *Redrawing the Boundaries: The Transformation of English and American Literary Studies*, ed. Stephen J. Greenblatt and Giles B. Gunn (New York: Modern Language Association of America, 1992), 252.

32. Regina M. Schwartz, *The Curse of Cain: The Violent Legacy of Monotheism* (Chicago: University of Chicago Press, 1997), 5.

33. See Lieu, *Christian Identity*, 15.

PART II

Textual Interpretation

4

The Dog-Woman of Canaan and Other Animal Tales from the Gospel of Matthew

Stephen D. Moore

Narrative time distorts severely and queerly in the Canaanite woman episode of Matthew's Gospel (15:21-28).[1] The unnamed woman is a grotesquely distended character, as we shall see, impossibly stretched between a remote past and a distant future. First, her name, which, of course, is not a proper name, but rather an archaic designation: "Just then a Canaanite woman from that region came out" (15:22).[2] Matthew has changed Mark's *gynē...Hellēnis, Syrophoinikissa tō genei* ("[the] woman . . . a Greek, Syrophoenician by birth"), terms already bristling with ethnic valence,[3] to *gynē Chanaia* ("a Canaanite woman"), an epithet more redolent of ethnic violence.[4] It has been suggested, perhaps implausibly, that "Canaanite" was a Phoenician self-designation when this Gospel was written.[5] What is more certain is that the term opens vertiginously onto a scriptural temporal trajectory that extends steeply backward through the conquest narratives and the exodus and wilderness narratives to the patriarchal narratives and the primeval history.

It is impossible in principle to say which of the approximately 170 instances of "Canaan" or "Canaanite" in Jewish scripture swirled about in our implied author's brain as he made his terminological substitution, but it is tempting to speculate. For instance, the Matthean Jesus encounters the woman in the region not just of Tyre, as in Mark 7:24, but of Tyre and Sidon (Matt. 15:21), and according to the postdiluvian genealogy, "Canaan [was] the father of Sidon" (Gen. 10:15; cf. 1 Chr. 1:13). Consequently, "the territory of the Canaanites extended from Sidon . . . as far as Gaza" (Gen. 10:19). In the Israelite myth of origins, however, the territory possessed by the Canaanites is always already destined for dispossession: "And I will give to you, and to your offspring after

57

you . . . all the land of Canaan, for a perpetual holding" (Gen. 17:8; cf. Exod. 3:8). How is this dispossession to occur? Deuteronomy 20:17 puts it succinctly: "You shall annihilate them" (cf. Zeph. 2:5). Their annihilation must be absolute, moreover, but why? Because their idolatry is a constant temptation for Israel (cf. Lev. 18:3). But does Israel enact the genocide enjoined on it? No, it does not, insists the tradition (see esp. Ps. 106:38).

Matthew's Canaanite woman is a representative figure, then, and what she represents is an unerased remnant, a polluted people (cf. 1 Esd. 8:69: "The people of Israel . . . have not put away from themselves the alien peoples of the land and their pollutions") whose very name connotes idolatry and hence abomination (more on which below). Yet the Canaanite woman pericope also symbolically enacts the completion of Yahweh's genocidal commission, although by means other than the sword. This is accomplished through temporal distortion—or *queer temporality*, to invoke a more theoretically charged term.

Queering Canaan

Coupling the term "queer" with the term "temporality" entails a temporary decoupling of queer theory from sex and sexuality.[6] A scant three years after the term "queer theory" was coined, Eve Kosofsky Sedgwick was already able to write: "[R]ecent work around 'queer' spins the term outward along dimensions that can't be subsumed under gender and sexuality at all: the ways that race, ethnicity, postcolonial nationality criss-cross with these and other identity-constituting, identity-fracturing discourses, for example."[7] One such dimension is that of time,[8] and, more recently, Rebecca Fine Romanow[9] has given the notion of queer temporality a more explicit postcolonial spin, arguing that the (post)colonial arena is a cultural and political pressure cooker productive of all manner of fractures and aberrations, temporal as well as geographical.

So how does queer temporality play out in the ethnically and colonially charged space conjured up in Matt. 15:21-28? To state it summarily, polytheism self-deconstructs spontaneously in this scene in the face of a Christian mission from the future that invades the woman's present and rewrites the mythic past. Midway through the scene, the polytheistic woman is already on her knees before the numinous figure who, other than Matthew's God, is the only sanctioned object of worship in Matthew's symbolic world ("But she came and worshiped him [*prosekynei autō*], saying, 'Lord, help me'"—15:25), having already hailed him with a messianic title ("Have mercy on me, Lord, Son of David"—15:22; cf. 1:1; 21:9).[10] The new Joshua is accomplishing what the old Joshua could not: "Now Joshua was old and advanced in years; and the Lord said to him, 'You are old and advanced in years, and very much of the land still remains to be possessed'" (Josh 13:1). In consequence, even the impersonal name from the distant past, applied to the woman at the outset ("a Canaanite woman from that region"), is drained of its primary (polytheistic) connotations as the episode unfolds and she is possessed by a Christology from the future—that of the Matthean community, retrojected back into the present of the historical Jesus as it tells and retells his tale.

Past and future are thus accessed in this scene. All that is inaccessible is the woman's present. Can the subaltern speak in this scene?[11] Not in the present tense, it would seem, except when articulating the plight of her daughter ("my daughter is tormented by a demon"—15:22). Even here, however, the woman is subsumed in an ethnic stereotype with its roots in the archaic past. Canaanites and demons go hand in hand; the idols that Canaanites worship are nothing other than demons, the tradition contemptuously claims (Deut. 32:15-17; Ps. 106:36-37; Bar. 4:7; 1 Cor. 10:20; Rev. 9:20).[12] In accordance with the deep logic of the narrative, therefore, as soon as the woman engages in sanctioned worship, thereby relinquishing her Canaanite identity, the Matthean Jesus is authorized to trigger the switch that will cause the demon to depart from her daughter.

By what narrative logic, however, is Canaan represented as a woman in this scene? The scriptural echo chamber activated by the term "Canaanite" again suggests possible answers.[13] Canaan is styled a slave from the outset in the primeval history: "lowest of slaves shall he be to his brothers" (Gen. 9:25; cf. 9:26-27). In the hegemonic gender ideology of the ancient Mediterranean world, slave and female occupied contiguous positions on the gender gradient, both imagined to be automatically at the disposal of a free elite male, to do with as he pleased (cf. Neh. 9:24, LXX, where the Canaanites are delivered to Israel "to do with them as it pleased" [*poiēsai autois hōs areston enōpion autōn*]). Confronted with such a paragon of masculinity, the only appropriate response from a social or ethnic inferior was fawning obeisance. In our pericope, slavish Canaan, represented as a woman, debases herself before Israel, represented by the Son of David, submissively picking up the humiliating dog epithet hurled at her (15:26-27).[14] The scene is thus intensely racialized and eroticized—and, again, temporally out of joint. The obeisance luridly on display represents a nationalistic fantasy less oriented to the actual conditions of the Roman-dominated present than the mythic conditions of the archaic past. The colonial cauldron has once again produced displacement and distortion in the temporal plane—"a 'queer,' nonnormative . . . temporality," as Romanov might phrase it.[15]

An important question remains, however, perhaps the most pressing question of all. Why *is* the Canaanite woman represented as a dog in this scene?

The Dog-Woman and the (In)human One

"Do not give what is holy to dogs," the Matthean Jesus earlier enjoined his audience (7:6), anticipating his initial refusal of miraculous aid to the Canaanite dog-woman. But why are dogs not worthy of what is holy? Ancient Mediterranean and ancient Near Eastern culture provides a chorus of similar-sounding answers. Sextus Empiricus, a philosopher and physician active in the late second and early third centuries C.E., voices an already ancient prejudice when he declaims, "[T]he dog . . . that animal reckoned the most worthless of all" (*Outlines of Pyrrhonism* 1.63). Neither is ancient Israelite or early Jewish tradition kind to dogs (for example, 1 Sam. 17:43; 24:14; 2 Sam. 9:8; 16:9; 2 Kgs. 8:13; Ps. 22:16, 20; Prov. 26:11; cf. Phil. 3:2; 2 Pet. 2:22; Rev. 22:15). All of this, however, is well-trodden ground, and so a fresh approach to the dog epithet is in order. Jesus' exchange with the woman participates in a more extensive Matthean discourse on human-animal relations and so may be contextualized within it. The Matthean Jesus is himself fully enmeshed in that discourse and partially constructed by it. The first question to consider, then, is this: What kind of creature is the Matthean Jesus? Oceans of ink have been spilled on his relationship to divinity. What of his relationship to animality?

The "Son of Man" title provides the most illuminating answer to that question. Already a major title for Jesus in Mark, *ho huios tou anthrōpou* occurs about twice as often in Matthew, as it also features prominently in Matthew's Q source. I have argued elsewhere[16] that a return to Daniel 7, the major source of the Son of Man title, enables an instructive reframing of human-animal relations in Mark. This is yet truer of Matthew, hence the brief recapitulation of my reading of Daniel 7 that follows.

Daniel 7 presents us with a cosmology that both anticipates and complicates the absolutized, hierarchical, human/animal dichotomy characteristic of modern Western philosophy since Descartes. On the one hand, Daniel 7 articulates an analogous dualism. The expression "son of man" (*bar 'ĕnāš*)—or, better, "one like a human being" (7:13)[17]—means, in this context, "one who is not a beast," the beast or beasts in question being those of Daniel's terrifying vision (7:3-8) with whom the *bar 'ĕnāš* is explicitly contrasted. On the other hand, the human in Daniel 7 is anything but "Cartesian man"—a deep interior repository of essentialized humanity constituted in absolute contradistinction to the animal. Instead, the human is a flickering, interstitial element in Daniel 7, a hyphen between the animal, the angelic, and the divine.[18]

The unstable positioning of the "one like a human being" in Daniel 7 invites a radical reconsideration of the *huios tou anthrōpou* title in Matthew no less than in Mark. Against the Danielic backdrop, one explicitly evoked in certain of the eschatological *huios tou anthrōpou* sayings in Matthew (24:30; 26:64; cf. 16:27-28; 19:28; 24:15, 27; 25:31), the title might be said to parse out fully only in relation to the nonhuman animals from which it acquires its meaning; for what does it mean to say that the Matthean Jesus is "the human being"—or "the human animal," as we might say today—if not that he is *not* a nonhuman animal or beast?

But it is not only the imperial beasts of Daniel's vision that the Son of Man is not. The Son of Man is also, and more immediately, not the more mundane beasts that populate his own discourse—metaphoric beasts, like the Danielic beasts, for the most part, and hence further human entities in animal masks. We hear of metaphoric sheep in particular (7:15; 9:36; 10:6, 16; 25:32-33; 26:31; cf. 2:6), including in the Canaanite woman pericope (15:24), but also of metaphoric fish (4:19; 13:47); swine (7:6); wolves, serpents, and doves (7:15; 10:16); other birds (13:4, 32); goats (25:32-33)—and, of course, dogs (7:6; 15:26-27). In contrast to Daniel's bestiary, then, the Matthean metaphoric beasts are non-imperial entities. Rome is not a beast in Matthew, in contrast to Revelation, say, or 4 Ezra, and so neither are its primary representatives. The centurion of Capernaum (8:5-13) is not an animal, nor is the prefect of Judea (27:2, 11-26, 58, 62-65) or the centurion at the foot of the cross (27:54). The text implies that the centurion of Capernaum is intimately related to the Canaanite woman: both are Gentiles who come to Jesus, hail him as "Lord," beseech him to heal their child, elicit a general statement from him concerning Israel, are lauded by him for their exceptional faith, and have their child healed from afar.[19] But whereas Jesus is able to encounter the centurion as a fellow elite male, he can only encounter the woman as a beast, as a dog, as a dog-woman. Why is this?

One possible set of answers to this question begins to emerge when Matthew is cross-read with the second volume of Derrida's *The Beast and the Sovereign*.[20] Derrida himself is reading *Robinson Crusoe*,[21] customarily hailed as the first English novel, in the lectures that comprise the volume, and finding that what Crusoe thinks of his animal companions is largely indistinguishable from what Descartes, Kant, and their philosophical progeny think of the animal in general.[22] What Derrida analyzes in *Robinson Crusoe* are the conditions of a "Cartesian-Robinsonian" existence,[23] but much of what he has to say seems to apply *mutatis mutandis* to the conditions of existence created by the Matthean Jesus through his own words and actions.[24]

Like Crusoe, the Son of Man seems to occupy an island on which there are "only men and beasts.... And when I say men, I mean men, not only humans but men without women and without sex. . . . [O]r, if you prefer, men without sexual difference and without desire, without obvious sexual concern as such."[25] This is so, in any case, until the final pages of the novel, Crusoe by then having left his island, when two women are finally mentioned; and until the final pages of the gospel, Jesus by then having departed this life, when the audience is finally informed, as if in afterthought, that Jesus' entourage had peripherally included women (Matt. 27:55-56). The (Robin)Son-of-Man state is essentially a first-stage Edenic state, post-Adam but pre-Eve.[26] Sexual difference has not yet erupted forcibly in the Son of Man's world. Like Crusoe, the Son of Man—or simply in this context, the Man[27]—seems to assume "some secret contract between sovereign euphoria, paradisiacal euphoria, and the absence of women."[28]

For sovereignty is indeed the issue here, and sovereignty is a solitary affair. On Crusoe's island "there is a sort of slave [Friday], there are some animals and nobody else."[29] On the Man's island, too, there are slaves of a sort. Disciples stand in the same relation to their Teacher as slaves (*douloi*) do to their Master, as the Man unequivocally states in 10:24-25 (cf. 8:9); while in certain of his parables the Man styles himself the master of the house (*ho oikodespotēs*) and those who serve him his slaves (13:24-30; 20:1-16; 24:45-51; cf. 12:29; 21:33-43).[30] And when the Man becomes undisputed sovereign of all, arriving "in his glory" to sit on "the throne of his glory," his slaves morph into the docile sheep that they always already were ("he will put the sheep at his right hand"—25:31-33; cf. 10:16; 26:31). "That's sovereignty, that's solitary and exceptional sovereignty: slave, animal, and no woman. No desire to come along and limit sovereignty."[31] Sovereignty begins with self-sovereignty, then, self-discipline, self-control. No other principle better encapsulates the elite Greco-Roman concept of masculinity.[32] How might such a sovereign relate to his inferiors? What Derrida says of Defoe's Crusoe applies equally well to the Matthean Man: "And the relation to savages as well as to women and beasts was the condescending, descending, vertical relation of a superior master to his slaves . . . sovereign to his submissive subjects—submissive or submissible, mastered or to be mastered, by violence if need be—subjected."[33]

Savages, women, beasts . . . the dog-woman of Canaan embodies all three contiguous categories, always and at once. She was long seen as a savage or heathen, and never more insistently, perhaps, than when the modern, European, Christian empires engulfed the non-Christian peoples of Africa, the Americas, and other regions in their civilizing, missionizing maw. Typical of learned construals of the Canaanite woman pericope from this period and the assumptions that informed them is that of the Oxford don Willoughby C. Allen in his 1907 commentary on Matthew: "It would seem, therefore, that the editor has rewritten Mk.'s narrative with a view to explaining how it was that Christ . . . should have extended his compassion to a heathen woman. He did not enter into a house on heathen soil. Rather the woman came out to Him. At first He paid no attention to her entreaty. . . . When she still importuned Him, He told her that the children's bread, that is, privileges intended for the Jews, should not be cast to dogs, that is, to heathen women like herself. . . . [A]s in the previous case of condescension to a heathen (8^{5-13}), faith forced the barrier of Christ's rule of working only among His own people. . . . Why does the editor lengthen the dialogue? Partly perhaps to heighten the effect. Not at once, and only because of the woman's earnest importunity, did Christ condescend to her. And partly, to explain the ambiguity of Mk 7^{27} 'Let first the children be fed.' There is no specific explanation given in Mk. of this 'children.' The reader is left, as the woman was, to apply it to the Jews as contrasted with the heathen (dogs)."[34]

Elsewhere I have argued that the term "heathen" in a nineteenth or early twentieth century biblical commentary readily conjured up a contemporary as well as an ancient reality—the "unsaved" dark-skinned mass of polytheistic humanity in need of Christ, in need of civilizing, and hence in need of colonizing.[35] Yet colonial-era commentaries like Allen's do serve to throw ordinarily unobserved features of Matthew's Gospel into cartoonish relief.[36] Like a classic colonial master, the Matthean Son of Man—a Man among un-men, so much so that men and women alike tend to morph into animals in his discourse, if not his presence—might seem to be the quintessential human being in Matthew, the very measure of the human, the Son of Humanity[37]—and never more conspicuously than when he is confronted by a woman who also happens to be a "heathen."

Yet matters are not quite so simple. The humanity of the Son of Humanity has already been thrown into question in the narrative—and by the Son of Humanity himself. A scribe pledging to follow him wherever he goes is warned: "Foxes have holes, and birds of the air have nests; but the Son of Humanity has nowhere to lay his head" (8:20). In his utter homelessness, his radical itinerancy, the Son of Humanity is more animal-like than a fox, more creaturely even than a bird. The latter formulation is especially significant, because elsewhere in this narrative the bird is singled out as a creature that is of less value than the human: "Look at the birds of the air. . . . Are you not of more value than they?" (6:26); "So do not be afraid; you are of more value than many sparrows" (10:31). In combination, these sayings place considerable strain on the humanness of the Son of Humanity.

Nowhere is the animality of the Son of Humanity more evident, however, than in the manner of his death and the metaphors used of it. "The Son of Humanity is going to be betrayed into human hands," he predicts (17:22), but what will ensue will threaten to undo his masculinity and even his humanity. The atrocious abuses to his person that he must endure (20:18-19; 26:67-68; 27:26-50) will threaten to cause him to slide off the lower end of the ancient Mediterranean honor/shame gradient altogether, beyond "slavish" femininity and into abject animality. That he will pass into death as an animal is suggested by his own interpretation of his death: "Then he took a cup, and after giving thanks he gave it to them, saying, 'Drink from it, all of you; for this is my blood of the covenant, which is poured out for many for the forgiveness of sins'" (26:27-28; see 20:28). The phrase "the blood of the covenant" evokes Exodus 24:8, and the blood there is that of sacrificed oxen (see 24:5). Through his words over the cup, the Son of Humanity identifies his impending slaughter as that of a sacrificial animal, whether the oxen of the Sinai covenant rite, which in Jewish tradition became a rite of expiation (see Heb. 9:19-22), or the paschal lamb whose substitutionary slaughter is evoked by the Passover seder at which the Son of Humanity is officiating (Matt. 26:1-2, 17-19). Either way, it is not on two legs but on four that the Son of Humanity goes to the soteriological slaughterhouse. In a reversal of the regular sacrificial sequence, the Son of Humanity is first eaten as an animal and only afterward slaughtered as an animal. As such, he is eaten while still alive. Even the metaphor describing his internment in the grave bespeaks his ingestion—his abject, abyssal, animalizing descent into the belly of the other: "For just as Jonah was for three days and three nights in the belly of the sea monster [*en tē koilia tou kētous*], so for three days and three nights the Son of Humanity will be in the heart of the earth" (12:40).

In the performative words uttered over the wine, then, and also over the bread ("Take, eat; this is my body"—26:26), the Son of Humanity enacts a still ill-understood abomination that thoroughly contaminates any clean line between humanity and animality. In effect, Derrida parses out the logic of this abomination in *Robinson Crusoe*, a novel obsessed with cannibalism.[38] To be swallowed by the sea through drowning or the earth through earthquake is a terrible thing. To be devoured by a fellow living creature is more terrible still—but not because the creature is more alien than the earth or the sea. The wild beast (or sea monster) that devours me is less different from me than the earth or the sea. Closer to me still, however, is the cannibal who eats me alive: only a fellow anthropoid can be anthropophagic. But the cannibal's "alterity is the more marked for being less marked."[39] The cannibal is more similar to the person being devoured than is the wild beast, but paradoxically the cannibal is also less similar, because the cannibal "eats his fellow, and thus becomes inhuman."[40] One would not say of the wild beast that it is "inhuman, inhumanly cruel."[41] "To have lost human dignity by being inhuman is reserved for humans alone, and in no way for the sea, the earth, or the beast. Or the gods. One does not say of beasts or of God that they are inhuman. Only humans are said to be inhuman."[42] And never more so than when they are devouring members of their own species.

How might all of this apply to Matthew's "Last Supper"? The inhuman abomination that is the execution by torture of the Son of Humanity—his savage scourging, his cruel crucifixion—is preceded by a still more inhuman abomination: his being eaten alive by those who are closest to him—as close as family, indeed ("And pointing to his disciples, he said, 'Here are my mother and my brothers!"—12:49; see 10:35-37; 12:50; 19:29; 25:40). At the Last Supper, through the performative magic of the "words of institution," the Son of Humanity surrounds himself with savage cannibals, who, however, are also his most intimate kin, who devour his flesh and drink his blood, no longer human but inhuman. But because they are acting on the orders of the Son of Humanity himself—the Human One[43]—he becomes the Inhuman One in this scene, the one who is neither human nor animal. The profoundly unstable relations between humanity and animality evident throughout the narrative here collapse altogether. This collapse is anticipated in certain of the narrative's earlier scenes, most obviously the two miraculous feeding episodes, with their routinely remarked eucharistic elements, their hungry, impatient anticipations of the Last Supper (see esp. 14:19-20; 15:35-36)—but also in the Canaanite woman episode.

"[E]ven the dogs eat the crumbs that fall from their masters' table," says the woman (15:27). "[I]t may even be that the bread should be considered a symbol of salvation (cf. the feeding stories)," muse Davies and Allison.[44] "That the table too is symbolic, intended to allude to the Lord's table (see 1 Cor. 10:21), is, however, too much," they add.[45] And yet they have led us to the table by raising the possibility that the bread is "a symbol of salvation": what can that mean other than that the torn bread may be taken to symbolize the broken, sacrificial body of the (In)human One offered to his disciples as the main course in his final meal with them? Davies and Allison also usher us to the table by their suggestion that the *kyriōn* ("masters"/"lords") of 15:27, usually assumed to refer to the Jewish people, might "[stand] in effect only for Jesus," the plural being "required by the logic of the preceding parable [that is, v. 26]. The one plural, 'dogs,' demands the other plural, 'masters'."[46] The woman's reply might then be paraphrased as: "Yes, Lord, yet even us Gentile dogs are permitted to gorge on the gobbets of flesh that fall from your sacrificial table."

This eucharistic construal of the woman's response would complete the narrative's construction of her as uncannily cognizant of Jesus' identity and mission ("Lord, Son of David . . . [S]he worshiped him"). But what else can she be said to know? She knows that the distinction between sheep and dogs to which Jesus appeals ("'I was sent only to the lost sheep of the house of Israel' . . . It is not fair to take the children's food and throw it to the dogs'") is a treacherously unstable one. The dog-woman's problem, Jesus would seem to be saying, is that she is not a sheep-woman. The more basic problem, she would seem to be replying, is that the sheep that Jesus has culled from the larger flock to follow him must soon morph into dogs so as to be able to heed his command that they devour his flesh and drink his blood (see 1 Kgs. 14:11; 16:4; 21:19, 23-24; 22:38; 2 Kgs. 9:10, 35-37; Ps. 68:23), while he himself must morph into a sheep or some other sacrificial animal in order that the ghastly meal may take place.

Yet it is not the meal but the woman who has most often been an object of disgust. The term "Canaanite" evoked revulsion for an ethnic other whose most abominable crime, whether real or imagined, was the ultimate "crime against nature": child sacrifice (Lev. 18:21; 20:2-4; 2 Kgs. 16:3; 23:10; 2 Chr. 28:3; 33:6; Jer. 7:31; 32:35; Ezek. 16:36). This iconic crime is no small part of the reason why John Chrysostom could say of the Canaanite woman that she calls to mind "those wicked nations, who overturned from their foundations the very laws of nature" (*Homily on Matthew* 52.1). Paradoxically, however, concern for her child is the dominant trait of the Canaanite woman in our episode, while Jesus' response to the child's plight is so uncaring, so callous, as to invite the term "inhuman." Much that is coded in the term "Canaanite," indeed, is more readily applicable to Jesus and his followers than to the woman. The text anathemizes her by projecting abomination onto her, "abominable" being a virtual synonym for "Canaanite" (see esp. Ezra 9:1, 11, 14; also Lev. 18:21-30; 1 Kgs. 14:23-24; 21:26; 2 Kgs. 21:2; Jer. 16:18; Ezek. 8:9-10). The real locus of abomination in the text, however, is the abominable death of the Son of

Humanity and the abominable interpretations of his death to which the text has recourse—preeminently, the anthropophagic devouring of his atrociously tortured body by those whom he earlier designated his true family: "Here are my mother and my brothers!" (12:49). At the heart of this abomination, then, is a savaging of conventional familial bonds: the mother and the brothers eat the living flesh and drink the living blood of the "beloved son" (3:17; 12:18; 17:5).

QUEERING THE LAST SUPPER

All of this returns us to the workings of queer temporality in Matthew's narrative. A major facet of queer temporality passed over in our earlier discussion is elucidated by Judith Halberstam: "Queer subcultures produce alternative temporalities by allowing their participants to believe that their futures can be imagined according to logics that lie outside of those paradigmatic markers of life experience—namely, birth, marriage, reproduction, and death."[47] And again: "[Q]ueer time . . . is . . . about the potentiality of a life unscripted by the conventions of family, inheritance, and child rearing."[48] By this definition, the Matthean Jesus would be an exemplar of an alternative temporality that invites the label "queer." His life, offered as a model to his disciples, is unscripted by the ancient Mediterranean institutions of marriage, biological progeny, conventional labor, or material inheritance. His conception and birth take place outside the conventional structures of marriage (1:18-25),[49] yet not so far outside as to fail to trouble them, to fissure them from within. As an adult, he himself eschews marriage and even sex, and hence biological sons and heirs. He seduces his male disciples into abandoning their own marriages (4:18-22; 8:14; 19:27-29; cf. 10:35-37), and holds eunuchhood up to them as an ultimate model (19:10-12; cf. 5:27-30).[50] The movement inaugurated by the Matthean Jesus, then, can be reconceived as a queer subculture productive of an alternative temporality that is profoundly anti-imperial, entailing as it does a present and a future imagined according to logics that lie outside the paradigmatic markers of Roman life experience. The Matthean Jesus and his disciples do not run on Roman time.

As if on cue, the scene that represents the most spectacular symbolic assault on the institution of the family in this narrative—the Last Supper, that most disturbing of family meals—also evinces the narrative's most spectacular example of queer temporality. The sacrificial meal is bloodless (which, of course, is why Christian tradition has been able to assimilate it so painlessly), but the torturous death from which the meal derives its efficacy is not. Although narratively anterior to the atrocious death, the meal so presupposes the slaughter that the slaughter can be said to precede the meal, as with any regular sacrificial rite. Time bends and warps once again in Matthew, as it already did in the Canaanite woman episode that anticipated this ghoulish meal, and again it twists around themes that make that bending queer: the natural, the normal, and the familial bonds and biological ties designed to hold them in place.

Notes

1. The number of biblical scholars practicing postcolonial criticism would be far fewer without the mentoring of Fernando Segovia. Although I have never had the privilege of studying formally with Fernando, his encouragement was crucial to me when I first began to engage with postcolonial theory. His example was no less important to me as my work in this mode developed—the example of somebody who refused to settle for constricted, formulaic forms of postcolonial analysis. I dedicate this essay to him with gratitude and admiration, even though the expanded lenses it employs would likely not be his.

2. The NRSV translation is used here and throughout, except where I modify it.

3. See Kwok Pui Lan, *Discovering the Bible in the Non-Biblical World*, The Bible and Liberation (Maryknoll: Orbis, 1995), 71–83; Jim Perkinson, "A Canaanite Word in the Logos of Christ; or the Difference the Syro-Phoenician Woman Makes to Jesus," *Semeia* 75 (1996): 61–86; and Hans Leander, *Discourses of Empire: The Gospel of Mark from a Postcolonial Perspective*, Literature, History of Ideas, and Religion (Göteborg: University of Gothenburg. 2011), 239–53.

4. See Leticia Guardiola-Sáenz, "Borderless Women and Borderless Texts: A Cultural Reading of Matthew 15:21-28," *Semeia* 78 (1997): 69–81; Musa W. Dube, *Postcolonial Feminist Interpretation of the Bible* (Saint Louis: Chalice, 2000), 147–53; and Surekha Nelavala, *Liberation beyond Borders: Dalit Feminist Hermeneutics and Four Gospel Women* (Saarbrücken: Lambert Academic, 2009), 61–95.

5. For example, see Ulrich Luz, *Matthew 8-20*, Hermeneia (Minneapolis: Fortress, 2001), 338.

6. Even though queer theory is, at base, the academic analysis of sex and sexuality, heterosex(uality) as well as homosex(uality). For a brief introduction to queer theory, see Stephen D. Moore, *God's Beauty Parlor and Other Queer Spaces in and around the Bible*, Contraversions: Jews and Other Differences (Stanford: Stanford University Press, 2001), 7–18. For a full-scale introduction, see Nikki Sullivan, *A Critical Introduction to Queer Theory* (New York: New York University Press, 2003). And for a critical retrospective, see Janet Halley and Andrew Parker, *After Sex? On Writing since Queer Theory*, Series Q (Durham: Duke University Press, 2010).

7. Eve Kosofsky Sedgwick, *Tendencies* (Durham: Duke University Press, 1993), 9.

8. See Judith Halberstam, *In a Queer Time and Place: Transgender Bodies, Subcultural Lives, Sexual Cultures* (New York: New York University Press, 2005), and Elizabeth Freeman, *Time Binds: Queer Temporalities, Queer Histories*, Perverse Modernities (Durham: Duke University Press, 2010).

9. Rebecca Fine Romanow, *The Postcolonial Body in Queer Space and Time* (Newcastle upon Tyne: Cambridge Scholars, 2008), 3–4.

10. The term *kyrios* flickers ambiguously in this scene, meanwhile (15:22, 25, 27), meaning both "sir" in the profane sense and "Lord" in the Christological sense.

11. See Gayatri Chakravorty Spivak, "Can the Subaltern Speak?" in *Marxism and the Interpretation of Culture*, ed. Cary Nelson and Larry Grossberg (Urbana: University of Illinois Press, 1988), 271–313.

12. See Louise J. Lawrence, "Crumb Trails and Puppy-Dog Tales: Reading Afterlives of a Canaanite Woman," in *From the Margins 2: Women of the New Testament and Their Afterlives*, ed.

Christine E. Joynes and Christopher C. Rowland, The Bible in the Modern World 27 (Sheffield: Sheffield Phoenix, 2009), 264: "[Epiphanius the Latin], like Hilary of Poitiers, imagines the woman as 'a mother of demon-possessed Gentiles' who suffer terribly from demon-possession having been 'led astray by idolatry and sin' and thus are nothing more than 'dogs who worship idols' and 'bark at God'" (*Interpretation of the Gospels*, 58). For differently focused explorations of the significance of demon possession in the Canaanite woman and Syrophoenician woman episodes respectively, see Elaine M. Wainwright, "Not without My Daughter: Gender and Demon Possession in Matthew 15:21-28," in *A Feminist Companion to Matthew*, ed. Amy-Jill Levine with Marianne Blickenstaff (Sheffield: Sheffield Academic, 2001), 126–37; and Laura E. Donaldson, "Gospel Hauntings: The Postcolonial Demons of New Testament Criticism" in *Postcolonial Biblical Criticism: Interdisciplinary Intersections*, ed. Stephen D. Moore and Fernando F. Segovia, Bible and Postcolonialism 6 (New York: T&T Clark, 2005), 97–114.

13. Answers different from those ventured by Dube, see *Postcolonial Feminist Interpretation*, 146–49. It is not that I disagree, however, with Dube's incisive analysis. Rather, it is the kind of question to which numerous viable answers are possible.

14. Augustine aptly paraphrased 15:27 as follows: "Yes, Lord, I am a dog, I desire crumbs" (*Sermon* 77.12).

15. Romanov, *The Postcolonial Body*, 3.

16. Moore, "Why There Are No Humans or Animals in the Gospel of Mark," in *Mark as Story: Retrospect and Prospect*, ed. Kelly R. Iverson and Christopher W. Skinner, Resources for Biblical Study (Atlanta: Society of Biblical Literature, 2011), 71–94.

17. "There is near universal consensus that the phrase 'one like a son of man' means simply 'one like a human being'." See John J. Collins, *Daniel: A Commentary on the Book of Daniel*, Hermeneia (Minneapolis: Fortress Press, 1993), 304.

18. A comment inspired by Jacques Derrida's fleeting analysis of Revelation's divine throne-room scene, see *The Beast and the Sovereign*, vol. 1, trans. Geoffrey Bennington, Seminars of Jacques Derrida 1 (Chicago: University of Chicago Press, 2009), 13. Derrida describes his own work on animality as "a summons issued to Descartes," see *The Animal That Therefore I Am*, trans. David Wills, Perspectives in Continental Philosophy (New York: Fordham University Press, 2008), 75.

19. W. D. Davies and Dale C. Allison, *A Critical and Exegetical Commentary on the Gospel According to Saint Matthew*, vol. 2, ICC (Edinburgh: T&T Clark, 1991), 558.

20. Derrida's ruminations on animality, especially in the "The Animal That Therefore I Am", reprinted with three related lectures in Derrida 2008 and now supplemented with Derrida, *The Beast and the Sovereign* (vol. 1; 2009) and *The Beast and the Sovereign*, vol. 2; Seminars of Jacques Derrida 2 (trans. Geoffrey Bennington; Chicago: University of Chicago Press, 2011), have been the principal philosophical catalyst for the emergent field of posthuman animality studies. For a brief introduction to the field, see Cary Wolfe, "Human, All Too Human: 'Animal Studies' and the Humanities," *PMLA* 124 (2009): 564–75, and for biblical engagements with it, see Matthew Chrulew, "Feline Divinanimality: Derrida and the Discourse of Species in Genesis," *The Bible and Critical Theory* 2.2 (2008); Moore, "Why There Are No Humans or Animals," and Jennifer Koosed, *The Bible and the Posthuman*, Semeia (Atlanta: Society of Biblical Literature, forthcoming).

21. Daniel Defoe, *The Life and Strange Surprising Adventures of Robinson Crusoe, of York, Mariner* (London: Taylor, 1719).

22. *The Beast and the Sovereign*, vol. 2, 278.

23. Ibid, 53.

24. This should not surprise us unduly, an historian might be imagined to remark, since Descartes's philosophical achievement in the area of human-animal relations was to hone an anthropocentrism whose essential elements had originally been formulated by Artistotle and the Stoics and widely disseminated in antiquity, on which see Gary Steiner, "Descartes, Christianity, and Contemporary Speciesism," in *A Communion of Subjects: Animals in Religion, Science, and*

Ethics, ed. Paul Waldau and Kimberley Patton (New York: Columbia University Press, 2006), 120–23. Philo, for instance, in his dialogue *On Animals*, follows the Aristotelian-Stoic line; see Ingvild Saelid Gilhus, *Animals, Gods, and Humans: Changing Attitudes to Animals in Greek, Roman, and Early Christian Ideas* (London: Routledge, 2006), 42–44.

25. In the case of the Son of Man, the little island has designs on bigger islands. Derrida is much taken with James Joyce's take on *Robinson Crusoe*—"the prefiguration of an imperialist, colonialist sovereignty, the first herald of the British empire, the great island setting off to conquer other islands, smaller islands (like Ireland) but above all islands bigger than it, like Africa, New Zealand or Australia," see *The Beast and the Sovereign*, vol. 2, 16, paraphrasing James Joyce, *Buffalo Studies* 1 (1964):1–25.

26. See *The Beast and the Sovereign*, vol. 2, 54. Appropriately enough, the Scholars Version translation of the New Testament renders *ho huios tou anthrōpou* as "the Son of Adam."

27. Adam's Hebrew name, *ha-'ādām*, means just that—"the man."

28. *The Beast and the Sovereign* (vol. 2), 54.

29. Ibid, 55.

30. See further Janice Capel Anderson and Stephen D. Moore, "Matthew and Masculinity," in *New Testament Masculinities*, ed. Stephen D. Moore and Janice Capel Anderson, *Semeia* 45 (2003): 79–89.

31. *The Beast and the Sovereign* (vol. 2), 55.

32. See Stephen D. Moore and Janice Capel Anderson, "Taking It Like a Man: Masculinity in 4 Maccabees," *JBL* 117 (1998): 249–73.

33. *The Beast and the Sovereign* (vol. 2), 278.

34. Willoughby C. Allen, *A Critical and Exegetical Commentary on the Gospel according to S. Matthew*, ICC (Edinburgh: T&T Clark, 1907), 169.

35. Moore, *God's Beauty Parlor*, 158–65.

36. See Leander, *Discourses of Empire*, 90–157, for postcolonial analysis of sixteen nineteenth-century commentaries on Mark, including their treatment of the Syrophoenican woman.

37. A translation of *ho huios tou anthrōpou* that some scholars and clergy prefer.

38. The vexed historical question of whether or to what extent cannibalism was, or is, a product of the European colonial imagination is beyond the scope of this essay. For explorations of the role(s) of cannibalism in colonial discourse, see Francis Barker, *et al.*, eds., *Cannibalism and the Colonial World* (Cambridge: Cambridge University Press, 1998); Barbara Creed and Jeanette Hoorn, eds., *Body Trade: Captivity, Cannibalism and Colonialism in the Pacific* (New York: Routledge, 2001); and Graham Huggan and Helen Tiffin, *Postcolonial Ecocriticism: Literature, Animals, Environment* (New York: Routledge, 2010).

39. *The Beast and the Sovereign* (vol. 2), 139.

40. Ibid., 142.

41. Ibid., 140.

42. Ibid., 141.

43. The Common English Bible consistently renders *ho huios tou anthrōpou* as "the Human One."

44. Davies and Allison, *A Critical and Exegetical Commentary*, 553.

45. Ibid.

46. Ibid., 555–56. See also Stephenson Humphries-Brooks, "The Canaanite Women in Matthew," *The Feminist Companion to Matthew* (ed., Amy-Jill Levine with Marianne Blickenstaff (Sheffield: Sheffield Academic, 2001), 143–44.

47. Halberstam, *In a Queer Time and Place*, 2.

48. Ibid.

49. See Thomas Bohache, "Matthew," in *The Queer Bible Commentary*, ed. Deryn Guest, Robert Goss, Mona West, and Thomas Bohache (London: SCM, 2006), 496.

50. Ibid., 507–11.

5

Sociology of the Sabbath in the Gospel of Mark

Stephanie Buckhanon Crowder

Joyce Carol Thomas, in her "Church Poem,"[1] inquires if the act of bending on Saturday becomes divine if it is done on the "Sabbath." She ponders if the preparation for the Sabbath is as sacred as the actual participation on the Sabbath. Are the efforts people undertake to get ready for church parallel to actual church attendance? Thomas posits that both the expectation and the arrival of the Sabbath are holy unto themselves. One must note that Thomas' poem defines "Sabbath" along the lines of one Christian tradition as that which occurs on Sunday. Thus for Thomas what happens on "Holy Saturday" sets the stage for "Holy Sunday."

Alice Walker makes a different move with the idea of Sabbath. Her *In Search of Our Mothers' Gardens* records: "Anybody can observe the Sabbath, but making it holy takes the rest of the week."[2] Whereas Thomas avers that the Sabbath is so sacred that preparation for it must begin a day early, Walker says that it is not the day or the timeliness of the event that produces holiness, but it is what happens after the Sabbath that reflects its sacrosanct nature or the nature of the one observing it. For Walker it is not the activity preceding the Sabbath that alludes to it, but it is what happens afterwards that mirrors its divine significance. Please note that in her effort, Walker, unlike Thomas, situates Sabbath within a twentieth-century Jewish context.

I begin this study of the Gospel of Mark with these two readings of the Sabbath due to my own interest in the use of biblical language in popular culture. In addition, the literature, although emanating from two African American authors, renders two different ideas on the Sabbath. The former is rooted in a Christian tradition; the latter is from Judaism. It is the second account that more closely aligns with the conceptual framework of the Sabbath in the Gospel of Mark. It is Mark's presentation of the Sabbath that will serve as the focus of my work. Thus, this essay seeks to answer the question, "What does one do on the Sabbath?"

My Culture and Identity

Fifteen years ago, I was hired by the American Diabetes Association (ADA) to be its Program Coordinator for African American Churches. I was hired primarily because I was a product of an African American Church and due to my ordained standing in the National Baptist and Disciples of Christ denominations. Thus, I understood many of the nuances of being in an African American Church.

My portfolio included recruiting congregations to sponsor Diabetes Sunday, an annual education awareness event held on the first Sunday in February. It was also my task to lead educational workshops and mail related material. What was appealing about the work was the manner in which the ADA sought to tell a new story but in a traditional manner. There was nothing novel about people gathering in churches for worship on Sundays, or on Saturdays if one were Seventh-Day Adventist. This the ADA understood. However, what was unusual was that for many churches, service would include a time to reflect not only on one's spiritual well-being, but also on physical health. Sunday worship, the Sabbath, became a forum for addressing the whole person.

A few years after transitioning from the ADA, I began serving as a Program Director for a federally-funded, faith-based, HIV/AIDS program. I was responsible for not only educating congregations on the dire statistics about HIV/AIDS, but also for partnering with churches to help them find ways to address this disease using their own infrastructure. The idea was to assist faith institutions in using what they already had in place to speak to a pressing community need. After all, there were and still are people with HIV/AIDS in the pews, pulpit, choir and serving in various ministries in the church.

Just as the American Diabetes Association did a decade earlier, now the Centers for Disease Control and Prevention (CDC) had begun to do in the twenty-first century. Both entities saw the power possibilities of engaging people about health issues on the Sabbath. Although the stigma, causes, and social ramifications related to HIV/AIDS hardly compared to diabetes, what was common then and now is the manner in which government and non-profit institutions have come to see the social, political, and human capital of churches. Without forthrightly acknowledging it, these non-religious structures see the value in "congregating" on the Sabbath. They have figured out what to do on the Sabbath—engage people in a dialogue about their health and physical well-being for the sake of spiritual growth and maturity.

As a biblical scholar and ordained minister, my vocation is in both the church and the academy. I believe that what I do on the Sabbath (Sunday for me) influences the what and the how of my teaching during the week. In turn, the time I spend researching and writing during the week compels me to broaden my theology and what I preach and teach on Sunday. My work in helping church attendees address diabetes, HIV/AIDS, and other health concerns and social issues is a natural progression and embodiment of my dual calling. It is through this hermeneutical lens that I preach, teach, practice, and write. As an interpreter and preacher of biblical narratives and as one who has labored with churches for health awareness and social justice, I have become curious as to the "original" purpose of the Sabbath. My work has spurred me to question whether talking about "sugar" or "the AIDS" from the pulpit is so unusual or is there perchance a biblical precedent for the Sabbath as meeting spiritual, communal, mental, emotional and yes, physical needs. Does the Bible answer the question, "What to do on the Sabbath?" According to the presentation in the Gospel of Mark, the answer is a resounding, "Yes!" The Gospel writer recontextualizes ideas of the Sabbath and demonstrates that its purpose is to provide healing from cultural, spiritual, political and physical disease. After expounding on the social location of Mark's community, this essay will provide a cursory overview of pre-Markan ideas on the Sabbath and then highlight various texts from the Gospel that mirror its reconfiguring of this sacred practice.

Culture, Identity, and Power in Mark's Community

The author of Mark penned the Gospel around 65–70 C.E., in the middle of the first Jewish-Roman War. Because of references to the destruction of Jerusalem in Mark 13, scholars maintain the writer alludes to the devastation of the Temple in 70 C.E. Hence, the earliest of the Gospels is a work rooted in conflict and chaos. The author does not mince words about the power dynamics at play. Mark clearly expresses the discomfort of the writer's community of believers. These followers of Jesus faced the conundrum of trying to live in a world in which the Roman, ruling elite were in direct conflict with Jewish leaders. The storyteller underscores the polemic of "giving to God" or "rendering to Caesar."

Not only does the Gospel point to political turmoil, but the writer shows intra-Jewish conflict as Jesus and his disciples challenge cultural traditions and mores. Whereas many maintain that there were also Gentiles in Mark's audience, the writer shows that there was disagreement over the ways of Jesus versus the traditional Jewish way. Therefore, while having to battle Roman imperialism on the one hand, Mark's community also had to face an internal struggle. In light of this double dueling, Mark reconstructs the Sabbath, a focal point of Jewish life, and allows it to reemerge as a means for addressing the community's political oppression and socioreligious marginalization.

CULTURE AND IDENTITY OF THE SABBATH BEFORE MARK

Before discussing how the Gospel writer reinterprets the Sabbath for the first century, establishing its historical development prior to Mark is significant. The Hebrew word "shabat" denotes not only the idea of resting, but it is the number "seven." Genesis (2:2-3) records God as resting on the seventh day. The children of Israel are to gather enough manna on the sixth day so that there is plenty to eat on the Sabbath (Exodus 16:22-30). The Ethical Decalogue (Exod. 20:8) records the only commandment that begins with "remember": Remember the Sabbath day and keep it holy. God forewarns Israel of the possibility of becoming too preoccupied or distracted lest the people forget to honor and observe a time set apart solely for God. Israel must remember. Israel must remember to keep a day set aside for God and God alone. The writer of Exodus continues to develop the urgency of seven/rest in explicating that people must observe Sabbath so that the land (34:21) and animals may also rest (21:10-12). Honor the Sabbath so that the "poor of your people may eat (v.11)." Here a day initially designed to pay reverence to God becomes a day to provide for the least of God's creation.

Moving from remembering God to remembering the land and the poor, the Exodus author compounds Sabbath as that which is not solely spiritual, but it is also a matter of justice and ultimately a representation of covenant—a perpetual sign between God, Moses and people (31:12). Just as the rainbow served as a sign of God's covenant with Noah, and circumcision was a sign of God's agreement with Abraham, here is now another sign of covenant between the divine and humankind. However, the Sabbath is not an occasional natural display in the sky or a fleshly act tethered to a male. The Sabbath as covenant is a day for everything God has created. It is covenant—supersized.

The Priestly editor of Leviticus later shows how this weekly observation yields a yearly focus. In addition to seventh-day rest, the community is now to dedicate itself, the land, slaves and all creatures to a seventh-year rest (Lev. 25:2-4). Furthermore, "seven weeks of years giving to forty-nine years" shall inaugurate a fiftieth year or jubilee year (25:9-10). This year of jubilee is a rest from indebtedness, slavery, and economic hardship. What began as a day for Israel to honor God is now a season where reverence for God ushers in respect and restitution for God's people. This is Sabbath maximized! Lowery asseverates that what is consistent from Genesis through Leviticus is God's provision in six days is enough for the seventh. Accepting this abundance is how humankind honors Sabbath, cessation and rest.[3]

In Deuteronomy's account of the Decalogue, Israel is not just to "remember" but to "observe." Ironically the people are to "observe" it by "remembering" that they were once slaves in Egypt (5:13-15). God through Moses instructs Israel to show mercy to aliens and slaves on the Sabbath just as the Lord God did the same for them during their bondage. Like the Priestly writer, the Deuteronomistic editor delineates the love of God expressed through love of humankind.

Other notations of the Sabbath are found in the prophets. Isaiah (1:13), Amos (8:5) and Hosea (2:13) connect it with lunar festivals and official cult celebrations. Ezekiel (20–22) records Israel as "defiled by the idols she has made" (22:5). Consequently the prophet declares a lack of Sabbath practice in Jerusalem. Scholars disagree on the prevalence of Sabbath observance during the exile. Some maintain that the continued recognition of this sacred time set the exiles apart from their captors. What is clear is that by the rise of Hellenization, the Sabbath is so essential within Judaism that Antiochus Epiphanes attempts to cease its observance along with that of circumcision.

From the aforementioned analysis of the Sabbath as noted in the Hebrew Bible, one can glean several insights. (1) God rests, and all created in God's image must rest; (2) God provides, and all of creation should honor that provision. A good God created and declared it all—good; (3) receipt of God's abundance and deliverance becomes embodied in the manner in which humankind treats the land, the poor, the alien, and the slave. Out of the abundance and mercy of God, people are to share and do for one another; and (4) there is a spiritual cord that connects economic obligation and social responsibility. Worship of the God of the Sabbath is the impetus for communal accountability.

In their work, "Reading Against Jesus: Nineteenth Century African Americans' View of Sabbath Law," Sadler and Powery incorporate some of these same motifs of justice. Because greedy slaveholders wanted slaves to work on the Sabbath, slaves had to recontextualize its ideas to suit their social location.[4] Many used the day as an opportunity to escape and thus physically live out the theological ideals of this observation as rest for the alien and slave. In a move parallel to slaves of the nineteenth century, members of Mark's community during the first century also reconfigure the meaning of the Sabbath.

The Sabbath in the Gospel of Mark

The context in Gospel of Mark is analogous to the politically laden setting in Exodus. The Israelites were fresh out of Egyptian bondage and in the middle of the wilderness when God first gave regulations regarding the Sabbath. They could probably still hear the slavemaster's whip and the thunder of Pharoah's chariots. Mark's community was living under Roman confines. Both groups were striving to remember the Sabbath through the framework of political subjugation. Mark's Jesus reinterprets the Sabbath in light of this first century oppression. He does so through the lens of healing. Jesus does not discard the historical groundings of this day set aside for the Lord. He does not throw out the baby with the bath water. Instead Jesus in Mark's account reorders the day and reminds those who would hear of its original spiritual-social obligation. Several passages in Mark all draw attention to the manner in which Jesus addresses the matter of "what to do on the Sabbath" (1:21; 2:23-28; 3:1-6, 6:1-6a; and 15:42—16:1).

Jesus and his newly minted disciples go to Capernaum, and on the Sabbath he begins to teach in the synagogue, the central sociopolitical and religious gathering place (1:21). Here a man with an unclean spirit cries out in agony. Jesus and the spirit have a conversation that results ultimately in his silencing and exorcising the demon. It is still the Sabbath when Jesus cools the fever of Simon's mother-in-law (1:30-31). Unlike the previous healing, this one does not involve a verbal exchange. Instead Jesus merely touches the woman and cures her. The disciples and Jesus end their Sabbath as he "cures many who are sick with various diseases and casts out many demons" (1:32-34). The Gospel writer is intentional in that Jesus' first acts of power occur on the day set aside to honor the provision of God. God through Jesus provides for the physical needs and well-being of God's people. This is indeed a cultural reminder for Mark's community.

On a Sabbath day, the disciples pluck heads of grain to meet their own physical needs (2:23). Unlike the three aforementioned accounts on the Sabbath, this action elicits a negative response from the Pharisees. What the disciples do is illegal on the Sabbath. Here Mark through his opponents recalls the Jewish law's prohibition not to work or harvest on the Sabbath (Exod 20:8-11; 34:21; Deut. 5:12-15). Jesus displays his knowledge of Jewish history by retelling David's action in the temple to abate his hunger (1 Sam. 21). Although his hermeneutics is a bit off key, as there is no reference to the Sabbath in David's case, Jesus trumps the Pharisees by basically telling them he and his disciples can do what they wish. The Sabbath is for humankind. The Son of Man is lord of the Sabbath (2:27-28). Consequently, Jesus not only declares his power over physical and spiritual ailments, but he also proclaims religious authority over Jewish leaders. He uses cultural history and tradition to reinterpret that same history and tradition in new day, a new age. It is his identity as "lord" that allows him to revise any past understanding and praxis of the Sabbath. It is his identity as "Son of Man" that subordinates the rules of the Sabbath to the needs of humankind. It is not only the Son of Man who has power over the Sabbath, but all humans have this power.[5]

In another synagogue healing, Jesus encounters a man with a withered hand (3:1). It is still the Sabbath and at this point the level of intensity and animosity surrounding Jesus and his "work" on this day has risen. Mark's Jesus continues to show his ability to verbally best his opponents. Instead of being on the defensive and waiting for an attack, Jesus is proactive and asks, "Is it lawful to do good or to do harm on the Sabbath, to save life or to to kill?" (3:4). The question is problematic on various levels. If his opponents respond that it is lawful to do harm, they will advocate lack of concern and ultimately violence. If they respond that it is lawful to do good, they in essence give Jesus permission to heal the man without legal repercussions or verbal assault. If those opposed to Jesus declare that it is lawful to kill on the Sabbath, they dishonor God and the sanctity of this day. On the contrary, if they aver that one must save life on the Sabbath, they once again affirm the labor of healing Jesus performs. Furthermore, they validate his new interpretation and practice on the Sabbath. In the end the Pharisees and those with them play it safe and say nothing (3:4).

For the first time in Mark's Gospel, Jesus responds with anger and subsequent grief (3:5). The hardness of the hearts of the opposition disturbs him. Nonetheless, he turns his attention and affection to the man in need. Jesus calls the man forward (3:3). This change in positioning indicates that the man is no longer decentered or marginalized. He is not a social outcast any more. Jesus then asks the man to stretch out his hand (3:5). Thus, the man has to acknowledge his frailty, and the people in the synagogue must look on him and his hand straightforwardly. It is perhaps an opportunity for the man and the community to come to terms with any hostility, shame or embarrassment they may have held. Mark uses the story to show how the Sabbath provides social restoration.

Like his first healing involving the exorcism of the unclean spirit, Jesus merely speaks, and the man's hand is restored (3:5). By saving a deformed hand, Jesus saves the man's ability to provide for himself. As one dwelling in an agrarian and fishing context, it is possible that man's inability to use his hand limited his power to provide for himself. Once again Mark helps to refocus the idea of the Sabbath as that which centers on God's provision and the need for humans to provide for each other. God through Jesus gives this man the means to care for himself and perchance for others. For Mark, the Sabbath is not the Sabbath for Sabbath's sake. It is a place, a celebration, an acknowledgement of not only social responsibility but of deliverance from economic hardship. Just as the slaves and aliens were to glean on the land on the seventh day and as the year of jubilee called for release from debt, Mark in this healing narrative also points to a fiscal cord that runs through Sabbath observation.

Nonetheless, one must not forget that this Gospel is rooted in religious and political disorder. Although the Pharisees and Herodians are silent in response to Jesus' question of what is lawful, they do not remain silent or suffer from arrested development. It is on this same Sabbath day that these leaders conspire not how to verbally respond to Jesus' rhetoric or how to simply silence him. Mark notes that the hardness of the hearts pushes these authority figures so that on the Sabbath they plot to destroy Jesus (3:6). It appears that in an indirect and perverse way they have answered the question of whether it is lawful to save life or to kill on the Sabbath.

In the Gospel's penultimate Sabbath story, Mark records Jesus attending the synagogue in his hometown of Nazareth (6:1-6a). Jesus is teaching, and people are astounded. What he says not only amazes them, but the "deeds of power by his hand" are just as stunning (6:2). Yet Jesus endures verbal abuse. This is not a result of his healing someone, but it is because of who he is. At issue is not the identity of Jesus as "Son of Man" or "Lord of the Sabbath." What is problematic is his family. Jesus' biological family and their lack of status cause trouble. Jesus is too plain, too ordinary. While elsewhere he is the healer, the restorer, at home he is just a carpenter. The same hands that touched Simon's mother-in-law and cooled her fever in Capernaum are the same hands used for maneuvering wood and tools at home, with a few exceptions. Jesus is no big shot in Nazareth.

Through this story Mark begins to set the stage for his further recontextualization of the Sabbath. Just as Mark's Jewish members would know the God of creation who rested on the Sabbath and provided enough manna on the sixth day for the seventh day, the writer now begins to unfold how God will provide for creation in another manner. God through the suffering Son of Man will offer salvation. Whereas earlier accounts of Sabbath activity in Mark note Jesus' power over physical dis-ease, social marginalization, economic disenfranchisement and political assaults, now the Gospel writer returns to the initial presentation of the Sabbath as that which honors God. Through the ensuing sacrifice of the Son of Man, Mark's community will recall its duty to revere God.

In another vein, the attacks on the healings or divine power of Jesus at this stage in his ministry prepare him for the betrayal and pain to come. He is amazed at the unbelief (6:6). The identity of Jesus begins to change from one who speaks with authority to one who will bleed and die. This Sabbath account in Mark refocuses the community's attention on the God of the Sabbath, not the Lord of Sabbath.

The Gospel of Mark makes its final mention of the Sabbath in the events surrounding the death, burial and resurrection of Jesus. The author records that on the day before the Sabbath, Joseph of Arimathea takes the body of Jesus, wraps it in linen and places it a tomb hewn out of a rock (15:42-46). After the Sabbath, Mary Magdalene, Mary the mother of James and Salome go to anoint Jesus' body. There is no mention of any activity on the Sabbath at this stage in Mark's work. While the writer has expounded on much Jesus and his disciples did on other days, now there is silence. There is inactivity. What should one do on the Sabbath? Be still. Be silent.

It appears that Mark indeed reframes the sense of sacredness of the day by purporting a cessation of action. The Genesis idea of Sabbath as rest and the Exodus mandate of a holy Sabbath now get re-visioned through the sanctimonious silence at the death of Jesus. God has worked out redemption for humankind. God has worked this out through Jesus. After God works, God rests. God's work is almost done. Let all the earth keep silent. Let all of creation rest and reflect on what God has done.

What to do on the Sabbath? Ask the founders of Chick-fil-A, and they will say eat burgers or go to some other eatery. After all, Chick-fil-A observes the Sabbath (on Sunday), and all of its restaurants are closed on that day. If one asks the owners of the Cupcake Collection in Nashville, they will say that on the Sabbath (Saturday), one should find some other sweet delicacy to savor. Their Seventh-Day Adventist faith calls them to honor this day of rest.

What should one do on the Sabbath? According to the Gospel of Mark, one should use the day to seek the healing and physical well-being of women, men and children. Whether it is healing from fever or from diabetes in this current time, the point is people need to be made well. The community must restore to economic ability those whose hands are "withered" due to no choice of their own. These persons must be restored so that they may provide for themselves and others. Today God calls humankind to seek the financial stability of our kindred who are "withered" due to job loss and fiscal disarray. On the Sabbath, according to Mark, one must work to include those who have been socially outcast and displaced. This also means women, men and children infected with and affected by our current HIV/AIDS crisis.

What to do on the Sabbath? Individuals honor the Sabbath by living through periods of suffering, distress and dis-ease. Even when a woman's own friends or a man's closest neighbors question their identity, Mark maintains that revering God on the Sabbath prepares both individual and community for redemption and salvation. Finally the Sabbath calls for periods of silence and inactivity. It calls God's creation to cease and desist and to let God's will and work be done.

Notes

1. *African-American Literature: A Brief Introduction and Anthology*, ed. Ishmael Reed (London: Longman, 1997), 450.

2. Alice Walker, *In Search of Our Mothers' Gardens* (San Diego: HBJ, 1983), 351.

3. Rick Lowery, *Sabbath and Jubilee* (Saint Louis: Chalice, 2000), 54.

4. Rodney Sadler and Emerson Powery, "Reading Against Jesus: Nineteenth Century African Americans' View of Sabbath Law," June 2005, http://www.sbl-site.org/Article.aspx?ArticleID=403.

5. Emerson Powery, "The Gospel of Mark," in *True to Our Native Land: An African American New Testament Commentary,* ed. Brian Blount, Clarice Martin, and Emerson Powery (Minneapolis: Fortress Press, 2007), 126.

6

———————

The Johannine Community

Power and Identity as a New Lens of Interpretation

Yak-Hwee Tan

In the field of Johannine Studies, the characterization of the Johannine community has been pursued by a number of scholars who have used various methodologies and approaches.[1] And they have made an invaluable contribution to the investigation of the Fourth Gospel. In their examination of the Fourth Gospel, some disclosed their agenda and identity, such as their sexual orientation, which bear upon their interpretation of the text. In the first part of this chapter, I will delineate some contributions regarding the history of Johannine Christianity, highlighting their methodologies and approaches that have ramifications in their representation of the Johannine community. I will then render some comments regarding their approaches.

Hereafter, I will seek to address the questions of power and identity regarding the characterization of the Johannine community especially in the light of the globalized world we live in. Finally, my concluding remarks will suggest that these questions might raised for biblical criticism in general, not simply the area of Johannine Studies.

THE JOHANNINE COMMUNITY: DIFFERENT APPROACHES

J. Louis Martyn's classic monograph *History and Theology in the Fourth Gospel* should be seen as a point of departure.[2] Martyn's new approach of reading the Fourth Gospel on several historical levels launched the study of the Johannine community anew. He argued that the story both of Jesus and the struggles of his believers are told when read at two levels.

Martyn hypothesized that the Johannine community was embroiled in an intra-religious and theological conflict between the Christians and the Jews.

83

As a result, the Christians were expelled from the synagogue. Martyn used a two-level reading strategy. At one level, the Fourth Gospel was said to present the story of Jesus as per the early part of the first century C.E.; at another level, the story of the Johannine community near the end of the first century C.E. That is to say, the Gospel's story of the *einmalig* (singular) event during Jesus' life on earth refers to the actual circumstances experienced by the Johannine community.[3] The story of the blind beggar and the events following his healing in John 9 showed the animosity of the Jewish authorities toward Jesus' followers and on another level, the story indicates the hostility lashed towards the Johannine community. As such, the story dramatizes the conflict between the synagogue and the church which led to their eventual separation. In the early period, the Johannine Christians were still involved in the life of the synagogue but they were expelled because of their confession in Jesus as both Messiah and God. For Martyn, the "literary history behind the Fourth Gospel reflects to a large degree the history of single community which maintained—over a period of some duration—its particular and somewhat peculiar identity."[4] Such is one approach to historical criticism, looking at the world "behind" the text.

Akin in certain respects to historical criticism, sociocultural criticism seeks to construct the social world "behind" the text, using concepts and models from social sciences such as sociology and anthropology. As in the case of the Fourth Gospel, scholars seek to construct the social world in which the community legitimizes its existence. In his article, "The Man from Heaven in Johannine Sectarianism," Wayne A. Meeks proposed that the "symbolic universe" reflects the "sectarian" character of the Johannine community, one that is anti-Jewish.[5] Meeks appealed to the motif of Jesus' "ascent and descent" in the Fourth Gospel and categories from the sociology of knowledge. According to John's Gospel, Meeks argued, the Jews, people of "this-world," were unable to understand and/or accept Jesus, the "one from above." This is seen in the encounter between Jesus and Nicodemus, a Pharisee and a leader of the Jews (John 3).[6] From a sociological perspective, the "ascent/descent" motif expresses the dialectic relationship between "the symbolic universe" and the community's historical experience vis-à-vis the Jews. That is to say, its "symbolic knowledge" of Jesus' other-worldliness bestows upon the Johannine community its identity in the light of the wider society which was Jewish in nature. Therefore, the community was able to demolish "the logic of the world, particularly the world of Judaism . . . progressively emphasizing the sectarian consciousness" of the community.[7]

Comments. Martyn's two-level reading of the Johannine community suggests that in order for readers to appreciate the struggles of the Johannine community, they must "see with the eyes and hear with the ears of that community."[8] Therefore, in order for the readers to obtain the meaning of the text, they must put aside their own presuppositions and use the appropriate methodological tools to extricate the text's historical and cultural contexts. In so doing, they can reproduce the world "behind" the text, the world of the biblical writer.[9] In a similar fashion, Meeks uses a socio-cultural approach to construct the community with respect to its socio-religious context. The identity of the real reader with his/her presuppositions is not brought to the fore.

THE JOHANNINE COMMUNITY: THE WORLD "IN" THE TEXT

Even though Martyn and Meeks used different methods to characterize the Johannine community, both were looking at the world "behind" the text with respect to the Jewish authorities. In other words, both argued for a situation that casts the Johannine community against Jewish society. R. Alan Culpepper, on the other hand, looked at the world "in" the text for his depiction of the Johannine community. And he must be credited for laying a foundation for the study of the Fourth Gospel using narrative criticism.[10] For his portrayal of the Johannine community, Culpepper examined the story's formal features, such as narrative time, plot, and implicit commentary, and how these interact with its characters. Jesus clarified or elaborated any misconceptions or misunderstandings the characters had of him. For example, the disciples inquired of Jesus regarding his "going away," and Jesus offered them an explanation with a metaphorical statement, "I am the way, and the truth, and the life; no one comes to the Father, but by me" (John 14:6).[11] The disciples have to be brought into a deeper faith with respect to the identity of Jesus. The disciples represent the Johannine community, and the story shows them as a community of little belief or unbelief, in need of a deeper faith from Jesus, the Revealer.

Culpepper's attention focused upon the artistry of the text and the "conventional literary codes" where meaning can be uncovered. He states, "the narrative components of the gospel interact and involve and affect the reader . . . [and the gospel] directs the production of its meaning."[12] Culpepper's analysis paved the way for the analysis of the world "in" the text.

In his earlier work Fernando F. Segovia contributed a detailed analysis of the Farewell Discourse, namely John 13:31—16:33.[13] For Segovia, the discourse is "an artistic and strategic whole with a highly unified and coherent literary structure and development, unified and coherent strategic concerns and aims, and a distinctive rhetorical situation."[14] By his careful and meticulous analysis of the structuration and rhetoric of the text, Segovia proposed that the Johannine community is seen as one having a special and privileged position in the world that entailed certain obligations and commitments. However, as members of the community, they would experience pressure from both inside and outside the community. As a result, their existence was in danger and hence, the urgent and immense need for exhortation and admonition to be steadfast.[15]

Comments. For both Culpepper and Segovia, the focus is upon the world "in" the text whereby the reader is able to make sense of the words, sentences and paragraphs of the text, having mastered the codes and conventions of the literary languages.[16] However, these interpretations of the Fourth Gospel do not account for the identity of the real flesh-and-blood reader(s) who is situated in his/her social location. Segovia later came to address the role of the real flesh-and-blood readers and its importance for the interpretation of the Fourth Gospel. Hence, he shifted his reading strategy towards cultural and ideological criticism, reading the Fourth Gospel from an intercultural perspective.[17]

The Johannine Community: The World "In Front" of the Text

Thus far, I have delineated diverse characterizations of the Johannine community by distinguished scholars who have used a variety of methods from the field of biblical criticism. With meticulous skill and professionalism, they dissected the world "behind" and "in" the text, without making known explicitly their own theological or ideological presuppositions. However, the depiction of the Johannine community has also been pursued by scholars from an ideological perspective, arguing that texts and authors as well as readers of the Bible are not neutral.[18] In other words, some ideological critics have argued that ideologies reside in text while others argued that ideologies reside in the people who read them. The emphasis is that people "construct" the meaning of the text, producing a proliferation of readings of the text that have been used as "weapon[s] of imperialism, sexism, and racism."[19] Therefore, ideological critics seek to read "against the grain" of such interpretations, to reconstruct the meaning of the text as well as disclose their diverse positioned and engaged social locations. A feminist reading strategy towards the characterization of the Johannine community models one such ideological approach.

Gail O'Day sought to show the significant role of women in the Johannine community.[20] We see this in the opening "sign" miracle in Jesus' ministry. It is a woman's initiative at the wedding at Cana that prompts Jesus to act (John 2:1-11). In addition, women provide Jesus' main conversation partners in three stories that reveal Jesus' identity and vocation and the nature of faithful discipleship (John 4:42; 7:53—8:11; 11:1-44). Moreover, Jesus' passion is watched over by the women, beginning with the anointing of Jesus' head by Mary and continuing with the women present at Jesus' death and Mary Magdalene's witness to the resurrection (John 12:1-8; 19:25-27; 20:1-18). O'Day further asserted that some theological themes in the Fourth Gospel are both liberating and transforming with respect to women's concerns, such as the "language of love."[21] She argued that the commandment to the disciples to love one another, modelled after Jesus' love for them (John 13:34-35), challenges both the men and women of the community to embrace discipleship and faith in a holistic way. The vine discourse includes no hierarchy among the branches, as their allegiance is only to the vine (John 15:1-11). As such, the vine metaphor exemplifies an egalitarian community that includes women and men and calls for equal treatment for women in the Christian community.[22]

O'Day described positively the Johannine community as one that includes women's participation in witness and discipleship. In her view the Fourth Evangelist "narrates a faith world that would not exist without women's participation in it."[23] However, Adeline Fehribach argued that the Fourth Gospel is couched with androcentric and patriarchal language that undermines the status of women.[24] Her historical-literary analysis of the Fourth Gospel shows how the Fourth Evangelist exploits female characters to further the plot of the story, that is, "to portray Jesus as the messianic bridegroom who was sent to establish the *familia Dei*" [family of God].[25] To illustrate her perspective, Fehribach argued that the portrayal of the mother of Jesus at Cana is positive because her assertiveness leads Jesus to perform his first "sign," turning water into wine (John 2:1-11). Jesus is fulfilling his destiny as promised by God. However, even though the mother of Jesus is depicted as a "mother of an important son" character type, she is shown to have misunderstood her son's importance. Apparently, Jesus' response to her points out that she does not know that Jesus' hour has not yet come. Ironically, she is denied of the kind of influence a "mother of an important son" would exercise over her son and concomitantly, her faith is questioned.[26]

As I have indicated, Segovia's approach to the Fourth Gospel has shifted from one that looks at the world "in" the text to the world "in front" of the text. Segovia's literary-rhetorical analysis demonstrates the relationship between the Word and God in terms of Jesus' journey between the other-world and the this-world and shows the structural flow that begins with the "other-world, to the this-world, and back to the other-world."[27] Segovia's literary-rhetorical analysis demonstrates the relationship between the Word and God with respect to the other-world and the this-world and showed the structural flow that begins with the "other-world, to the this-world, and back to the other-world."[28] In addition, Segovia observes the Gospel's ideological stance in the *difference* between the two worlds. The this-world is in "darkness" and needs enlightenment by the Word who is the Light and who is at the beginning of the world, the other-world (John 1:9). However, this *difference* is challenged because the Word becomes "in-carnated—human-ized; in believers, humanity becomes in-spirited—divin-ized" (John 1:14).[29] Such a "crossing over" to the this-world has a number of ramifications. One ramification involves power; that is, access to and knowledge of God are found only in those who believe in the Word, the "children of God" (1:12). Moreover, those who fail to be part of the community are also considered as enemies who have aligned themselves with the Roman empire or Judaism.[30] Therefore, Segovia argues that John 1:1-18 is not an abstract theological poem but a concrete expression of the reality that encompasses political, religious, and cultural as well as intellectual relationships. Moreover, Segovia highlights the dynamics of inclusion and exclusion that beckon for a critical response to one's own convictions as well as to the Fourth Gospel.

Comments. The two feminist readings of the Fourth Gospel disclose not only diverse interpretive methods but also the hermeneutical stance of the biblical scholars who bring "particular assumptions about the relationships among author, text, and reader and about the ways that people do and should interpret texts."[31] Even though O'Day and Fehribach have been informed by their gender identity as evidenced in the titles of their article and book respectively, their interpretations are different. Therefore, scholars who use ideological criticism demonstrate varied and multifaced identities and assumptions.

Furthermore, Segovia's assessment of the convictions and interests readers bring to the text invites us to question how texts and interpreters relate to matters of power and identity. As delineated above, the varied characterizations of the Johannine community offered by scholars disclose that on the one hand without an author there is no text, but on the other hand without a reader a text does not communicate.

POLITICS AND POETICS OF LOCATION: POWER AND IDENTITY

There will be diverse interpretations so long as there are diverse readers, who bring distinctive concerns and assumptions to the work of interpretation and who employ particular critical methods to address their concerns.[32] However, there is another aspect to consider in the process of interpretation, namely, the connection between power and knowledge. This connection was first propounded by Michel Foucault: "We should rather admit that power produces knowledge . . . that power and knowledge directly imply one another that there is no power relation without the correlative constitution of a field of knowledge, nor any knowledge that does not presuppose and constitute at the same time power relations."[33]

In other words, power and knowledge are not only interdependent but also serve to reinforce each other.

POWER, KNOWLEDGE, DISCOURSE

In calling attention to the interconnectedness between power and knowledge, Foucault also questioned the unspoken rules that determine the nature of a discourse as well as the identity of the authors who order such a discourse. According to Foucault, a "discourse" may be defined as "some material medium" whereby all ideas are ordered, organized, and patterned by unspoken rules.[34] As such, the powerful and/or knowledgeable have the power to construct and regulate knowledge and, more precisely, to construct the *kind* of knowledge concerning the "powerless." However, power functions in a capillary fashion and does not proceed from some central or hierarchical structure. Power is never inactive. In short, power is always, already, everywhere.[35] To put it another way, power resides not only within the discourse but also in the individual; the poetics and politics of the discourse/text at work and the *politics* and *poetics* of location go hand in hand.

Mary Ann Tolbert argued that the *politics* of location emphasizes the "multiplicity, complexity, and contextuality of human experience" and questions the writing of the text and its ideology. The *poetics* of location, on the other hand, analyzes the text understood as "constitutive reality," raising the question of language of power and the construction of positive or negative representation of others.[36] A politics of interpretation calls attention to the diverse relationships and commitments of authors and readers, while a poetics of interpretation investigates how biblical texts embody, promote, or resist certain configurations of power.

In a similar fashion, Susan Stanford Friedman has employed the phrases, *rhetoric of space* and *rhetoric of location*, to discuss the question of *locational feminism*. She argued that *locational feminism* is not static but is dependent on its location which is conditioned by time and space. Locational feminism acknowledges its historical and geographical grounding, but it also "changes, travels, translates, and transplants in different spacio/temporal contexts."[37] Though Friedman's approach concerns feminism, I find her argument on space and location applicable to the question of social location and the biblical text. One's interpretation of the biblical text is "simultaneously situated in a specific locale, global in scope, and constantly in motion in time and space."[38] Space and location are no longer seen as solely physical or temporal; they are not fixed, but shifting. Since space and locations are no longer fixed, the meanings of events or issues can be constructed in diverse contexts across time and space. Meanings are no longer static but have become fluid because of other determining factors, such as the social location of the "real reader." That is to say, one's perspective is always *locational.* This is evident in the rise of biblical scholars from parts of the world other than the West who are engaging in the task of biblical interpretation, including myself.[39]

As one whose heritage is Chinese and Confucian but who became a Christian during her youth at a Christian mission school and whose education has been primarily Western, Christian, and Eurocentric in character, I cannot deny that my encounters with the West and Christianity have produced an "in-between" person. That is, my identity is no longer an essentialized one but one that embodies a clashing of classes, nationalities, religions, and ethnicities. As such, the hermeneutical stance of my reading of the Johannine community is shaped by the *politics* and *poetics* of location, a re-presentation of the community as one that is in flux.

Re-presenting the Johannine Community: A Postcolonial Perspective

In the farewell discourse, Jesus, like a departing/dying hero, issues words of encouragement, warning, and admonition to his followers, providing them with a sense of self-definition as a community.[40] In view of his the impending departure to the world-above, Jesus warns the disciples against the hatred of the world-below because of the disciples' alliance with him and not with the world-below (John 15:18-16:3; cf. 13:1). The "world-below" refers to the encompassing reality of the Roman Empire, which includes diverse political, social, cultural, and religious conditions.[41] At the same time, Jesus exhorts the disciples to stand firm because the coming Paraclete will teach them many things (John 14:15-17, 25-26; 15:26-27; 16:4b-15). The disciples are further encouraged by the revelation that Jesus is going ahead to prepare a place for them (John 14:1-4; 16:1-14). Lest the disciples grow apathetic because of Jesus' assurances, they are admonished to remain in Jesus, to bear fruit, and to love one another (John 15:1-17). As such, the disciples are caught in a flux—"caught in two worlds."[42]

The binary opposites of Self and Other are depicted metaphorically as the vine and the branches respectively. The hegemonic identity of Jesus, the Self, is upheld in that he claims exclusivity in the light of other allegations as well the demand of complete allegiance from his disciples, the Other (John 15:1, 6). In the face of the Roman imperial reality, Jesus emerges as the new Self. By drawing the disciples to himself, he creates an alternative community in resistance to the imperial rule. On the other hand, the disciples will encounter harsh realities with respect to the "world-below" because of their alliance with Jesus. The disciples know Jesus' sender, but the "world below" does not, even though the "world below" has witnessed Jesus' works in their midst. As such, the identity of the disciples as the Other is inverted with respect to the "world-below."

On the one hand, the Farewell Discourse constructs the identity of the Johannine Community in terms of *difference*; on the other hand, it re-presents the identity of the Johannine community as fluid. In their collision with the Roman Empire, a "contact zone" is created where disparate cultures meet, clash, grapple with each other.[43] The "contact zone" emerges when the colonized or subjugated group re-presents information which the colonizers have selected and designed concerning them (the colonized).[44] In the case of the Johannine community, the identity of the community is full of contradictions and ambiguities: they could "slide" into either world, that is, the "world-above" or the "world-below," the world of the imperial Roman Empire. The Johannine community, hence, proves to be a challenge to either world. But more importantly, the fluid nature of the community means that they are defined neither by the "world-below" nor by the "world-above." In other words, the self-definition of the Johannine community is grounded upon their own understanding of their relationship to these two worlds, a relationship that is always fluid in nature.

My characterization of the Johannine community illustrates my interrogation of the text and of real readers, demonstrating the significant role of social location in the task of interpretation. Therefore, in the light of the characterization of the Johannine community, both the text itself and its readers are called into question. This process brings me to discuss the role of social location in the task of interpretation.[45] Behind each interpretation really stands the world of the real readers "who are neither neutral nor impartial but as inextricably positioned and engaged within their own different complex social locations."[46] The multidimensional context of readers' experiences and agendas, such as one's sexual orientation, socioeconomic class, race and ethnicity, ideological stance, and so forth, creates differences and particularities in their approaches to the reading of the texts. In short, the questions of power and identity are critical for the interpretation of the biblical text, not least the Fourth Gospel.

Globalization has created inroads whereby borders between nations are becoming more accessible. At the same time, it has brought about the intensification of cyber technology and its related processes, contributing to "a shift from temporal to spatial modes of thought."[47] In other words, the rhetoric of historical narrative and other discourses which are produced for pedagogical ends are challenged by their implication in networks of power.[48] Underlying the rhetoric of historical narratives are ideologically conditioned presuppositions. Therefore, readers need to challenge and investigate these underlying presuppositions. This strategy of interrogation lies within one's reach because the fluid nature of space and location has created a "social space" whereby power and identity may be exercised by real, flesh-and-blood readers.

Segovia's critical analysis of the shifting paradigms in biblical studies names three phases: the first phase defined by historical criticism and the second phase shaped by literary criticism and (socio)cultural criticism.[49] Attention to the agenda and identity of real, flesh-and-blood reader(s) is located in the third phase. Recognition of real readers and their diverse interests challenges anew standard questions in biblical criticism, particularly the characterization of the Johannine community.

Furthermore, the world that we live in is "glocal" in nature, meaning that the "local and global are co-complicit, each implicated in the other."[50] In other words, the particularities of the local, such as its material culture, are not only linked with the local but are also connected politically and economically with the global. This mutual implication precludes tendencies to homogenize one or the other.[51] Therefore, the idea of a univocal interpretation of the biblical text is undermined with respect to both critical methodologies and real readers. The notion that texts are fluid also enables interpreters, who are conditioned by their social locations, to reinterpret and re-present their own identities and realities and readings of the texts anew. In short, accounting for power and identity represents a critical dimension for contemporary biblical interpretation.

Notes

1. My first encounter with Fernando F. Segovia was in the course that I enrolled in when I was a graduate student at Vanderbilt University. In this course he introduced the methods and

theories in the study of New Testament Studies and my "eyes were opened" to see the array of methods and approaches where one could use in the examination of biblical texts. Moreover, for someone like me who delights in the study of the Fourth Gospel, Fernando F. Segovia's passion for the Fourth Gospel radiates in his lectures and discussions in and outside the classroom; it is infectious. Fernando F. Segovia's contribution to biblical studies, therefore, is not only an academic quest but also a personal dedication for what he does; an example which we could emulate. His contribution to the academy, I am certain, will continue to linger in years to come. Segovia is an accomplished scholar not only in the field of Johannine Studies but is also a foremost pioneer in the field of postcolonial biblical criticism, proposing a "postcolonial optic" in reading the biblical text. And I count it an honor and privilege to write a chapter for this volume in honor of an esteemed scholar, teacher and friend.

2. J. Louis Martyn, *History and Theology in the Fourth Gospel*, 3rd ed. (Louisville: Westminster John Knox, 2003).

3. Ibid., 30.

4. J. Louis Martyn, "Glimpses into the History of the Johannine Community," in *The Gospel of John in Christian History: Essays for Interpretation* (New York: Paulist, 1978), 90–121.

5. Wayne A. Meeks, "The Man from Heaven in Johannine Sectarianism," *JBL* 19 (1972): 44–72.

6. Ibid., 58–59.

7. Ibid., 70.

8. Martyn, *History and Theology*, 18.

9. Fernando F. Segovia, "'And They Began to Speak in Other Tongues': Competing Modes of Discourse in Contemporary Biblical Criticism," in *Decolonizing Biblical Studies: A View from the Margins* (Maryknoll: Orbis, 2000), 3–33. See also A. Berkeley Mickelsen, *Interpreting the Bible* (Grand Rapids: Eerdmans, 1963), 170.

10. R. Alan Culpepper, *Anatomy of the Fourth Gospel: A Study in Literary Design* (Philadelphia: Fortress Press, 1983).

11. Ibid., 152–65.

12. Ibid., 6.

13. Fernando F. Segovia, *The Farewell of the Word: The Johannine Call to Abide* (Minneapolis: Fortress Press, 1991).

14. Ibid., 284.

15. Ibid., 283–308.

16. W. Randolph Tate, *Biblical Interpretation: An Integrated Approach*, rev. ed. (Peabody: Hendrickson, 1997), 152.

17. Fernando F. Segovia, "Inclusion and Exclusion in John 17: An Intercultural Reading," in *What Is John?"* vol. 2, *Literary and Social Readings of the Fourth Gospel*, SBLSymS 7, ed., Fernando F. Segovia (Atlanta: Scholars, 1998), 183–209; see also, "John 1:1-18 as Entrée into Johannine Reality: Representation and Ramifications," in *Word, Theology, and Community in John*, ed. John Painter, R. Alan Culpepper, and Fernando F. Segovia (Saint Louis: Chalice, 2002), 33–64.

18. For an introduction to ideological criticism, see The Bible and Culture Collective, "Ideological Criticism" in *The Postmodern Bible* (New Haven: Yale University Press, 1995), 272–308; and Tina Pippin, ed. *Ideological Criticism of Biblical Texts, Semeia* 59 (1992).

19. Tina Pippin, "Ideology, Ideological Criticism and the Bible," *Currents in Research: Biblical Studies* 4 (1996): 60.

20. Gail R. O'Day, "John," in *Women's Bible Commentary: Expanded Edition with Apocrypha*, ed. Carol A. Newsom and Sharon H. Ringe (Louisville: Westminster John Knox, 1998), 381–93.

21. O'Day, "John," 390–93. O'Day discussed the theological themes under the various headings, "the language of love," "the vine metaphor" and "father language of God," and asserted that these themes addressed both the concerns of women and men, even though they are not directed at women per se.

22. Ibid., 391–92.

23. Ibid., 382.

24. Adeline Fehribach, *The Women in the Life of the Bridegroom: A Feminist Historical-Literary Analysis of the Female Characters in the Fourth Gospel* (Collegeville: Liturgical, 1998).

25. Ibid., 20. The pericopae that Fehriback analyzes are: The Mother of Jesus at Cana (2:1-12); The Samaritan woman at the well (4:1-41); Mary and Martha of Bethany (11:1-46; 12:1-11); The Mother of Jesus at the Cross (19:25-28); and Mary Magdalene at the tomb (20:1-18). She omits the story of the adulterous woman (7:53-8:11) because the story did not appear until the fourth century C.E.

26. Ibid., 42–43.

27. Segovia, "John 1:1-18 as Entrée into Johannine Reality," 37.

28. Ibid., 37.

29. Ibid., 55.

30. Ibid. 56. The other ramifications involve religion, ethnicity and race, and gender.

31. Beverly J. Stratton, "Ideology," in *Handbook of Postmodern Biblical Interpretation*, ed. A. K. M. Adam (Saint Louis: Chalice, 2000), 123.

32. See Mary Ann Tolbert's article, "Politics and Poetics of Location," in *Reading from This Place*, vol. 1: *Social Location and Biblical Interpretation in the United States*, ed. Fernando F. Segovia and Mary Ann Tolbert (Minneapolis: Fortress Press, 1995), 305–17. Tolbert argues that the complex relations between modernism and postmodernism have ramifications for biblical interpretation, such as "politics of location" and "poetics of location."

33. Michel Foucault, *Discipline and Punish: The Birth of the Prison*, trans. Alan Sheridan (New York: Random, 1977), 27.

34. Bill Ashcroft, Gareth Griffiths and Helen Tiffin, *Key Concepts in Post-Colonial Studies* (London: Routledge, 1998), 71.

35. Michel Foucault, *Power/Knowledge: Selected Interviews and Other Writings 1972–1977*, ed. Colin Gordon, Leo Marshall, John Mepham, and Kate Sopher (New York: Pantheon, 1980), 98.

36. Tolbert, "The Politics and Poetics of Location ," 311–17.

37. Susan Stanford Friedman, "Locational Feminism: Gender, Cultural Geographies, and Geopolitical Literacy," in *Feminist Locations: Global and Local, Theory and Practice*, ed. Marianne Dekoven (New Brunswick: Rutgers University Press, 2001), 15.

38. Ibid., 15.

39. See R. S. Sugirtharajah, ed., *Voices from the Margins: Interpreting the Bible in the Third World*, 2nd ed. (Maryknoll: Orbis, 1995); Musa W. Dube, *Postcolonial Feminist Interpretation of the Bible* (Saint Louis: Chalice, 2000).

40. See Yak-Hwee Tan, *Re-presenting the Johannine Community: A Postcolonial Perspective* (New York: Lang, 2008).

41. Segovia, "Inclusion and Exclusion in John 17," 183–209.

42. See also Yak-Hwee Tan, "The Johannine Community: Caught in 'Two Worlds" in *New Currents Through John: A Global Perspective*, ed. Francisco Lozada, Jr. and Tom Thatcher (Atlanta: Society of Biblical Literature, 2006), 167–79.

43. Mary Louise Pratt, *Imperial Eyes: Travel Writing and Transculturation* (London: Routledge, 1992), 4. Pratt seeks to show the connection between travel writing and forms of knowledge and expressions, how their interaction and intersection have bearing upon the production of "the rest of the world" for European consumption.

44. Ibid., 7.

45. See Francisco Lozada Jr., "Social Location and Johannine Scholarship: Looking Ahead," in *New Currents Through John: A Global Perspective*, ed. Francisco Lozada Jr. and Tom Thatcher (Atlanta: Society of Biblical Literature, 2006), 183–97. In his article, Lozada explores the question of the reader's social location by reviewing three works on the Gospel of John that use social location in various ways. The three works under examination fall under the theoretical framework of cultural studies.

46. Fernando F. Segovia, "Cultural Studies and Contemporary Biblical Criticism: Ideological Criticism as Mode of Discourse" in *Decolonizing Biblical Studies: A View from the Margins* (Maryknoll: Orbis Books, 2000), 46–47.

47. Friedman, "Locational Feminism," 18.

48. See Edward W. Said, *Orientalism* (New York: Vintage, 1979). Said argues that Orientalism is a discourse invented by European culture to manage and produce the Orient.

49. Segovia, "Cultural Studies and Contemporary Biblical Criticism: Ideological Criticism as Mode of Discourse," 36.

50. Friedman, "Locational Feminism," 31.

51. Ibid., 30.

7

Negotiating Difference

Theology and Ethnicity in the Acts of the Apostles

Eric D. Barreto

Race and ethnicity are powerful forces.[1] Racial and ethnic notions have forged communities and torn neighbors asunder. Racial and ethnic identities have helped people face the world's challenges with solidarity. Racial and ethnic prejudice has precipitated both mere dislike and violent warfare. Race and ethnicity are inevitable features of human life whenever and wherever we gather to form communities of "fictive kinship."[2] Whether for good or ill, race and ethnicity are inescapable.

Too many biblical scholars have, however, tended to neglect or otherwise marginalize the presence, function, and importance of ethnic difference in the texts of the Bible. Though many are motivated by the hope that the gospel might bring to pass a world in which racial and ethnic animus are a remnant of the distant past, such neglect has left this central feature of human life underexplored. Moreover, theological analysis of ethnic difference has too often not examined the complexities and even contradictions present when we engage in discourse of race and ethnicity, devolved into simple binaries, or simply neglect this central notion of identity.

The Acts of the Apostles is a natural home for exegetes hoping to make sense of the rich ethnic diversity of God's people. At root, Acts narrates the intrusion of the gospel into the myriad populations that dotted the landscape around the Mediterranean in antiquity. Propelled by persecution and the Spirit's guidance, these first followers of Jesus carry the gospel message to the very ends of the earth. A number of cultural boundaries are crossed in Acts, but at no point does Luke narrate the cessation of ethnic difference. Instead, the text invites us to enter a world in which ethnic difference and faithful unity coexist.

97

What Role Did Race and Ethnicity Play in Early Christianity?

In both biblical scholarship and Christian theology more broadly, the description and reconstruction of the earliest days of the Christian church as a movement that strived for the end of racial and ethnic differences is widespread. Recently, Denise Kimber Buell concluded,

> Most historical reconstructions published in the last twenty years depict earliest Christianity as an inclusive movement that rejected ethnic or racial specificity as a condition of religious identity. "Christianity swept racial distinctions aside," proclaims Frank Snowden, Jr., a classicist whose influential scholarship has helped to reframe the way we think about race in antiquity. Similarly, Anthony Smith, writing for anthropologists as well as historians, states that earliest Christianity "helped to…transcend existing ethnic divisions." And the feminist theologian Rosemary Radford Ruether asserts that "class, ethnicity, and gender are . . . specifically singled out as the divisions overcome by redemption in Christ." These are only three examples, ranging across three disciplines, but they are typical in making the rejection of the relevance of race or ethnicity a defining feature of earliest Christianity.[3]

These depictions emerge from a clearly positive desire to see the end of the ethnic and racial strife that pervades our world and our shared histories. However, by denying the continued importance of racial and ethnic differences among the earliest Christians, such reconstructions advocate an inaccurate portrayal with significant impact today. In our hope to make racism a relic of the past, we may strive too quickly and move too easily into a mode of forgetfulness or denial. By denying the reality of difference, we may end up only exacerbating the problem of prejudice.

Especially problematic has been the tendency of biblical scholars and Christian theologians alike to draw a fundamental binary between a nationalistic, ethnocentric Judaism on the one hand and a universal, ethnic-free Christianity on the other.[4] In this way, Christianity becomes an open association of all peoples wherein their differences are no longer of importance, in stark contrast to a purported Judaism with rigid lines of ethnic demarcation. Though such exegetical decisions may seem innocuous at first, they have misshaped our theological and historical imagination.[5] Both Christianity and Judaism in antiquity traded on the cultural leverage that ethnic discourse provides.[6] Moreover, both recognized that the negotiation of our ethnic differences is an irreplaceable component of our social fabric.

If we read the New Testament with an eye towards ethnic discourse and pay attention to the importance of ethnic differences in antiquity and today, we will discover a deeply theological and sophisticated engagement with human differences. The theological question of inclusion and exclusion is central to much of the New Testament. How can the many peoples of the world together worship the one God of Israel? What does it mean that the story of God's interaction with God's chosen people extends to the rest of the world? To answer these important questions, the author of Luke-Acts turns to ethnic discourse, to the consideration of human differences not as obstacles to unity to be transcended but theologically vibrant sites for God's actions in the world.

The author of Luke-Acts views our differences as a gift from God to be treasured, not a difficulty to be overcome. Ethnic and racial differences are not the problem that curses the human family. Instead, prejudice and racism inject our differences with the sinful notion that our differences lead to superiority and inferiority or the distorted belief that our differences are merely cultural cues for determining who is in and who is out, rather than emblems of God's gift of diversity.

What Role Do Race and Ethnicity Play in the Acts of the Apostles?

Luke cannot help but think of ethnicity when composing Acts. After all, the travel itinerary of Acts' main protagonists covers a broad swath of the ancient world. As Acts 1:8 indicates, these earliest proclaimers of the gospel move from Jerusalem, to Judea, to Samaria and finally to the very edges of the world. From its very first chapter, therefore, Acts narrates the crossing of ethnic and cultural boundaries. Acts guides us through some of the great cities of antiquity, finally finding Paul preaching unencumbered at the urban seat of Roman power. The negotiation of ethnic boundaries is part of the very narrative fabric of Acts.

Examples of these negotiations abound. I will focus on Acts 16 in the next section; however, I would like to highlight just a few other elements of the narrative of Acts as a means of introduction.

The extended scene of the promised outpouring of the Spirit in Pentecost is a powerful story. Jesus promises his disciples to send a gift to them both at the conclusion of Luke's Gospel (Luke 24:49) as well as the opening verses in Acts (1:8). That promise comes to fulfillment in Acts 2 right as the city of Jerusalem is teeming with visitors from around the world. Tongues of fire descend upon the gathered faithful as the Holy Spirit grants the power to speak in other languages. Such a miracle baffles the *Ioudaioi*[7] gathered for the festival from every corner of the Roman Empire. In 2:5–11, Acts outlines the ethnic identities of all these peoples in detail. Whether Luke is here imitating some other forms of ancient literature is unclear though entirely possible. What may be clearer, though, is the nature of the scene he paints.

Despite their sharing of a faith that draws them from great distances, these gathered masses are not homogenous; they are not all entirely alike. It is this scene of ethnic and linguistic diversity in which the Holy Spirit makes a grand appearance. Each person hears the gospel proclaimed in her own language. The Holy Spirit does not speak with one language but with all the languages of the human tableau. If you have had any experience with foreign languages, the enormity of this feat is even starker.

Remember that languages do not correlate exactly. That is, you cannot speak a new language by looking up individual words in a dictionary and translating them accordingly. One has to learn the language at a deeper, syntactical level. Moreover, language and culture are inextricably tied together. So, the Holy Spirit's translation of the gospel must cross not just linguistic boundaries but cultural ones as well. In this scene, the differences among people are not made void or ended. The Holy Spirit does not force all those gathered in Jerusalem to hear the gospel in a universal heavenly language. Instead, the Holy Spirit accommodates and lives into the multiplicity of human language and culture as a direct expression of the gospel's wide reach over all the peoples of the world.

To be sure, the story of Babel lies in the background here (Gen 11:1-9).[8] That story sought to comprehend how human cultural and linguistic diversity came about. Here, Luke pursues a similar though not identical thought. How can the good news of Jesus be proclaimed in a world rife with ethnic and linguistic diversity? How can the gospel find expression in other tongues and cultures? What will bind these believers together? Pentecost suggests that this sharing occurs in the very midst of ethnic diversity with the Spirit's intervention as a binding agent. The Spirit permits all to hear the gospel in their own vernacular and in their own cultural contexts without requiring our differences to be brought to an end. The Parthians and Medes, Cretans and Arabs that filled Jerusalem that fateful Pentecost day did not leave their ethnic identities behind in order to follow the Messiah. Instead, the Spirit spoke in the multiplicity of human languages to draw all near to God.

The theological problems and opportunities afforded by the multiplicity of peoples populating the world emerge powerfully in a number of critical narrative moments in Acts, inviting even further investigation of the early church's negotiation of ethnic boundaries and the theological import of such moves.

The encounter of Peter and Cornelius (chap. 10) begins to erode the rituals and mores that kept Jew and Greek from breaking bread together and thus embracing full fellowship. Peter's acceptance of Gentile believers as sisters and brothers in faith lags behind the powerful moving of the Spirit. The conclusions of the apostolic council in Acts 15 further engage in ethnic discourse by paving a theological path by which both Jew and Gentile could draw near to God. In neither case does difference come to an end. Instead, God provides a way to live into these differences in a faithful way.

Earlier in the narrative (8:26-40), Philip's encounter with the Ethiopian eunuch signaled the expansive ambitions of God and God's church.[9] The Ethiopian eunuch's identity is caught in a web of complex discourses around ethnicity, gender, and sexuality. He is a foreigner from an exotic land, a powerful and wealthy individual. But his status as a eunuch both provides the means by which he could become rich and powerful but sets him up for approbation according to some ancient texts.[10] For modern readers, that an African here plays an important role in the earliest days of the church provides a hedge against the racist assumptions perniciously present in church, scholarship, and the wider culture alike.

In addition, the powerful, looming shadow of Rome also precipitates a number of questions about identity, especially when so many of the peoples depicted in Acts are colonial subjects of a hegemonic empire. The negotiation of their ethnic identity is complicated by the hegemony of Rome's imperial might.

The kind of analysis of ethnic discourse I propose could be conducted with a number of important passages in Acts. In this essay, however, I would like to turn our attention to an important but often neglected chapter. In Acts 16, rich stories, the crossing of cultural boundaries, and profound ethnic negotiations intersect.

Negotiating Jewishness and Romanness: Acts 16 as a Test Case

Acts 16 narrates the aftermath of the consequential conclusions of the Jerusalem council in chap. 15.[11] Faced with complex questions about the composition of God's people and Gentiles receiving the good news, the leaders of the early days of the Jesus movement reach a consensus. Gentiles need not embrace fully the dictates of Jewish religiosity—especially circumcision and eating practices—though they ought to abide by certain cultural regulations probably dealing with pagan religious practices (15:28-29).

Acts 15 thus narrates a critical turn in the narrative that has been brewing since much earlier. That the Gentiles would be welcome amid the followers of Jesus was augured at least as early as the prophetic songs of the opening chapters of Luke's Gospel. In Acts, the ambiguously identified Ethiopian eunuch (8:26-40) and the conversion of the centurion Cornelius and his household (chap. 10) signaled an openness to Gentiles that would only receive official ecclesial sanction in Acts 15. With the conclusions of the apostolic council, we might safely assume that the question of inclusion had been fully settled, that the dividing line between Jew and Greek had been clarified and transcended. Acts 16 quickly challenges this seemingly clear consensus.

Negotiating Identities on Timothy's Body (16:1-5)

The opening verses of Acts 16 are both brief and enigmatic. Much is left unsaid in this rather controversial moment of Pauline biography in Acts. In verse 1, we are introduced to Timothy, a disciple whose father was Greek and whose mother was *Ioudaias* and a "believer" (pistēs). His reputation is generally sterling, but he faces one significant obstacle to the work Paul hopes to accomplish alongside him. "The Jews who were in those places" (16:3) know that his father was Greek and thus are suspicious of Timothy's fealty to Jewish religious and ethnic practices. To preempt this concern, Paul has Timothy circumcised. Lest we think that this circumcision violates the conclusions of the apostolic council, verse 4 recounts that Paul and Timothy successfully communicate its decision.

This brief narration leaves many gaps in the story. Why was Timothy not circumcised as a child? Some scholars have theorized that his father might have prohibited it or that local cultural pressures "de-incentivized" it. But Luke provides no clarification. Moreover, what was the ethnic status of Timothy prior to his circumcision? What was his ethnic status following his circumcision? Notice that at no point does Acts attach a single clarifying ethnic term to Timothy. Much scholarship has wondered whether Timothy would have been considered to be a Jew or a Gentile in antiquity.[12] Yet the narrative suggests that this question may miss a wider point. Timothy never receives a clarifying ethnic appellation because his ethnic identity remains irreducibly mixed. He remains—even after his circumcision—the product of a mixed marriage and thus both Jewish and Greek.

In the end, Timothy embodies an ethnic seam running through the end of Acts, representing the ethnic divide between Jew and Greek with which the church in Acts needed to grapple. Evidence for this conclusion can be found in Timothy's fleeting appearances in the closing chapter of Acts. Paul's role in the circumcision of Timothy never emerges again even when he is accused of teaching Jews to forsake their ancestral ways (for example, 21:21). But Timothy's presence is noted four times in the final chapters of Acts (17:14; 18:5; 19:22; 20:4). In none of these instances does Timothy play a prominent role in Luke's storytelling; he is only one among Paul's entourage, but his presence is powerfully symbolic. In these lists of Paul's companions, Timothy is not a stranger, an alien, or an outsider whose presence requires justification. As I have argued elsewhere, "He is no longer under the critical gaze of those who would question his fractured ethnic identity. Instead, he is wholly a part of a movement that does not erase one's ethnic origins but finds ways to embrace these differences. . . . He shows that ethnic incertitude is no obstacle to the gospel and that ethnic purity is not requisite for membership in the multiethnic people of God."[13]

A Roman Citizen? (16:16–40)

Ethnic controversies continue later in Acts 16 with the arrival of Paul and his retinue in Philippi. Paul has already discovered a place of prayer populated by faithful women on the outskirts of the city and found success in proclaiming the gospel to Lydia and her household. On his way to the place of prayer, Paul would regularly encounter a mantic girl whose prophetic abilities were exploited by her master for economic gain. Driven to the edge of impatience, Paul reacts apparently without too much forethought. He ejects the spirit and precipitates an impending tumult.

The business syndicate brings Paul and Silas before the local authorities accusing them, not of ruining their enterprise,[14] but of destabilizing the fragile social, cultural, and political fabric of this Roman colony. They posit a stark contrast. These "Jews" are asking us to do something that we "Romans" ought not do. The ethnocentric accusation is unmistakable, as Richard Pervo recently concluded: "The owners were shrewd enough to mask their avarice with a potent brew concocted from the ultimate resort of the scoundrel, a dose of old-time religion, and a garnish of racism."[15]

The accusations are so effective that Paul and Silas end up at the receiving end of a brutal physical attack and are imprisoned. A miraculous earthquake and the conversion of a guard fill the long narrative night. The next day brings seeming liberation. For unknown reasons, the local authorities decide to release Paul and Silas, but Paul has been affronted by the previous day's events, and he refuses to leave quietly. He makes a bold declaration that I think has been poorly translated recently.

Most modern translations record Paul's claim of Roman citizenship in 16:37-38.[16] However, the same ethnic terminology (*Rōmaios*) is used in these verses as in the accusation leveled against Paul and Silas earlier in verse 21. The addition of a claim to citizenship is not entirely misplaced. The rights of citizenship are certainly in view here. But pointing in these verses solely to a claim to Roman citizenship misses a key narrative theme. Paul's claim to be "Roman" is a direct refutation of the scurrilous accusation brought against him and Silas. The claim is not solely juridical or legal but ethnic in nature. Paul's assertion advances a bold claim that he and Silas are not contraveners of the local culture, but are truly at home in these Roman environs. In claiming to be Roman, they do not therefore challenge the accusation of verse 20. They indeed are "Jews" but that ethnic identity does not naturally lead to the conclusion reached by the sinister business syndicate.

Scholars have frequently seen in this story a glimpse into Pauline biography. This may be the case, but such a focus may miss the narrative and theological implications of Paul's claim. Paul is not merely claiming political rights due to a citizen but undercutting wholly the baseless accusation lobbed their way. Paul and Silas are not a threat to this Roman colony, for they indeed are Romans! In this way, Luke narrates how the early church negotiated a space in the midst of the teeming ethnic diversity of the ancient world. Paul and Silas are both Jewish and Roman. These two identities are not at odds, and they along with other believers do not have to sacrifice their ethnic and cultural identities in order to be faithful followers of Jesus.

Race, Ethnicity, and Readings of Scripture

That race and ethnicity matter in the study of the Bible is made evident by a number of recent efforts to understand how these admittedly difficult notions helped shaped biblical texts.[17] Fundamental to how we view ourselves individually is how we group those who are like us and those who differ from us.

How then might Acts illuminate the complex negotiations of ethnic difference that define so much of our world today? That Acts engages in ethnic discourse does not by itself solve the theological and ideological problems we face as we strive towards cultures and communities of faith that welcome and embrace differences. Tat-siong Benny Liew is right to call attention to the many sharp edges we find in the book of Acts as Luke grapples with difference.[18] Liew is precisely right that "the problem of community integration in Acts is entangled with matters of language and ethnicity."[19] Furthermore, for Liew, Luke's purportedly inclusive impulses also carry exclusionary requirements.[20] Simply, Luke's use of ethnic discourse and thinking is not an unalloyed good, especially when readers of Acts see the promotion of a facile universalism.

I would agree that something far more complex than such a facile universalism is part of the narrative fabric of Acts. Such complexity requires a careful and critical perspective. Acts cannot serve as a mere handbook for resolving today's many ethnic conflicts. Neither is it irrelevant to our work today.

While I concur that the negotiations of difference in Acts are complex and potentially able to contravene efforts to embrace difference, I do not concur with Liew that, in the end, Acts grapples problematically with ethnic difference. The vision of the world Acts propounds is one in which ethnic differences are taken seriously but are not presumed to be inherently problematic in the creation of communities of faith. In narrative form, Acts forwards a powerful theological argument that faithful unity and ethnic diversity are neither at odds nor mutually exclusive. Luke cannot fathom a world in which our differences are transcended or effaced but narrates a church in which ethnic differences are taken seriously but not allowed to divide people between the inferior and the superior. The cultural contexts have certainly shifted in the intervening centuries, but analogous pressures today demand an equally robust theological response.

Notes

1. A previous version of this essay appeared in *WW* 31 (2011): 129-37. I would like to thank the journal's editor and my colleague Fred Gaiser for kindly permitting the essay's republication. Fernando Segovia and his work have been critical influences in my scholarship and vocation as a theological educator since my days in seminary when I read his *Decolonizing Biblical Studies: A View from the Margins* (Maryknoll: Orbis, 2000) in one sitting. My approach to biblical studies has not been the same since. For his work, influence, and mentoring, I am most grateful.

2. "Fictive kinship" is a phrase used to define ethnic identity by Jonathan Hall, *Ethnic Identity in Greek Antiquity* (Cambridge: University of Cambridge Press, 1997).

3. Denise Kimber Buell, "Rethinking the Relevance of Race for Early Christian Self-Definition," *HTR* 94 (2001): 453. See also Buell, *Why This New Race? Ethnic Reasoning in Early Christianity* (New York: Columbia University Press, 2005).

4. See Denise Kimber Buell and Caroline Johnson Hodge, "The Politics of Interpretation: The Rhetoric of Race and Ethnicity in Paul," *JBL* 123 (2004): 235–51.

5. For the disastrous results of such a truncated imagination about ancient peoples, see Susannah Heschel, *The Aryan Jesus: Christian Theologians and the Bible in Nazi Germany* (Princeton: Princeton University Press, 2008).

6. See, for example, Laura Nasrallah and Elisabeth Schüssler Fiorenza, eds., *Prejudice and Christian Beginnings: Investigating Race, Gender, and Ethnicity in Early Christian Studies* (Minneapolis: Fortress Press, 2009).

7. There is considerable debate in biblical studies around the best translation of *Ioudaios*. Some scholars advocate for "Judean," partly as a corrective of previous scholarship that lumped all "Jews" together as opponents of Jesus and Christians more broadly but also as an acknowledgment that the term is primarily an ethnic, not just a religious marker. See, for example, Steve Mason, "Jews, Judaeans, Judaizing, Judaism: Problems of Categorization in Ancient History, " *JSJ* 38 (2007): 457–512. In contrast, other scholars have advocated retaining the term "Jews" despite its attendant problems because it preserves a vital connection between ancient and modern adherents to this system of belief and ethnic classification. See, for example, Amy-Jill Levine, *The Misunderstood Jew: The Church and the Scandal of the Jewish Jesus* (San Francisco: HarperSanFrancisco, 2006), 87–117.

8. See Theodore Hiebert, "The Tower of the Babel and the Origin of the World's Cultures," *JBL* 126 (2007): 29–58.

9. See Clarice Martin, "A Chamberlain's Journey and the Challenges of Interpretation for Liberation," *Semeia* 47 (1989): 105–35.

10. See, for example, Deut. 23:1; Lev. 21:16-20; Sir. 20:4, 30:20; and 1QSa 2.5-6. To complicate matters further, ancient Jewish reflections regarding eunuchs were not universal. In Isaiah 56:3, for instance, the inclusion of eunuchs becomes a marker of the arrival of God's reign. See also Wis. 3:14.

11. For a fuller treatment of Acts 16, see Eric D. Barreto, *Ethnic Negotiations: The Function of Race and Ethnicity in Acts 16* (Tübingen: Mohr Siebeck, 2010).

12. See, for example, Shaye Cohen, *The Beginnings of Jewishness: Boundaries, Varieties, Uncertainties* (Berkeley: University of California Press, 2001), 363–77.

13. Barreto, *Ethnic Negotiations*, 117.

14. Compare the complaints of Demetrius, the Ephesian artisan of statues of Artemis, in 19:25-27. There the economic loss that Paul's preaching would cause is at the forefront.

15. Richard I. Pervo, *Acts: A Commentary* (Minneapolis: Fortress Press, 2009), 406.

16. See, for example, RSV, NRSV, NIV, and TNIV. In contrast, see KJV, NKJV, ASV, and NASB.

17. See, for example, Mark G. Brett, ed., *Ethnicity and the Bible* (New York: Brill, 1996); Buell and Hodge, "The Politics of Interpretation," 235–51; Charles H. Cosgrove, "Did Paul Value Ethnicity?" *CBQ* 68 (2006) 268–90; and Dennis C. Duling, "Ethnicity, Ethnocentrism, and the Matthean Ethos," *BTB* 35 (2005): 125–43. For two recent theological explorations of race and ethnicity, see J. Kameron Carter, *Race: A Theological Account* (Oxford: Oxford University Press, 2008) and Willie James Jennings, *The Christian Imagination: Theology and the Origins of Race* (New Haven: Yale University Press, 2010). For a fuller bibliography, see Barreto, *Ethnic Negotiations*, 195–99.

18. Tat-Siong Benny Liew, "Acts," in *Global Bible Commentary*, ed. Daniel Patte (Nashville: Abingdon, 2004), 419–28.

19. Liew, 422.

20. As Liew concludes, "Acts has an ethnicity problem" (422). On this last point Liew and I disagree a bit. See below.

8

Naming the Powers

Cultural Studies and the Politics of Representation in Western "Pauline Studies"

Abraham Smith

The Bible puts an end to this strife when it says: "There is neither male nor female in Christ Jesus" [Gal 3:28] . . . When Paul said, "Help those women who labor with me in the Gospel," he certainly meant that they did more than to pour tea.[1]
—Julia Foote Moore, nineteenth-century AME Zion preacher

Misogynist, homophobic, racist, xenophobic, elitist—Paul seems to serve as a mirror for our own anxieties about religion, politics, domination, and justice.[2]
—Davina Lopez

INTRODUCTION

Neither homogenously formed nor consensually defined, cultural studies is best viewed as an interdisciplinary "theoretical-political project" that seeks both to *democratize culture* (those "persistent forms or patterns of thought" shared by a given group's members) and to *interrogate all cultural productions* (that is, cultural practices, operations, and formations).[3] As a "theoretical-political project," moreover, one principal way in which cultural studies seeks to *intervene* (to make changes) in the world is to interrogate the *politics of representation*, that is, to examine carefully the *"effects and consequences* of representation," the operations of power and ideological commitments associated with the re-presentation of events, histories, and subjectivities.[4]

107

Thus, to examine the politics of representation within any discourse is to examine not only "how language and representation produce meaning [which is the task of poetics or semiotics] but how the knowledge which a particular discourse produces connects with power, regulates conduct, makes up or constructs identities and subjectivities, and defines the way certain things are represented, thought about, practised and studied."[5] As Ola Söderström has acknowledged, cultural studies raises the question "who has the power to produce authorised representations of the world and what/who are the legitimate objects/subjects of scientific representation?"[6] Cultural studies also asks the following questions: How do dominant institutions or dominant conceptualizations underwrite certain representations rather than others? How do the iterations of select representations or choices of representations mark patterns of inclusion or exclusion of human groupings? And how are representations inflected in the different moments or sites of our "cultural circuits," that is, in the various moments or sites in which meaning is produced in a given culture: "in the construction of identity and the marking of difference, in production and consumption, as well as in the regulation of social conduct"?[7]

Given these brief remarks about cultural studies, I wish to raise the following questions about Western "Pauline studies": How would the use of a *politics of representation* as an analytic mark a critical intervention in Pauline studies? That is, to what extent can such an analytic reveal operations of power and ideological commitments in the systemic patterns of reflections on Paul in the West? How are Paul, his letters, and the communities to which Paul wrote re-presented in the evolution of what is called Western "Pauline studies"? To what extent are the frames of discussion connected to larger dominant constructions of Jews, of *ta ethnē* (or "the Gentles"), of Christian scriptures, and of what counts as important in Western conceptualizations? Thus, how do our figurations of Paul, his letters, and the communities to which he wrote help us to *name and identify the powers*, the prevailing narratives that underwrite and thus control our "rituals of receptions," that is, our "culturally ordered" deployments of the bible as "cultural capital" in public/social policy arguments, our traditions of hermeneutical strategies for reading or otherwise appropriating the bible, and our traditions of what the bible is (and thus the authority the bible has).[8]

Toward such a cultural studies intervention, the chapter proceeds in three steps. *First*, the chapter examines the evolution of what is called Western "Pauline studies" by charting how such discourse has re-presented "Paul," "Judaism," *ta ethnē*, and Paul's "context" of empire. *Second*, the chapter examines a relatively recent critique of the prevailing politics of representation inherent in much of the discourse of "Pauline studies." That is, the recent critique of the "heroic Paul" seeks to excavate a key discursive framing that seems persistently to govern our re-presentations of Paul, his letters, and the communities to which he wrote. *Finally*, the chapter returns to the question of "rituals of reception" to ask how we might reframe our investigations in a way that democratizes the space in which Paul, his letters, and the communities to which he wrote are appropriated. That is, the chapter seeks to show that for most readings or appropriations of Paul, his letters, and the communities to which he wrote, there are dominant institutions or constructions that control our "rituals of reception." Thus, unless these "instruments of power" or control are addressed, much of what biblical studies professionals do may not really matter.[9]

The Politics of Representation and Three Stages in Western "Pauline Studies"

So, how has Paul been re-presented? What are the images used to understand Paul? In the discourse on Paul, his letters, and the communities to which he wrote, moreover, which human groupings are depicted as villains and which are depicted as heroes? As we shall see, such questions may be difficult to answer because images of Paul are sometimes contradictory of each other. According to Calvin J. Roetzel, "[t]hroughout history a kaleidoscope of images of the apostle Paul has continually offered fresh combinations."[10] For example, tradition portrays him as "a man of small stature, with a bald head and crooked nose, in a good state of body."[11] Later, in accordance with what is known as the "western introspective," Protestant reformers presented Paul as "a guilt-ridden victim of a burdensome law" while seventeenth-century Rembrandt (in what was actually a self-portrait) presents Paul as "wiry, deeply reflective, introspective."[12] With respect to some nineteenth-century black women (though not all), Paul is presented as an ally who would have been able to lose his apparently subordinationist rhetoric had he been acquainted with the travails of black women.[13] By contrast, many nineteenth-century slavers saw Paul as an ally in their support for the so-called "peculiar institution."[14] Thus, so myriad and contradictory are the portraits of Paul that some scholars see him as a mysterious, even protean figure.[15]

What accounts for the mystery? The mystery about him is not solely a factor of disputable texts within the body of epistles attributed to Paul, though many scholars do acknowledge a distinction between *vintage jazz Paul* (that is, the undisputed Pauline texts [1 Thessalonians, Galatians, 1 and

2 Corinthians, Philemon, Philippians, Romans]) and *jazz fusion Paul* (that is, the disputed Pauline letters [2 Thessalonians, Colossians, Ephesians, 1 Timothy, 2 Timothy and Titus]) among the thirteen letters that bear his name. Nor is the mystery singularly related to attempts to align Paul's chronology and thought with canonical Acts, the latter being one among many of the earlier interpretations of Paul. Nor does the temporal distance between Paul and contemporary interpreters alone render Paul enigmatic because an early interpreter also chimed in on the difficulty of making sense of Paul. That is, the writer of 2 Peter opined about Paul's letters: "there are some things in them hard to understand" (3:16).[16]

The enigmatic Paul, though, may come into clearer focus if we measure Paul's ostensible egalitarian vision (read within his own "ethnoracial discourse") against any signs of a comparable social program on a variety of fronts.[17] That Paul was a Jew is indisputable and that he welcomed openly and passionately his Gentile converts into the family of God seems clear. On other social relational fronts, though, one looks in vain for an equal passion. So, although there are three pinnacles in the egalitarian ethos of Gal. 3:28 ("There is no longer Jew or Greek, there is no longer slave or free, there is no longer male and female; for all of you are one in Christ," NRSV), signs of a "practical program" in his letters are evident only for the race/ethnicity front, not for class/status nor for sex/gender.[18]

To be sure, when Paul writes to Philemon, he levies some "social and community pressure" but without making an explicit exhortation for Philemon to free Onesimus.[19] And while 1 Cor. 7:21-24 may certainly be read to encourage enslaved persons to seek freedom when an opportunity arises, far too much ambivalence results—at least in scholarship—in centuries of efforts to parse Paul's truest thoughts about slavery based on the wording of this passage.

Likewise, with regard to Paul's stance toward gender, we might ask: Where is that passion and intensity that we can see when he seems to make a case against using ethnic distinctions as markers for inclusion in the family of God? Again, to be sure, he seems anti-conventional when he admonishes the unmarried to remain celibate (1 Cor. 7:7-8), as was he, but why does he resort to a conventional patriarchal bias in 1 Cor. 11:2-16 (with his dictum of woman as created "for the sake of man" [1 Cor. 11:9])? That patriarchal bias depends on "the [similarly patriarchal] Genesis [2:18] account of creation," and Paul's concession to patriarchy is worse in 1 Cor. 14:33b-36, if, in fact, he wrote it.

Furthermore, Paul's seeming ambivalence in furnishing a social program for all three parts of the egalitarian ethos of Gal. 3:28 likely opened the door to what may be called accommodationist readings in the disputed Pauline texts, especially in the Pastorals (1 Timothy, 2 Timothy, Titus), as, for example, in 1 Tim. 2:11-15, in which "Paul" is presented as saying categorically that women are prohibited "not only from speaking in church but also teaching and exercising any kind of authority over males."[20] In yet other accommodationist readings, Colossians (Col. 3:4-4:7) and Ephesians (5:21-6:9), for example, the egalitarian Paul is domesticated again through association with ancient "household codes" (aka the *Haustafeln*).[21] Thus, the information we have about Paul—even the earliest information—does not seem to offer a consistent portrait, if one can (or should) be found. Understandably, then, from about the eighteenth century on, Western biblical scholars, presumably having embraced the legacies of democratic bible study bequeathed by the Reformation and the High Renaissance, have sought to advance their own understandings of Paul.[22] With the broadest of strokes, the evolution of Pauline studies in the West could be viewed as proceeding in three stages.

In the first stage, from the formative days of modern critical biblical studies, the traditional conceptual apparatus for understanding Paul and his assemblies was informed by a Protestant-Roman Catholic debate about personal faith. In accordance with a Protestant theology informed by Augustine and Luther, Paul was seen as the bold proclaimer of "justification by faith" while Judaism was seen as a religion of merits, a projection in part based on Protestant views of Roman Catholicism.[23] Likewise, Paul was separated from his own native Judaism and assumed to be the creator of a superior "new, universal, and spiritual religion," namely Christianity, while Judaism itself, at least in the tradition of Georg Wilhelm Friedrich Hegel's [and F. C. Baur's] racialized discourse, was seen as the separatist, parochial and inferior "other."[24]

This traditional perspective, though, had a misguided view of Paul and a misguided view of Judaism. With respect to the former, the traditional perspective saw Paul as one who converted from Judaism to Christianity, though Paul himself never prefers the diction of a "conversion" for himself, only a "call." Krister Stendahl, who famously wrote about the conversion/call debate, argued that the idea of Paul's conversion was superimposed on Paul from a much later period. That is, it emanates from "a later, individualized development in Western consciousness and psychology."[25] Thus, Paul was not influenced by the aforementioned "Western introspective" consciousness. With respect to Judaism, the traditional perspective also erred because it read Paul's intra-Jewish conflicts (such as what occurs in Galatians when Paul passionately advocates the inclusion of Gentiles in the family of God) through the prism of "modern Protestant-Catholic or Christian-Jewish conflicts."[26] The result was that ancient Judaism was made to appear legalistic and Christianity (as Paul understood it, according to this perspective) was made to appear as law-free. As we can see, power dimensions associated with the politics of representation operated during this period. Indeed, in this era, Paul and Judaism seemed used as sites largely through which Protestants sought to work out their own social identity but in ways that deformed others.

In the second stage, Pauline studies would be informed by the "New Perspective," which radically changed the scholarly representations of both Paul and Judaism. The term "New Perspective," an expression coined by J. D. G. Dunn in 1983, refers to a perspective that first came to light in the work of Krister Stendahl and E. P. Sanders.[27] According to Matlock, the New Perspective is neither totally "new" nor a single idea. While it represents a recent shift in Pauline scholarship, its emphasis—as with the so-called traditional or "old perspective"—is still soteriological and thus "broadly traditional."[28] Furthermore, it "signifies not a singular settled position but a broad family of related interpretive tendencies."[29] Barry Matlock identifies two pillars as axioms. One pillar is "that Paul was not really concerned about individual sin, guilt, and forgiveness, but rather that communal and social concerns having to do with Jewish and Gentile relations, practical concerns arising from Paul's mission, were his primary context and focus."[30] Paul, in fact, remains a Jew, not a convert to another religion. He still sees himself as a Jew but now one with a special call upon his life, a mission to the nations (or Gentiles). A second pillar is "that the Judaism of Paul's day was not a 'legalistic' religion of meritorious 'works-righteousness,' so that Paul's 'opponents,' and his position over against them, must be reassessed."[31] Thus, the New Perspective is a collection of perspectives that seeks to read Paul and the Judaism of his age apart from what the New Perspective calls a "'Lutheran' reading of Paul and Judaism."[32] It is clear, moreover, that the New Perspective is informed by the tragedy of the Shoah, the post–WWII "emergence of organized Jewish-Christian dialogue," and by attempts to show the lingering effects of constructions of ancient *genē* (families, races, kinds) on modern conceptualizations of race and ethnicity.[33]

The third stage of Western Pauline studies is known as an empire-critical approach to Paul, an approach that may be applied to many biblical texts, not just those bearing Paul's name. Such an approach not only looks at the ways in which Western biblical studies itself is tied to empire but also examines the relations between biblical writers and empire.[34] With respect to empire-critical approaches to Paul, there seem be three major assumptions. First, for empire-critical approaches, the dichotomy between religion and politics is false and one must not view ancient Judaism and early Christianity as religions alone nor must one view the Roman Empire as a political sphere alone.[35] Second, the study of Paul should shift from a "history of ideas approach toward a history of people and movements over time, especially people who have been and/or dominated and marginalized and associated movements."[36] Third, scholars must not only see Paul as called (as opposed to converted), but they should see how he is called to politics, that is, he is called to encourage "religio-political resistance to the Roman Empire through declaring a crucified Christ as savior from the evil [old] age."[37]

The empire-critical approaches do not suggest that Paul, in standing in "opposition to the Roman imperial order," was a "rabble-rousing revolutionary," a thesis that simply cannot be aligned with Rom 13:1-7.[38] If resistance, though, may be manifested across a spectrum of forms, some of which are subtle or indirect, then, Paul and the communities to which he wrote, in accordance with the spectrum of resistance practices of their time, deployed a variety of "arts of resistance."[39] Such "arts" could include, for example: (1) traditions that incorporated political diction and presupposed a "critique of this age and its values," including those of the Roman imperial order;[40] (2) the cultivation of "assemblies" (*ekklēsiai*) whose orientations resisted—on many fronts—the ideologies of the cultures around them;[41] and (3) the subtle political critique of local accommodationist practices through admonitions of community self-sustenance apart from the Roman patronage systems on which most of the urban cities of Paul's world depended.[42]

While the empire-critical approach has unmasked empire in Western Pauline studies and has highlighted some of Paul's counter-imperial discourse, Davina Lopez points out how sometimes this approach has failed to see how empire and politics are very much "gendered, sexualized, and racialized," and thus the empire-critical prism has not understood the "complex interconnectivity of status, race, gender, and sexuality" that was embedded in the Roman imperial machinery against which Paul fought.[43] Likewise, the empire-critical prism has not noticed the multiple venues through which the ideology of Roman domination manifested itself in representations.[44] Thus, Lopez advances a gender-critical optic that is informed by literary and visual representations. With such an optic, according to Lopez, one can get a clearer perspective on Paul's understanding of being called to *ta ethnē* or what is often called "the Gentiles" (Gal. 1:15-16). That is, Paul is called to join the subordinate position of the *ta ethnē*, those nations that have been conquered ("feminized") by the Romans, in accordance with the gendered and sexualized subordinating logic of Roman imperial ideology.[45] Thus, in effect, Lopez' methodology proffers a critique to the traditional perspective on Paul, the New Perspective on Paul, and even the empire-critical approach to Paul because all three perspectives failed to identify *ta ethnē* (the Gentiles) apart "from a construct dependent on differences from Jews."[46] Thus, all three approaches were trapped in a binary bind through which they understood the Gentiles only "in terms of what they are not," namely, Jewish.[47]

Visible then in this short description of Western Pauline studies (and the story could be told in a different way as well) is the way that re-presentation is connected to larger discursive frameworks, either those that operate in the ancient world (as we are able to reconstruct them) or those that affect how we ourselves identify Paul, Judaism, or *ta ethnē*. In the case of our discursive frames, moreover, binding binaries often force out of the discussion insights that ought to be considered or they trap us into representations that may not adequately and concretely treat the evidence that is available before us. And, obviously and most importantly, such binaries can have dangerous consequences for those who are marginalized in any given society and within any given period of human history.

The Politics of Representations and the Critique of the "Heroic Paul" in "Pauline Studies"

Not discounting the benefits of the New Perspective and of empire-critical approaches to Paul, a key challenge lingers, namely, the need to shift away from what may be called the "heroic Paul." In a recent essay in *The Colonized Paul: Paul through Postcolonial Eyes*, Melanie Johnson-DeBaufre and Laura S. Nasrallah proffer a critique of the "heroic Paul," that is, a critique of "an interest in Paul-the-individual."[48] They argue that even "politically engaged scholars" maintain this interest, though, in doing so, such scholars "replicate . . . [Paul's] self-authorizing rhetoric and Acts' heroic depiction of him, rather than presenting him as one significant voice among many."[49] Furthermore, they note that the "heroic Paul" (for example, the "self-sufficient traveler" or the "larger-than-life hero") should be "de-centered" so that the early messianist assemblies may be represented not as passive recipients of Paul's letters or as subjects of Paul (in the role of a colonizing missionary) but as a network of civic assemblies fully capable of contesting Paul's leadership on any given score.[50]

For Johnson-DeBaufre and Nasrallah, new strategies of appropriation must be deployed to move "beyond the 'heroic Paul.'"[51] Such strategies, in effect, could provide new frameworks for "Pauline studies," with examinations of Paul's letters and their afterlives (such as canonical Acts and the *Acts of Thecla*) now being viewed as "sites of vision and debate," sources for portraying "diverse communities," and scenes for demystifying subordinationist and domesticating logic whether it be found in Paul, his earliest interpreters, or his continuing legacy.[52]

Two of the principal benefits of the essay by Johnson-DeBaufre and Nasrallah are that: (1) they help us to see the extent to which our politics of representation will always be informed by larger, persistent frameworks of conceptualization; and (2) such frameworks of conceptualization have damaging effects or ethical consequences. With respect to the persistence of patterns of conceptualizations, representations of the "heroic Paul," while prominent as early as canonical Acts, continue to this day because history far too often is framed as the history of "great men." Even our courses (mine included) perpetuate a focus on "Paul-the-individual" with such titles as "Paul and his Rhetoric" or "The Pauline Epistles" as if the goal is to provide a "paradigmatic human . . . for contemporary meditations."[53] According to Barry Schwartz, this search for paradigms, which may be traced back in the West at the least to a "culture of deference" in the eighteenth and nineteenth centuries, still holds some sway today.[54] Thus, to change this representation of Paul requires a rethinking of historiography itself, that is, a rethinking of the framework in which histories (or historical representations) are written. As Schwartz remarks, "Historiography, shaped by egalitarian social structures, describes past events as collective rather than individual achievements."[55] With respect to the damaging effects of representations, Johnson-DeBaufre and Nasrallah, informed by "an ethics of interpretation," call attention to how "ideologies of colonization" (such as giving voice only to "a few heroic men") perpetuate or blindly support the kinds of values that eventually came to be associated with "triumphalist Christianity."[56]

I would add, moreover, that as long as Paul or any portion of the bible or its cast of explicitly mentioned (or even overlooked) characters are viewed as paradigms, along with the socio-historical structures from which they cannot be extracted, it is inevitably impossible to see ourselves fully taking a role as critics of the bible and its mores. The issue I am addressing, of course, is that our roles as interpreters are invariably tied to what we think the bible does or to what we think we can expect to get from it and from its (explicit and implied) world.[57] So, if we are to *name the powers*, more is involved than the "heroic Paul." The larger grid of conceptualization that controls our politics of representation may be the "rituals of reception" that we bring to the bible itself.[58]

PAUL, THE POLITICS OF REPRESENTATION, AND RITUALS OF RECEPTION

According to Fernando F. Segovia,[59] the conjunction between cultural studies and biblical studies occurred at a time when biblical criticism began to take on a multitude of voices and directions.[60] Such voices were varied because of the inclusion of non-male, non-Western, and non-heterogendered individuals in the biblical profession.[61] Such directions were also varied because biblical criticism began to consider the "situated and interested nature of all reading and interpretation."[62] Accordingly, a virtual death knell was sounded against critical traditional approaches that failed to consider the bible's effective history, that is, its reception in history.

Examinations of the bible's receptions in history, though, need not be directed exclusively toward scholars of the bible, though scholarly self-reflection is a worthy pursuit. Within this conjunction between cultural studies and biblical studies, as Segovia has envisioned it, biblical criticism ideally would embrace a "*diversity in readings*," featuring "the academic type of reading" but also "other traditions of reading—the theological or churchly, the religious or devotional, the cultural or popular."[63]

This interest in a "diversity of readings," then, leads to my final comments on Western "Pauline studies." The larger question for Western "Pauline studies" may not be about the politics of representation simply with respect to Paul, his letters, or the communities to which he wrote as much as it is about the politics of representation related to the larger discourse of the bible. There is, then, a need to bring under closer scrutiny prevailing rhetorical uses *of* the bible by various communities of practice, prevailing hermeneutics or strategies of appropriation that are used *on* the bible, and prevailing domains of convictions *about* the bible.[64]

PREVAILING RHETORICAL USES OF THE BIBLE

In the several centuries that have passed and gone since the biblical books were compiled over a period of some seven hundred years, Christians have used these texts, including Paul's letters (both undisputed and disputed), to victimize "children, women, Jews, the disabled [or better, those located as disabled], witches, people of color, slaves, scientists, criminals, heretics, and even animals, nature, and the environment."[65] It appears, then, that biblical texts have a rhetorical appeal such that Christians (and others) frequently cite them to support arguments on the social and public policies of their day. In effect, these texts are attributed some sort of cultural capital in decision-making processes and in how certain groups define themselves against others. What is interesting to note, moreover, is that some of the same basic steps taken to make villains out of one human grouping in one historical period are used to create another, newer set of villains in another historical period. So, for example, if nineteenth-century Christians could take a handful of isolated texts to build "a flimsy edifice of interpretation, judgment, and rejection" to support slavery and to deny suffrage to women, then, yet other handfuls of texts pasted together would be used by the Nazis to fan the flames of anti-Jewish sentiment and violence or by white South Africans to sanction apartheid or by twenty-first century Christians to repress sexual minorities.[66] And so, *bully-gesis* continues. Thus, the biblical texts have become not simply stories, chronicles, and letters. They have become texts that figure into consistent, recurring patterns of caricaturization, victimization or demonization. These texts, in effect, are made to mirror the politics of those who appropriate them, to participate in the binaries that are perennially used to control and wield power over others.

PREVAILING HERMENEUTICAL STRATEGIES ON THE BIBLE

The biblical texts alone do not have cultural capital in the politics of representation. To name the powers is to identify yet other ways in a politics of representation is at work, especially in the deference given to *some* hermeneutical strategies over yet others. For example, if institutions such as churches and schools embrace historical criticism and literary criticism but never introduce cross-cultural hermeneutics as a valid strategy of appropriation, are we not in fact representing such an approach as limited or lacking in value?[67] If our institutions and schools never learn about indigenous reading practices (as, for example, those used by Native Americans, the Aborigines in Australia, and the Maoris in New Zealand), exactly what value are we assigning to these approaches?[68] That is, there is an implicit politics of representation embedded in our choices of hermeneutical approaches.

Thus, in a recent work, Musa Dube argued that theological studies in academic institutions (and I would add in churches as well) needs a "curriculum transformation," that is, a transformation that takes seriously the ways in which our pedagogy perpetuates the view that some approaches—for example, "Latin American and Hispanic, Asia and Asian American, African and African American, Native American and Palestinian," are deemed derivative or peripheral while other approaches are deemed central.[69]

PREVAILING DOMAINS OF CONVICTIONS ABOUT THE BIBLE

One other set of powers that controls the politics of representation in biblical discourse is the set of prevailing domains of convictions that function like pre-interpretive perspectives for any set of readers/appropriators of biblical texts, namely, what they think the bible is, what they think the bible does, or the authority they think it has (which, of course, is always an ascribed authority).[70] Such convictions are not solipsistic but are very much "culturally ordered."[71] One such conviction, which has the backing of most denominational bodies, for example, is the doctrine of biblical authority. The doctrine, which is of relatively recent vintage, attributes authority to the bible as a normative source for making "beliefs, activities or positions credible."[72]

Yet another ideological commitment that often goes unexamined is the view that the bible is the "Word of God." However innocent the expression may seem, it is not. In fact, this confessional claim often breeds bibliolatry (or worship of the bible), if not also the assumption of the ascendancy of Jewish scriptures and Christian scriptures over other scriptures, foundational narratives, or charter stories (such as the canonical texts of Chinese Buddhism to the Hindu Vedas to the Mayan Popol Vuh) that operate outside the pale of Western cultures.[73] Such an ideology also perpetuates in our own times the scriptural imperialism of earlier imperialists who imposed their presence, their languages, and the bible's literary canon onto the colonized through a variety of mission institutions and with an insistence that the bible is a "universal standard for all cultures."[74] So, beyond the operations of powers that creates villains and heroes in Pauline studies, there are conceptualizations of the bible itself that impact identity formation and the ways in which certain human groupings are re-presented.

Likely shaping these "rituals of reception" for many Western Christian readers (including so-called biblical studies professionals) are what Mary Ann Tolbert would call "the institutional voices of the Christian church, in all of its many divisions."[75] These voices often control "not only the publication of biblical interpretations but also the education of those who read the Bible—from scholars to pastors to congregants."[76] These voices also control who is allowed to become ordained—in the name of Paul; who can minister and who is simply proscribed to become a "tea-pourer"—in the name of Paul; and which new group becomes the latest victim in a long litany of monsterization—all in the name of Paul. So, the greater work to be done likely lies not in the parlor conversations of biblical scholars (including the so-called Pauline scholars) but in creating venues through which we may begin to demystify the propaganda ports of these institutional voices. If there is to be an intervention in Western

"Pauline studies," it must go beyond Paul to the wider parameters of biblical discourse itself. It must assess every moment in our "cultural circuits," that is, "in the construction of identity and the marking of difference, in production and consumption, as well as in the regulation of social conduct."[77] It will come only when we recognize, as James Baldwin did many years ago, that "people are trapped in history and history is trapped in them."[78]

Notes

1. Quoted in *Afro-American Religious History*, ed. Milton Sernett (Durham: Duke University, 1985), 209.

2. Davina C. Lopez, *Apostle to the Conquered: Reimagining Paul's Mission* (Minneapolis: Fortress Press, 2008), xi.

3. On cultural studies as a "theoretical-political project," see John Beverly, *Subalternity and Representation: Arguments in Cultural Theory* (Durham: Duke University, 2004), 17. On culture as "persistent forms," see David Chaney, *The Cultural Turn: Scene-Setting Essays on Contemporary Cultural History* (London: Routledge, 1994), 2.

4. Stuart Hall, "Introduction," in *Representation: Cultural Representation and Signifying Practices*, ed. Stuart Hall (London: Sage, 2011), 6.

5. Hall, 6.

6. Ola Söderström, "Representation," in *Cultural Geography: A Critical Dictionary of Key Concepts*, ed. David Atkinson, Peter Jackson, David Sibley, and Neil Washbourne (London: I.B. Tauris, 2005), 13.

7. Hall, 4.

8. James S. Bielo "Introduction: Encountering Biblicism," in *The Social Life of Scriptures: Cross-Cultural Perspectives on Biblicism*, ed. James S. Bielo (New Brunswick: Rutgers University, 2006), 5–7.

9. Wherever the words "bible" or "biblical" appear in this chapter, I am referring to what Christians have labeled as their bible with full recognition of the contested nature of the term and of the inherent divisions within Christianity about this nomenclature and over what it includes. The term "instruments of power" emanates from Mark D. Jordan, *The Ethics of Sex* (Oxford: Blackwell, 2002), 151.

10. Calvin J. Roetzel, *Paul: The Man and the Myth* (Minneapolis: Fortress Press, 1999), 8.

11. Ibid., 8. This description, which ties physiognomics (or physical structure) to ethical behavior obviously reflects the culturally determined view that the collection of indices of physiognomics would have been viewed as positive in the second century CE world that produced the description. See Bruce J. Malina and Jerome H. Neyrey, *Portraits of Paul: An Archaeology of Ancient Personality* (Louisville: Westminster John Knox, 1996), 139–45.

12. Roetzel, 8.

13. *Maria Stewart: America's First Black Woman Political Writer* (ed. Marilyn Richardson; Bloomington: Indiana University, 1987), 68.

14. On these slavers, see Albert Raboteau, *A Fire in the Bones: Reflections on African-American Religious History* (Boston: Beacon, 1995), 19.

15. The idea that Paul was a Christian Proteus emanates both from Amos Jones Jr., *Paul's Message of Freedom: What Does It Mean to the Black Church?* (Valley Forge: Judson, 1984), 16; and Wayne A. Meeks, ed., *The Writings of Saint Paul*, A Norton Critical Edition (New York: Norton, 1972), 437. As Jones writes (16), "Proteus, a sea god [in *The Odyssey*] had the uncanny ability of

changing forms at will and escaping the grasp of his would-be captors." The same seems to be true of Paul.

16. For these ideas, see Abraham Smith, "Paul and African American Biblical Interpretation," in *True to Our Native Land: An African American Commentary on the New Testament*, ed. Brian Blount, Clarice Martin, Cain Felder and Emerson Powery (Minneapolis: Fortress Press, 2007), 31–42.

17. Denise Kimber Buell and Caroline Johnson Hodge, "The Politics of Interpretation: The Rhetoric of Race and Ethnicity in Paul," *Journal of Biblical Literature* 123 (2004): 235-241.

18. Demetrius Williams, *An End to This Strife: The Politics of Gender in African American Churches* (Minneapolis: Fortress Press, 2004), 36.

19. Williams, 34.

20. Ibid., 57.

21. On the domestication of Paul's erstwhile egalitarian ethos, see Clarice J. Martin, "The Haustafeln (Household Codes) in African American Biblical Interpretation: 'Free Slaves' and 'Subordinate' Women," in *Stony The Road We Trod: African American Biblical Interpretation*, ed. Cain Hope Felder (Minneapolis: Fortress Press, 1991), 206–31.

22. See Richard Pervo, *Profit with Delight: The Literary Genre of the Acts of the Apostles* (Philadelphia: Fortress Press, 1987), 12. Compare John J. Collins who writes: "While the Reformation encouraged Christians to read the Bible for themselves and used it as a counterweight to Catholic tradition, it was not until the eighteenth century and the Enlightenment that biblical criticism began to emerge in its modern form, and it developed hand in hand with critical historiography in the nineteenth." John J. Collins, *The Bible after Babel: Historical Criticism in a Postmodern Age* (Grand Rapids: Eerdmans, 2005), 4–5. The Protestant Reformation's *sola scriptura* doctrine gave impetus to both the democratic study of scripture and the historical meaning of scripture. The High Renaissance humanists provided the earliest and perhaps the crudest tools for biblical interpretation. See William Baird, *History of New Testament Research* (Minneapolis: Fortress Press, 1992), xvi–xix.

23. For a sterling critique of this view of Paul, see Buell and Hodge, 239–41.

24. Richard A. Horsley, "Introduction," in *Paul and the Roman Imperial Order*, ed. Richard A. Horsley (Harrisburg: Trinity International, 2004), 1. On Hegel and Baur, see Shawn Kelley, *Racializing Jesus: Race, Ideology, and the Formation of Modern Biblical Scholarship* (London: Routledge, 2002), 76–77; John M. G. Barclay, "'Neither Jew nor Greek': Multiculturalism and the New Perspective on Paul," in *Ethnicity and the Bible*, ed. Mark G. Brett (Boston: Brill, 2002), 197; Magnus Zetterholm, *Approaches to Paul: A Student's Guide to Recent Scholarship* (Minneapolis: Fortress Press, 2009), 33–67.

25. Quoted in Lopez, 121. On Stendahl, see Krister Stendahl, "The Apostle Paul and the Introspective Conscience of the West," *Harvard Theological Review* 56 (1976): 199–215.

26. Lopez, 121.

27. On Dunn, see James D. G. Dunn, "The New Perspective on Paul," *Bulletin of the John Rylands University Library of Manchester* 65 (1983): 95–122. On the contribution of Sanders, see E. P. Sanders, *Paul and Palestinian Judaism: A Comparison of Patterns of Religion* (Minneapolis: Fortress Press, 1977).

28. Barry Matlock, "Almost Cultural Studies: Reflections on the 'New Perspective' on Paul," in *Biblical Studies/Cultural Studies*, ed. J. Cheryl Exum and Stephen D. Moore (Sheffield: Sheffield University Press, 1998), 435.

29. Matlock, 435.

30. Ibid.

31. Ibid.

32. Ibid., 436. For a good overview of the New Perspective, see Kent L. Yinger, *The New Perspective on Paul: An Introduction* (Eugene: Cascade, 2011).

33. Zetterholm, *Approaches to Paul*, 9; Love L. Sechrest, *A Former Jew: Paul and the Dialectics of Race* (New York: T&T Clark, 2009), 10. For a critique of the New Perspective, see Caroline

Johnson Hodge, *If Sons, Then Heirs: A Study of Kinship and Ethnicity in the Letters of Paul* (New York: Oxford University, 2007).

34. A notable example is Neil Elliott's *The Arrogance of Nations: Reading Romans in the Shadow of Empire* (Minneapolis: Fortress, 2008) and a spate of books that emerged out of the Paul and Politics Group of the Society of Biblical Literature. On a critique of the connection between empire and biblical studies, see Lopez, 10.

35. On the critique of scholarship that presupposes a "dichotomy between politics and religion, see Lopez, 9.

36. Ibid.

37. Ibid., 123.

38. Richard A. Horsley, "Introduction," in *Paul and the Roman Imperial Order*, ed. Richard A. Horsley (Harrisburg: Trinity International, 2004), 3.

39. On the different paths by which resistance might take place, see James C. Scott, *Domination and the Arts of Resistance: Hidden Transcripts* (New Haven: Yale University, 1990).

40. J. Paul Sampley, *Walking between the Times: Paul's Moral Reasoning* (Minneapolis: Fortress Press, 1991), 108.

41. On Paul's development of *ekklesiai* as an alternative movement, see Richard A. Horsley, "Submerged Biblical Histories and Imperial Biblical Studies," in *The Postcolonial Bible*, ed. R. S. Sugirtharajah (Sheffield: Sheffield, 1998), 165.

42. Abraham Smith, "Unmasking the Powers: Toward a Postcolonial Analysis of 1 Thessalonians," in *Paul and the Roman Imperial Order*, ed. Richard A. Horsley (Harrisburg: Trinity International, 2004), 54. Here I am principally drawing on my own essay: Abraham Smith, "Paul and African American Biblical Interpretation," 31–42.

43. Lopez, xii.

44. Ibid., xii–xiii.

45. Ibid., 4–6.

46. Ibid., 5.

47. Ibid.

48. Melanie Johnson-DeBaufre and Laura S. Nasrallah, "Beyond the Heroic Paul: Toward a Feminist and Decolonizing Approach to the Letters of Paul," in *The Colonized Apostle: Paul through Postcolonial Eyes*, ed. Christopher D. Stanley (Minneapolis: Fortress Press, 2011), 161.

49. Johnson-DeBaufre and Nasrallah, 162–68.

50. Ibid., 170–71.

51. Ibid., 173.

52. Ibid.

53. Ibid., 161.

54. Barry Schwartz, *Abraham Lincoln and the Forge of National Memory* (Chicago: University of Chicago, 2000), 305. Note also that Stephen Moore and Yvonne Sherwood argue that early biblical criticism, though initially interested in proffering a critique of the bible's morality, grew in time to embrace what had been accepted before the emergence of the rationalists, namely, that "the Bible and morality were synonymous." Stephen Moore and Yvonne Sherwood, *The Invention of the Biblical Scholar: A Critical Manifesto* (Minneapolis: Fortress Press, 2011), 59.

55. Schwartz, 304.

56. Johnson-DeBaufre and Nasrallah, 170, 174.

57. Compare Moore and Sherwood (63) on this point.

58. Bielo, 5.

59. This chapter is dedicated to Fernando F. Segovia.

60. Fernando F. Segovia, "Cultural Studies and Contemporary Biblical Criticism as a Mode of Discourse," *Reading from this Place*, vol. 2: *Social Location and Biblical Interpretation in Global Perspective*, ed. Fernando F. Segovia and Mary Ann Tolbert (Minneapolis: Fortress Press, 1995), 5. Compare Fernando F. Segovia, "The Bible as a Text in Cultures: An Introduction" in *The Peoples'*

Bible, ed. Curtiss P. DeYoung, Leticia Guardiola-Saenz, Wilda Gafney, George Tinker, and Frank Yamada (Minneapolis: Fortress Press, 2008), 25–29.

61. Ibid., 26–27.

62. Segovia, "Cultural Studies," 5.

63. Fernando F. Segovia, *Decolonizing Biblical Studies: A View from the Margins* (Maryknoll: Orbis, 2000), 99.

64. I owe the specific language about domains, hermeneutical strategies, and rhetorical appeals to Bielo, 4–5.

65. Adrian Thatcher, *The Savage Text: The Use and Abuse of the Bible* (Malden, MA: Blackwell, 2008), 5–6.

66. Ibid.

67. See, for example, the edited collected by D. N. Premnath, *Border Crossings: Cross-Cultural Hermeneutics* (Maryknoll: Orbis, 2007).

68. Most of these practices are noted by Musa Dube, "Post-Colonial Biblical Interpretations," in *Dictionary of Biblical Interpretation*, ed. John H. Hayes (Nashville: Abingdon, 1999), 300–302. To Dube's list, I have added Delores Williams' proto-gesis hermeneutics. See Delores Williams, "Hagar in African American Biblical Appropriation," in *Hagar, Sarah, and Their Children*, ed. Phyllis Trible and Letty M. Russell (Louisville: Westminster John Knox, 2006), 171–84. Williams (174) asserts that proto-gesis (as opposed to exegesis) draws on cultural studies, uses pertinent genre-specific interpretative strategies to unearth a biblical cultural deposit deeply sedimented in one's own community, and yet remains in dialogue with historical critical discussions.

69. Musa Dube, "Curriculum Transformation: Dreaming of Decolonization in Theological Studies," in *Border Crossings: Cross-Cultural Hermeneutics*, 125.

70. Note that Brad R. Braxton defines *biblical authority* not as a textual property but an attributed value by specific interpretive communities. See Brad R. Braxton, *No Longer Slaves: Galatians and African American Experience* (Collegeville: Liturgical, 2002), 37. Accordingly, engagement with a biblical text does not mandate a community's automatic assent to the text's assumed values. Likewise, Braxton views *biblical inspiration* as a "byproduct of a religious text's *usefulness* in a religious community" (34). Thus, historically, beyond early religious communities' assumption of divine revelation as a valid claim, biblical inspiration *was possible* only through several processes occurring in those communities, namely, the composition, codification and canonization of texts deemed useful or valuable to the communities (32-34). And, for contemporary religious communities, biblical inspiration *is possible* only because these communities both respect the documents' foundational utility and deem them as yet having theological relevance for contemporary audiences (31–37).

71. Bielo, 5.

72. Mary McClintock Fulkerson, "Church Documents on Human Sexuality and the Authority of Scripture," *Interpretation* 49 (2001), 51.

73. On "scriptural imperialism," as opposed to territorial imperialism, see R. S. Sugirtharajah, *The Bible and the Third World: Precolonial, Colonial and Postcolonial Encounters* (Cambridge: Cambridge University, 2001), 52. Vincent Wimbush seems to treat a similar idea. See his "'Naturally Veiled and Half Articulate': Scriptures, Modernity and the Formation of African America," in *Still at the Margins: Biblical Scholarship Fifteen Years after Voices from the Margins*, ed. R. S. Sugirtharajah (London: Continuum, 2008), 56–68.

74. Musa Dube, "Post-Colonial Biblical Interpretations," 299–303.

75. Mary Ann Tolbert, "What Word Shall We Take Back?," in *Take Back the Word: A Queer Reading of the Bible*, ed. Robert E. Goss and Mona West (Cleveland: Pilgrim, 2000), x.

76. Tolbert, xi.

77. Hall, 4.

78. James Baldwin, *Notes of a Native Son* (Boston: Beacon, 1984), 163.

9

___

"Talkin' 'Bout Somethin'"

Beyond a Positivistic Reading of Paul

Jennifer G. Bird

> In order to break the hold of androcentric biblical texts over us, it is
> necessary to uncover the mechanisms and incoherences of such texts,
> to see the inconsistencies of our sources, to elaborate the androcentric
> projections and political-theological functions of such texts and their
> contemporary androcentric interpretation.[1]

As this is a contribution to a volume interested in reshaping biblical scholarship
by attending to the ways culture, identity and power influence how we engage
biblical texts, I begin this chapter with a brief discussion of some aspects of my
own identity.[2] As someone living in the United States who can select "white"
for my ethnicity, I am aware that I have certain social and economic privileges
simply due to the happenstance of where I was born, the color of my skin and
the countries my ancestors came from. As a female, I am simultaneously aware
that my voice is granted authority and respect differently than that of males.
Some of my experiences growing up in a lower-middle class family have taught
me not to take for granted housing and daily sustenance. Being predominantly
heterosexual, I find human sexuality and how we choose to express it to be
more accurately described as falling somewhere on a continuum instead of into
one of two categories. I point out these components of my identity because of
the role the bible has had in shaping our understanding of national identities,
wealth and poverty, sexuality, and gender roles. But I also think that we would
collectively benefit from acknowledging how these aspects of ourselves and our
cultures inform how we read and interpret the bible. In the interest of simplicity

123

for this chapter, I will foreground a feminist critical voice, noting that it will at times intersect with some of these other ideological concerns.

The quotation at the beginning of this chapter dates from 1985, reminding us that we are going on thirty years of sound, critical feminist biblical scholarship, yet the primary point—the primary call to action—within this scholarship has still to be taken to heart by a stunningly large portion of biblical scholars. This call to action can be summarized in the following way: Since biblical texts and the interpretations of them have been written by and for males, we, as responsible, critical thinkers in the twenty-first century, must acknowledge and grapple with the numerous ways this male-centered perspective has affected the content of the biblical texts and the realms of scholarship on them.

For the realm of Pauline studies, as this chapter seeks to engage, this call to action is still relevant, even within the sub-disciplines that allegedly are striking new ground. I will engage a recent edited volume on Paul, *Paul Unbound: Other Perspectives on the Apostle*, as a means of elucidating this point.[3] Three questions outline the main body of the chapter: (1) If we continue to use the categories already established for "proper" Pauline studies and simply add new layers to them, how can we say we are doing something new? (2) Who is it that inhabits the realm of "respected" scholarship? (3) And why is it that so many scholars only dance around the claims—or worse yet, merely implied conclusions—in their scholarship that if made clear and taken seriously *could* truly shake up what is thought to be normative about Paul? In conclusion, bolstered by a challenge directed to all biblical scholars by Vincent Wimbush in his 2010 Society of Biblical Literature presidential address, I will end the chapter with suggestions for a way "forward" in Pauline studies that is not simply another layer added to the same structure but is interested in a restructuring altogether.

What About This Is New?

In the "Introduction" to *Paul Unbound*, editor Mark Given explains that the book's aim is to be relevant to and yet go beyond "traditional theological and historical concerns."[4] The title is intended to allude to Prometheus—who was bound for years because he offered humankind fire, thus helping them—in that Paul has been somewhat bound by tradition and theology, and "these chapters reflect some of the ways in which the study of Paul has in recent years been liberated from a variety of traditional or conventional perspectives."[5] These ideals are noteworthy, and in my opinion commendable. But they are not as easily accomplished as is claimed.

Several of the chapters of this book offer helpful political and economic data that shape our understanding of what Paul did and the people he actually engaged with, in particular a chapter by Steven Friesen that I discuss below. But offering these contributions is not the same as letting Paul go, loose and free from traditional perspectives. Additionally, the subtitle suggests that what is presented in this volume are cutting-edge, new perspectives on Paul. What makes this suggestion confusing is that most of the chapters are written as summaries of recent scholarship, which is helpful in its own way, but do not make clear when the author assumes that she or he is stepping beyond the traditional boundaries. Saying that something is new does not make it so.

The first chapter in this volume is by Warren Carter, "Paul and the Roman Empire: Recent Perspectives," in which he reviews three books edited by Richard Horsley that were products of the "Paul and Politics" Group of the Society of Biblical Literature.[6] Carter's primary claim ought to pique the interest of any reader: Horsley's books "offer a significant challenge to much previous and current work on Paul and advocate an innovative and exciting approach that cannot be ignored in studies of Paul."[7] While I realize he is reviewing some of the work that has been done on these dynamics, the way he handles his review is strikingly centered on scholarship that maintains the overall framework of Pauline studies.

For instance, Carter highlights several features of the work contained in these three volumes. The first is that in addition to the three "overlapping and comprehensive societal structures and cultural traditions, namely, the assemblies of Christ believers, Israel, and the Roman Empire" that Paul engages, scholars are now bringing the "legacy of debate and interpretation concerning Paul" into the fray.[8] Carter asserts that the political is theological. On this level, pointing out that much of the language Paul used theologically was initially political is new and ground-breaking for many scholars. But this does not do anything to unsettle the theological implications of, for instance, serving a God who is Lord and master. This basic theological assertion has been problematized by feminist theologians for several decades now. So, while it is shocking for some to see the political implications of their theological beliefs, the reversal of political loyalty can still be simply another power-play: Paul's Lord trumps the Lord in Rome. This new twist still concedes the authority of Paul, perpetuates it, and reinscribes it.

Carter engages two scholars whose work, if taken seriously, *could* influence a change in the framework, Elisabeth Schüssler Fiorenza and Davina Lopez. But Carter summarizes their contributions in such a way that a person who is not really paying attention might miss their implications. Schüssler Fiorenza challenges the "correctness" ascribed to Paul, when scholars side with Paul over against his opponents from the outset, subsequently taking that same authority when they affirm Paul's words.[9] "Schüssler Fiorenza and [Antoinette] Wire make the point that attention to Paul must not tune out the other voices, especially those of women and slaves, in the assemblies of which his is only one voice."[10] It seems Carter summarizes them nicely. But is he paying attention to what they are saying? Paul's voice is but one in a conversation of more than just two. Paul faced many positions about how things should run and what people should think. What Carter does not acknowledge here is that we need to go beyond imagining that differences of opinion existed to challenging the voice that "won" in the end: Paul's. He is correct because his voice is canonized, not because he necessarily *was* correct.

Lopez's work implies that gender constructions based upon the Pauline corpus ought to "challenge and reconfigure" the male dominant/female submissive construction of gender. If Lopez is correct and Paul was challenging the dominant/submissive construction of gender, it is worth the time to pause and consider how many relationships within church structures would be changed in applying this insight. The claims being made by both Schüssler Fiorenza and Lopez have profound implications for Pauline studies and our current social constructions based upon the Pauline corpus. I do wonder what Carter's chapter would have looked like if he had spent more time discussing work that has the potential to genuinely "loose" Paul from the fetters of tradition and theological certainty.

Carter does state that the imperial framework of Paul's words needs to be highlighted and problematized.[11] I do agree with him, but here I have two responses to his brief comment. The first is to note that some scholars have done precisely that in their work.[12] Does this mean that he is unaware of this work or that he was bound by time and space and could not engage it here (there is no reference to it in the footnotes)? What does this tell us, as readers of Paul and the scholarship about him, concerning the political motivations of our colleagues? The second response to his statement about needing to address the imperial framework of Paul's words is that for someone new to this realm of study the implications of "exposing Paul's imperialism" are not necessarily clear. Indeed, not simply the labels used, "Lord? Savior? Son of God? Christ?," but also the framework of Paul's thought—male-centered and imperial-friendly—the tone of his assertions and commands in his letters, and the dualism of his thought all need to be challenged, or do I mean "changed"? They are certainly all perpetuated today.

Another chapter worth noting in this "tell me which part is new" section is the one contributed by Deborah Krause, "Paul and Women: Telling Women to Shut Up Is More Complicated Than You Might Think."[13] She offers an overview of feminist scholarship on Paul, in particular how it has moved from addressing specific "problematic" passages for women to investigating Paul's letters contextually with women in mind. This is an important shift. She thus concludes something similar to other contributions in the *Paul Unbound* volume: Paul's writings are "not so much a reservoir of Paul's ideas about women as they are artifacts of discourse about human relationships, gender, religious experience, and power at work in Paul's churches and the world in which they lived."[14]

> They are witnesses to the struggle that women and men have engaged to define the nature of the church's leadership, the shape of human community within the church, and the intersection between religious experience and the authority to speak of it.[15]

To this end, Krause suggests that Paul's letters ought not to be sought for comfort as much as for courage to continue the struggle.[16] Krause takes up two of the most problematic passages for women, 1 Cor 14:34-36 and 1 Tim 2:12-15, and shifts the light on them ever so slightly so that the reader can see how they both give an indication of the struggle that is happening regarding women's ability to speak in the ekklēsia. She suggests that we read them as a man's attempt to control the speech of women, rather than as a description of what was already happening. Yes, this does seem to be the point: there were women speaking up and assuming leadership roles and some men were not comfortable with it and sought to control them. Unfortunately, this is precisely how many communities do handle these passages already, using them to "legitimately" curb the participation of women in church congregations today. The texts indicate there was a struggle going on, and that struggle for power between males and females continues. Period. I am at a loss as to how in leaving the discussion here, without also somehow unsettling the authority of biblical texts entirely, this is an empowering reading for women. Krause has done nothing to upset the apple cart of Paul's privilege and power, thus she does nothing to unbind him. Rather, I would suggest she, perhaps unwittingly, re-binds him.[17]

As Elisabeth Schüssler Fiorenza reminds us, since "it is not 'biological' sex difference but patriarchal household and marriage relationships that generate the social-political inferiority and oppression of women," then we must challenge the authority of scripture that has this kind of prescription for women.[18] Regardless of who penned the restrictive prescription—Paul or someone in his wake—the command has been afforded unquestioned authority simply because it is in the canon. This is the level on which something new needs to be said and done.

One of the striking characteristics of some of the recent scholarship on Paul that claims to be doing something new or breathing fresh air into the field is that there is a simultaneous need to disagree with Paul without letting go of his authority.[19] Any approach that does not unsettle or uproot the problematic passages in Paul but allows them to remain, supposedly now just fallow, is perhaps underestimating the power of scripture to continue to define our realities today. The fact that the difficult passages remain is something we can no longer overlook. In addition, it is not just a few phrases here and there that are at issue. These *are* androcentric texts; they *do* promote ideas and theological beliefs from a kyriarchal world view; they *do not* accord women equal status or representation; they *do* embody first century biases; they absolutely *do* promote heteronormativity; Paul's rhetoric *is*, as often as not, manipulative, judgmental or otherwise of an ilk we would do well not to perpetuate; and his writings *can and do* justify abusive and exploitative relationships, both within male/female pairings and within the structuring and running of ecclesial bodies. It is a curious business, needing yet hating Paul. When we do not seek to reframe Paul and his writings entirely, but simply add a feminist interpretation to them, the effect is much like dipping something in chocolate: it might taste a bit better, but the androcentric texts at the core remain the same.

Thus, I was not convinced that either of these two chapters, or any of the others, falls outside the umbrella of being in service to the church and theology. There are new twists on the same basic ideas or structures; there is nothing challenging enough to cause a shift or effective liberative change. Just as the field of biblical studies in general has tried to "add and stir" when it comes to incorporating new perspectives and voices from "the margins and periphery," and thus do everyone a disservice for being somewhat disingenuous, so too are we falling short if we think that simply adding new perspectives will change the understanding of what is normative in Pauline studies.

Who Inhabits This World?

Feminist studies therefore maintains that established scholarship as androcentric scholarship is not only *partial* insofar as it articulates only male experience as human experience, but that it is also *biased* insofar as its intellectual discourse and scholarly frameworks are determined only by male perspectives primarily of the dominant classes.[20]

In the two chapters in *Paul Unbound* that discuss Paul and the Law and Paul's "opponents," what interests me more than the content itself is that the voices in this dialogue are almost exclusively those of white males.[21] The inquisitive student of Paul and all things related might want to ask why this is the case. What is it about the debate that does not draw women and people of various ethnicities to it? Is it that discussing and dissecting the Law is not relevant to them? (No) Is it that there are women and people of various ethnicities who *are* writing on these topics but are not being taken into consideration? (Perhaps) Given the numerous subfields on Paul to choose to engage, perhaps these other scholars prefer to put their energies elsewhere. I do not expect to be able to explain this situation but merely to draw attention to the political implications of it.

Given the importance of Paul for Christian doctrine and belief it *is* worth the time to reflect on why the traditional Pauline topics are so predominantly directed by white males, or perhaps more to the point, to consider the implications that the topics predominantly filled with "pale male" scholarship are considered to be the most important topics. Given the power and authority that Paul and his writings confer on those who interpret them, it *is* worth our time to consider the power implications of certain topics being predominantly populated by white males. There should be no confusion as to why those topics tend to be seen as the "weightier matters" whereas a focus on Paul and gender constructions, for instance, is often deemed secondary or peripheral to important Pauline issues.

To be sure, it does matter how we interpret Paul in relation to his own Judaism. Paul's views of the Law and of God's covenant with Israel were of import in the first century and remain so to this day. What perhaps needs to be noted here, though, is that all of these conversations about legalistic upholding of the Law or ethnic inclusion in the covenant conceal the deeper issue, which is that Paul did indeed "create" something new and, intentionally or not, it led to the supersession of Judaism by Christianity, from the perspective of the Church. None of the debates regarding how to properly interpret Paul's motivations or view of the Law will change this fact. Making Paul into someone innocent of wrongdoing will not change what did develop out of Paul's thought and writings.

One may want to ask why these males "protesteth too much," then, and why they have not been as invested in addressing the manifold other injustices that have been carried out based in part on Paul's words. In saying this I do not intend to make light of any manifestations of anti-Semitism. I do, however, wish to direct our attention to the centuries of harm, violence, abuse and exploitation of millions of people—especially of females, but also of people of various races and ethnicities—that his writings have also contributed to. Or to come at the issue from a different perspective, what do we get from clearing Paul's name of any connection to anti-Semitism? What is it that people are after in *needing* to find Paul innocent on any topic: the law, the covenants, sex/sexuality, leadership and so on? It is all related to the need to ultimately be able to claim Paul as authoritative.

This brings us full circle in this discussion of how the authority ascribed to Paul and his writings is also given to those who agree with him. The gender, ethnicity, social standing and places of academic training of the scholars involved in any discourse will influence how that discourse is framed and what is deemed important or central to it. For people who engage biblical texts for the sake of personal edification, sermon preparation or scholarly endeavors, take note of the voices you trust to guide you in making sense of Paul's words.

Who Will Be Brave Enough To Speak?

> Paul is so inherently interesting that anyone who writes about Paul should feel an appropriate sense of intimidation, lest one's words detract from the writings and accomplishments of Paul himself.[22]

I include this quotation from the preface of another book as a way of indicating how powerful and authoritative Paul continues to be, even here at the beginning of the twenty-first century. Thomas Phillips's fondness for Paul stands in stark contrast to the questions I regularly hear from engaged students: "Why do we still see Paul as authoritative?" and "Why do we assume that Paul is correct about everything?" While Phillips is certainly more educated on the matter than my students are, I do not think that he is more invested in his admonition than these students are in their line of questioning. They are less invested in maintaining Paul's place of prominence, however. They are willing to name what is there in Paul's words. Many scholars dance around these difficult issues instead of taking them head-on, perhaps because of how far and wide the reverberations might be felt. I suggest that it is time to stop avoiding and start saying what is apparent to us.

Steven Friesen's contribution to the volume, "Paul and Economics: The Jerusalem Collection as an Alternative to Patronage," is a fascinating example of this dynamic.[23] He makes several strident claims but he does not hold his reader to having to think them through thoroughly. For instance, he states that "In our reconstructions [of Paul's churches] we must compensate for the historical invisibility of the poor."[24] Yes, this is indeed an important contribution or challenge to scholars of early Christianity. It is worth our time to sort through the implications of a thoughtful understanding of the prominence of the poor in the Jesus movement and early churches. Friesen's careful data collection and analyses of the people Paul refers to in his letters suggest that the early churches did not have people from the upper echelons of wealth as we are often lead to believe. Furthermore, according to Acts it was *only* the wealthy that Paul interacted with. This distinction between Paul's version and Acts' on this matter is more than a minor point; it has huge implications for how we envision the earliest churches and what we claim Paul's *modus operandi* was, not to mention the challenge to the authority of scripture that this indictment brings.

But it is Friesen's closing comments that I find most curious:

> There are other topics to explore in the context of systematic deprivation and Paul's churches. We could look at the Lord's Supper as a meal shared among the poor, or Paul's manual labor as a refusal to commodify his apostolic calling . . . all three of these experiments [including the collection as a counter to patronage] apparently failed. . . . Perhaps it was necessary for Paul's boldest economic initiatives—the ones that abandoned the Roman system of inequality—to fail in order for an evolving Pauline Christianity to become over the course of time an integrated part of that system of inequality.[25]

I cannot help but wonder if he has flipped the order of cause and effect here, as that is what I take him to be suggesting in his article. Regardless, his point is made, and it is one I appreciate. But while the way he "says it slant" may make it more palatable for some, I fear that it will allow too many to ignore the implication altogether.

Jerry Sumney's chapter, "Paul and His Opponents: The Search," also has bold implications somewhat tucked away in plain sight. One of the main points he makes is that there were teachers that Paul opposed who nonetheless thought that they were carrying on his tradition. This indicates for us two things: Paul was considered authoritative, and there was already diversity in the way his teachings were interpreted.[26] More to the point, "the churches were still defining the range of diversity they would deem acceptable."[27] Certainly this clutch of points has been made before, but the fact that respected biblical scholars, such as Sumney points out, do not seem to have fully considered them ought to raise some questions for us. It is not just a matter of it being too recent of a development for them to be expected to be familiar with it. There is something deeper at stake. Suggesting that Paul's way was not the only way, which these points do indicate, raises the issues of power and control, whose voices "counted" and whose did not.

While Sumney is only dealing with identifying Paul's opponents, his cautionary remarks regarding how we read Paul's polemics perhaps ought to apply anytime Paul makes strong claims and asserts his authority with powerful words. "Interpreters in recent decades more readily recognize and take account of the fact that Paul's characterizations of those he opposes are often tendentious, particularly in polemical contexts. Similarly, when Paul is defending himself, he often presents the charges others make about him in a dramatic and exaggerated form to lead his readers to dismiss those charges out of hand or to make them easier to refute."[28]

Not only are these important observations about Paul's tone and his use of rhetoric in general, but do they not also suggest that the very label "opponents" ought to be reconsidered? The dualistic framework here, of Paul versus others, creates or sustains an assumed antagonism within the movement instead of allowing for accepted variations. It sets us up to need to find "the" correct doctrine or practice. As Sumney suggests, one of the benefits of more carefully identifying Paul's "opponents" is that "we will be able to recognize a breadth of diversity among early believers that disallows simplistic and false frameworks such as the 'orthodox church' and the 'heretics' for the first-century church."[29]

Beyond simply embracing variety in the early church understandings of what was "allowed" and what was not, we come back to the reality that Paul's legacy and assumed correctness have deep roots, psychically, ecclesiastically and theologically. I suggest that we have to make the bold implications of our findings quite clear, or they will not penetrate the established models for how to understand all things Pauline.

Concluding Commentary

Vincent Wimbush opened his 2010 Society of Biblical Literature presidential address with the following challenge for all those who undertake critical engagements of the bible. I have chosen to quote him at length in order to convey the urgency of his message and so as not to dismiss that his driving concern is about race/racism. While it was not my intention to engage the specific form of his challenge in this chapter, the underlying power dynamics that Wimbush speaks of are of particular interest to me from a feminist standpoint and do concern us all.

> I stand before you this evening with yet another challenge, imploring the Society—and by extension, all critical interpreters—to start and to sustain "talkin' 'bout somethin'." Here is the challenge plainly put: there can be no critical interpretation worthy of the name, without coming to terms with the first contact—between the West and the rest, the West and the Others—and its perduring toxic and blinding effects and consequences. The challenge remains for this Society and all collectivities of critical interpreters in general to engage in persistent and protracted struggle, not symbolic or obfuscating games around methods and approaches, to come to terms with the construal of the modern ideologization of language, characterized by the meta-racism that marks the relationship between Europeans and Euro-Americans and peoples of color, especially black peoples. What might it mean to address in explicit terms the nature and consequences of first contact for the unstable and fragile big tent that is our Society? What might it suggest for the ongoing widely differently prioritized and oriented work we do in our widely different settings and contexts with our nonetheless still widely shared absolutist and elitist claims and presumptions about such work? It would make it imperative that we talk about discourse and power, slavery and freedom, life and death.[30]

I have sought to highlight in this chapter a certain amount of complacency within Pauline studies, regardless of the "critical" method that any given scholar brings to the engagement. The world needs us to be about the business of "talkin' 'bout somethin'," instead of being comfortable with mere nuances on the status quo counting as a "fresh voice" within Pauline studies.

Instead of accepting as truth and standard what is said in a given passage, responsible biblical scholarship would then wrestle with the implications of the content. If taken seriously, if put into practice, what does that idea, command, or custom lead to? Is the result something beneficial? Does it contribute to creating spaces and relations of equality, mutuality, and respect for all people? Or does it put restrictions on some, for reasons that we can understand in its as-close-as-we-can-get-to-it original context but that we no longer need to acquiesce to? If it is the latter, it is time to find a way to say, categorically, that it is not authoritative anymore.

I suggest that we start to take more seriously the ethics of interpretation and the afterlives thereof.[31] When the focus is on what Paul says or meant for the sake of accurate application we tend to overlook the side effects of uncritically engaging and teaching Paul and his letters. What results is that a positivistic approach is undertaken, for the sake of "mutual benefit," "building up the Church," Christ-centered discipleship, and so on. It is relatively inwardly focused: either on the individual or the local church body. What about the Body worldwide? What about the engagement with humankind? What about the way Paul and his writings shape our worldviews, set the tone we take in engaging someone with whom we disagree, or initiate intense "us vs. them" paradigms for the Church and scholarly discourse? Ought not our current scholarship engage Paul and his "legacy" at the level of how well it plays in the sandbox of life? Instead of spending hours upon hours determining the correctness of a given understanding of an element of Paul's thought, why not engage the ethical and moral implications of assuming that Paul is the best voice to listen to on any given topic? To be sure, biblical scholars have learned well at the feet of Paul and by his example; we have become too good at imitating him, in his rhetorical devices no less than in his theological claims and assertions of correctness.[32] It is high time that we find new examples to model our faith and scholarly discourses upon.

My life-long church attending, undergraduate students put a fine point on the urgency of the matter. I asked them to consider, throughout a semester course on Paul, the effects of teaching and preaching Paul's writings uncritically. Though they joked around all semester about the tone of Paul's assertions, which they deemed to be arrogant, at the end of the semester not a single one of them reflected on the effects Paul's arrogance might have on those who take up his writings uncritically. They could consider such issues when pressed on it in seminar, but it had not penetrated their overall framework for how they think about Paul.

I think that it is no longer sufficient to acknowledge that our social values have changed since the first century when the texts of our religious communities have not. Put differently, it is about time for us to confront, instead of explain away, the reality that people can turn to Paul's contributions to "God's word" and find judgmental ideals, justification for power-over relations between men and women, and rhetoric that contributes to creating oppressive communal structures, to name but a few manifestations of leaving Paul's writings unchallenged. Their situatedness cannot be excused; it must be engaged directly. Instead of finding ways to make Paul palatable and understandable, I suggest that it is time for us to challenge Paul and his interpreters on the very idea of granting Paul such authority. If what is called God's word is to lead to embrace and empowerment, to fullness of life, to the end of relations of domination and exploitation, and to authentic and loving communities,[33] then let it be so.

Notes

1. Elisabeth Schüssler Fiorenza, "Remembering the Past in Creating the Future: Historical-Critical Scholarship and Feminist Biblical Interpretation," in *Feminist Perspectives on Biblical Scholarship*, ed. Adela Yarbro Collins, SBL Biblical Scholarship in North America 10 (Chico: Scholars, 1985), 61.

2. It is indeed an honor and privilege to be able to contribute to this volume honoring Fernando F. Segovia, who was my advisor at Vanderbilt University. He is exceptionally gifted as an advisor. With great humility and unending attention to detail, Fernando teaches his students how to do the work in their own voices instead of in a version of his. It is my hope that I am similarly inspiring for the students entrusted to me.

3. Mark D. Given, ed., *Paul Unbound: Other Perspectives on the Apostle* (Peabody: Hendrickson, 2010).

4. Mark D. Given, "Introduction," in *Paul Unbound: Other Perspectives on the Apostle* (Mark D. Given, ed., Peabody: Hendrickson, 2010), 1.

5. Ibid., 1.

6. Warren Carter, "Paul and the Roman Empire: Recent Perspectives," in *Paul Unbound: Other Perspectives on the Apostle*, ed. Mark D. Given (Peabody: Hendrickson, 2010), 7-26. The three books he reviews: Richard Horsley, ed., *Paul and Empire: Religion and Power in Roman Imperial Society* (Harrisburg: Trinity International, 1997); Horsley, *Paul and Politics: Ekklesia, Israel, Imperium, Interpretation* (Harrisburg: Trinity International, 2000); and Horsley, *Paul and the Roman Imperial Order* (Harrisburg: Trinity International, 2004).

7. Carter, "Paul and the Roman Empire: Recent Perspectives," 8.

8. Ibid., 18.

9. Ibid., 20–21.

10. Ibid., 19.

11. Ibid., 24.

12. For example, Joseph A. Marchal, "Military Images in Philippians 1-2: A Feminist Analysis of the Rhetorics of Scholarship, Philippians, and Current Contexts," in *Her Masters Tools? Feminist and Postcolonial Engagements of Historical-Critical Discourse*, ed. Todd Penner and Caroline Vander Stichele (Atlanta: Society of Biblical Literature, 2005), 265-86 ; idem, *The Politics of Heaven: Women, Gender and Empire in the Study of Paul* (Minneapolis: Fortress, 2008); Elisabeth Schüssler Fiorenza, "1 Peter," in *A Postcolonial Commentary on the New Testament Writings*, ed. Fernando F. Segovia and R. S. Sugirtharajah (New York: Continuum, 2007), 380-403; idem, *The Power of the Word: Scripture and the Rhetoric of Empire* (Minneapolis: Fortress, 2007); Jennifer Bird, *Abuse, Power and Fearful Obedience: Reconsidering 1 Peter's Commands to Wives* (London: T&T Clark, 2011).

13. Deborah Krause, "Paul and Women: Telling Women to Shut Up Is More Complicated Than You Might Think," in *Paul Unbound: Other Perspectives on the Apostle*, ed. Mark D. Given (Peabody: Hendrickson), 161-174.

14. Ibid., 172.

15. Ibid.

16. Ibid., 173.

17. Ibid., 161–74.

18. Schüssler Fiorenza, "Remembering the Past in creating the Future," 58.

19. Sandra Hack Polaski's recent volume, *A Feminist Introduction to Paul* (Saint Louis: Chalice, 2005), does a good job of straddling the fence in this way. She very clearly wants to disagree with several parts of the Pauline corpus, but all the while she is maintaining Paul's overall authority.

20. Schüssler Fiorenza, "Remembering the Past in creating the Future," 56, italics original.

21. A. Andrew Das, "Paul and the Law: Pressure Points in the Debate" in *Paul Unbound: Other Perspectives on the Apostle*, ed. Mark D. Given (Peabody: Hendrickson, 2010), 99–116.

22. Thomas E. Phillips, *Paul, His Letters, and Acts*, Library of Pauline Studies (Peabody: Hendrickson, 2009), preface.

23. Steven J. Friesen, "Paul and Economics: The Jerusalem Collection as an Alternative to Patronage," in *Paul Unbound: Other Perspectives on the Apostle*, ed. Mark D. Given (Peabody: Hendrickson, 2010), 27–54.

24. Ibid., 42.

25. Ibid., 51-52.

26. Jerry L. Sumney, "Paul and His Opponents: The Search," in *Paul Unbound: Other Perspectives on the Apostle*, ed. Mark D. Given (Peabody: Hendrickson, 2010), 58.

27. Ibid., 59.

28. Ibid.

29. Ibid., 66–67.

30. Vincent L. Wimbush, "Interpreters—Enslaving/Enslaved/Runagate," *JBL* 130, no. 1 (2011): 9.

31. Elisabeth Schüssler Fiorenza, *Rhetoric and Ethic: The Politics of Biblical Studies* (Minneapolis: Fortress Press, 1999).

32. Elizabeth A. Castelli, *Imitating Paul: A Discourse of Power* (Louisville: Westminster/John Knox, 1991).

33. Elizabeth A. Johnson, *She Who Is: The Mystery of God in Feminist Theological Discourse* (New York: Crossroad, 1998), 30–31. Elisabeth Schüssler Fiorenza, *Bread Not Stone: The Challenge of Feminist Biblical Interpretation* (Boston: Beacon, 1984), xiii.

PART III

Cultural Interventions

10

Multiple Locations–Belongings and Power Differentials

Lenses for a Liberating Biblical Hermeneutic

Eleazar S. Fernandez

When I was in the Philippines, I was simply a Filipino. When I settled in the United States, a change in my identity happened. I became a person of color, a racial ethnic minority. Then at one point I had the privilege to teach in Yaoundé, Cameroon, and something strange happened. I found it difficult to believe, but for the first time in my life I was called white. In one of my public lectures someone asked me during the question and answer time if I was speaking as a Filipino or as an American. I was tempted to say, as I often do, that I am a racial ethnic minority in America, but I thought that saying so is only partly true. The question, it seemed to me, called for a more nuanced response, a response that takes account not only of my minority status but also of my privileged location in relation to others. Being a racial ethnic minority is only one of the many locations (identities) and belongings I assume in the web of social relations. I am not always and everywhere the oppressed racial minority. These multiple locations and belongings and, therefore, multiple positions in power differentials, I later on realized, have informed my approach to the reading of texts.

This essay attempts to articulate a way of reading texts (whether written texts, social contexts, physical bodies, and so on) or a reading strategy that seeks to be perennially transformative. Such a reading strategy, therefore, must make several crucial refusals. It must refuse to claim a single location as the only liberating location from which to read a text and to trivialize other locations; it must refuse to make a claim that it has arrived at a permanent liberating content under the guise of having possessed the essential meaning of the text or of having articulated the point of view of the poor. Moreover, it must refuse to make the claim that a particular sacred text is essentially as well as inherently liberating. A central claim of this essay is that shifting multiple locations and belongings as well as power differentials must be taken seriously if a hermeneutic strategy is to maintain its self-critical and liberating stance. Real flesh-and-blood readers assume a variety of positions—in relation to time, geography, geopolitics, diaspora location, social location, religion, ethnicity, gender, sexuality, and so on—in the power-knowledge nexus that inform their readings and cultural or religious discursive productions in the global market. This power-knowledge nexus is pervasive globally as well as locally, and it assumes multiple shapes.

Naming the crucial place of shifting multiple locations and belongings as well as the power differentials in any act of reading is, however, only one aspect of the strategy. Deconstructive naming must pave the way for the imaginative constructive task, one that not only celebrates competing and, many times, conflicting interpretations, but is also committed to the construction of an alternative tomorrow. In other words, my reading strategy is not simply a postmodernistic celebration of multi-locational reading; it is a reading strategy that, in the spirit of liberation discourse, is committed to emancipatory praxis. Moreover, it is a preferential reading, a reading intended to let muted voices speak up.

The next few pages articulate my reading strategy. To test its validity and fruitfulness as a reading strategy, I will show how it bears on the intertwined issues of global diaspora and the Israeli-Palestinian situation, a topic which I had the privilege to address at a conference in Bethlehem, Palestine in August of 2011.

A Revised Liberation Hermeneutics: Postcolonial Critique

The main insights of liberation hermeneutics continue to hold a central place in my reading approach, but my approach has also undergone transformation, particularly with insights from poststructuralism and postcolonial discourse. While I criticize some expressions of liberation hermeneutics from a postcolonial lens, I affirm Elizabeth Schüssler Fiorenza's point that liberation hermeneutics and postcolonial discourse are not "exclusive oppositions."[1] Still, a distinction must be made. With ideas from postcolonial and, particularly, feminist discourse, I have become more critical of the biblical text itself, not just of the interpretation of the text. While liberation hermeneutics is prophetic in responding to themes of social justice, the way it construes the Bible and the reading strategies it employs tend to be conservative. Liberation remains, as Marcella María Althaus-Reid said in her essay, "Gustavo Gutiérrez Goes to Disneyland," a "theme park" of Western theology.[2] Liberation hermeneutics seems to have forgotten that "[a]s a collective memory, the *Bible is constrained and determined by the culture in which it was produced*, and its contents remain unfinished and uncertain."[3] It seems to have forgotten to critique the text as "text" and "history" and its ideological function in society both past and present.[4] Though a liberationist-advocacy form of reading highlights the importance of context and the flesh-and-blood readers who are always positioned (the question of social location) and interested (the question of social agenda), it relates to the biblical text as a mine for moral prescriptions that can be used to authorize an advocacy stance.[5] Following a linear trajectory from text to issues, liberationist readings can easily fall into textualism. In a context that questions only interpretations of the Bible but not the Bible's ambivalent history—including its production, translation into various languages, and dissemination—textualism reinforces what R. S. Sugirtharajah calls Christian "scriptural imperialism."[6] With the exception of the scholar-expert who is the active one-way interpreter, the culture of the subaltern flesh-and-blood readers remains passive; it does not talk back to the Bible.

I continue to affirm some of the main tenets of liberation hermeneutics, particularly God's identification with the poor or the weak in any society as well as a commitment to rigorous socio-economic criticism; however, I must say that unlike the early versions of liberation hermeneutics, I no longer see the poor as "a unified and homogenous revolutionary subject." The poor do not constitute a homogenous special class that will drive history forward, but instead is composed of individuals from various walks of life who are struggling for a more dignified life.[7] The poor or the subaltern's experience of oppression cannot be reduced on the sole basis of economics or class. There are multiple expressions of marginalization, and they relate to one another in an interlocking fashion.[8] This understanding is predicated on a nuanced understanding of power, something that is not constrained by deterministic materialist analysis.

Power in its various articulations is a crucial concept in my reading strategy. Here I adopt Michel Foucault's notion of the power-knowledge nexus.[9] The traditional clear-cut division between power and knowledge needs radical overhauling. This division often serves as a mask: it does not expose the productive role of power and it allows knowledge to present itself as truly immaculate, unstained or unspoiled by power.[10] The relationship between knowledge (truth) and power is not a relationship of cause and effect respectively, but they co-produce. Power is not only negative and coercive, it is also productive: it produces knowledge; it creates regimes of truth. My reading strategy sees context and text, production of texts, readings of texts, and readers of (con)text as always-and-already imbricated in the power-knowledge nexus.

IMPERIAL POWER-KNOWLEDGE NEXUS AND ITS BEARINGS ON BIBLICAL DISCOURSE

We may name the global expression of hegemonic power-knowledge nexus as empire. The Roman Empire was the context in which the Christian New Testament took shape. That same Roman Empire became the cradle of Christianity. The rise and fall of empires provides a significant lens for understanding the context, content, and production of the biblical text. Even as the early Christians resisted empire and created what is considered religious resistance literature, in many ways this literature, following Schüssler Fiorenza, *"re-inscribed the structures of domination* against which it seeks to argue"; that is, early Christian literature re-inscribed imperial ways of thinking and structures of domination.[11] Thus, it is not enough for a hermeneutics that seeks to be liberating to be satisfied with the claim that the Bible and, in particular the New Testament, is an anti-imperial document. This form of anti-imperial studies often ends up trying to "rehabilitate Christian writings."[12] While I celebrate anti-imperial/resistance discourse or literature because it supports my political stance, in many ways it has not carried the historical project of criticism far enough. And, to pursue the argument, the assertion that the gospel is counter-imperial refuses to examine how imperial language is re-inscribed in the sacred text and how it functions today. With imperial language inscribed as gospel language and, as a consequence, acquiring performative status, imperial language shapes identity and contemporary praxis.[13] As such, knowing the imperial context of the biblical formation and the pervasive power of empire in our present context is crucial. In other words, following Schüssler Fiorenza, it is also imperative that biblical and theological emancipative work have two foci: "the Roman Empire as the context and social location of Christian scriptures, on the one hand, and contemporary forms of empire and global possibilities for resistance, on the other."[14]

Empire has undergone transformation up until its most recent expression. The ancient Roman Empire embodied what Walter Wink calls the "Domination System," which he describes as a "network of Powers."[15] "No matter what shape the dominating system of the moment might take (from the ancient Near Eastern states to *Pax Romana* to feudal Europe to communist state capitalism to modern market capitalism)," Wink goes on to say, "the basic structure has persisted now for at least five thousand years, since the great conquest states of Mesopotamia around 3000 B. C. E."[16] While we can say that continuities exist, it may be that the basic structure is also evolving. I am of the opinion that a significant shift is now altering how empire is constituted and visualized. Wink provides a worthy starting point in talking about power as "network," but we need to further refine our understanding of it. Here, Michael Hardt and Antonio Negri's account of empire is useful.[17] Without discounting the imperial acts of some nations, like the United States, Hardt and Negri contend that "[t]he contemporary global order can no longer be *understood adequately* (my emphasis) in terms of imperialism as it was practiced by the modern powers, based primarily on the sovereignty of the nation-state extended over foreign territory." Instead, they argue, "a 'network power,' a new form of sovereignty, is now emerging, and it includes its primary elements, or nodes, the dominant nation-states along with supranational institutions, major capitalist corporations, and other powers."[18]

Geopolitics as Power-Knowledge Nexus: Diaspora, Shifting Locations, Victims, and Victimizers

If empire has the ability to re-inscribe its power-knowledge nexus, particularly power differentials, in what are considered sacred texts, it re-inscribes how we see the world as well. As something productive, it develops a system of order and classification that gets accepted over time as "reality." This is true with "geography." While no one can exist without geography, on closer scrutiny, geography is really geopolitics or, to be more precise, is experienced as geopolitics. Geopolitics, at least in the global sense, is a creation of empire. Empire maps the areas of the world into various political-economic regions for its own purposes. Whether through conquest, creating boundaries to form nation-states, or imposing spheres of global market activity, imperial hands are at work. We may take the case of Asia and the Middle East or Near East. What is Asia and what makes up Asia? Where is the boundary of Asia? Can we not say that what is currently referred to as the Middle East is Western Asia (and part of North Africa)? Asia has something to do with the Middle East because the Middle East is Western Asia. Moreover, a great portion of the Christian New Testament books, though commonly understood as Middle Eastern texts, were written in Asia or written for communities there.[19]

Not only does imperial geopolitics create or define boundaries and geopolitical regions for its own purposes, it also disperses or diasporizes people. If geopolitics is a creation of empire, we may say that diaspora is a creation of empire. Normally, following the practices of ancient empire, the sequence is:

exploration, conquest, colonization, exploitation, and dispersion. The empire that diasporizes people from one location often creates a diaspora mess somewhere else when the diasporized settle, or are resettled by, imperial powers. Aside from aspiring to go or settle in the country of their imperial masters (for example, Asian Indians and Jamaicans in Britain, Surinamese in The Netherlands, Martinicans in France, and Filipinos in the United States), colonized diasporas often end up in the former/current colonies of their colonial masters, such as Asian Indians in Kenya, Fiji, and Guyana (former colonies of Britain), and Vietnamese in New Caledonia (administered by France). Diaspora and settlement may bring conflict in the host countries. The tension between Indo-Fijians and the native Fijians is an expression of imperial mess. The Kanaks of New Caledonia also view France's action to resettle more Vietnamese refugees as a devious move to suppress the Kanaks' struggle for independence. From the Kanaks' point of view, what France is doing is "genocide by substitution."[20]

The diaspora of the Jews, the establishment of the State of Israel, and the plight of the Palestinians are all part of imperial mess. The history of the Jewish people is largely a history of diaspora, a diaspora that, in many respects, has been triggered by the comings and goings of imperial powers.[21] If the Jewish diaspora could not be adequately understood apart from empire, nor can the creation of the State of Israel. Nor could the return of the Jewish diaspora to Israel be understood adequately apart from empire and its geopolitical interest. By extension, the creation of the State of Israel that has led to the dispersal of the Palestinians cannot be understood apart from empire and its geopolitics. To be sure other factors need to be taken into account, but imperial geopolitics provides the larger frame. Determined to play the dominant role in the region, Britain and later on the United States supported the Jewish Zionist aspiration for the creation of the State of Israel as a surrogate state. This support for Israel's creation was reinforced by the creation of allies docile to the interests of Britain and the United States among Arab states.

Multivalent Reading: Myths of Exodus and Liberation

The Exodus narrative provides another specific case of how the power-knowledge nexus and shifting location inform one's reading. It tells us that there is no such thing as the text speaking for itself, for every reading is always located reading within the web of power relations. Exodus has provided the central narrative that has played in the imagination of oppressed communities, and it has been the darling narrative of liberation hermeneutics. Yet the same narrative has captivated the utopian imagination and informed the political practice of conquerors, imperial nations, and xenophobic groups. The Exodus paradigm has not escaped from nation-states that use the narrative to rally nativistic and virulent nationalism. Cromwell invoked Exodus to overthrow the British monarchy during the British Civil War, while Dryden used it to rally behind the monarchy during the Restoration. On the one hand, the American revolutionaries invoked Exodus against the British colonizers, and, on the other hand, they invoked conquest when they seized the land of the Native Americans.[22]

Most interpreters, I would say, do not read the whole Exodus narrative. They focus on the first half and get stuck there. They need to un-stick themselves and continue reading to the second half of the Exodus narrative to discover that the whole narrative includes Eisodus (entry into the promised-land). The whole narrative is Exodus/Eisodus. The jubilation of the Exodus is not complete without the Eisodus. No one can continue with Exodus excitement for the long haul; the Exodus people must become an Eisodus people. The people who flee must find a place to settle. Otherwise, as the Israelites did in their complaint to Moses, they would rather go back to the flesh pots in the land of Egypt. It is at this point when Exodus turns into Eisodus that the narrative also becomes problematic, because the Exodus of liberation turns into the Eisodus of conquest, occupation, dispossession, and displacement of the local inhabitants. "If people were not deprived of engagement with the second half of the Exodus paradigm," as noted by Michael Prior, "they would not escape morally unscathed from their communal encounter with the whole biblical paradigm. . . . Combining the Exodus from Egypt with the Eisodus into the land of the Canaanites and others as the narrative requires, the biblical paradigm would more appropriately *justify the behavior of the conquerors*."[23] I hope that readers "would not escape morally unscathed" when they read the whole narrative, but I am not that optimistic. As Prior knows, readers construct or invent ways of reading to justify their actions, including concepts such as *terra nullius* (empty space), civilizing pagans, and God's "election."[24]

A different way of reading, however, makes the Exodus/Eisodus-Liberation/Conquest even more problematic, which cannot be easily rehabilitated by asking readers to read the whole narrative. The issue is not simply about sound exegesis, but about the narrative itself. As a narrative, "the biblical claim of the divine promise of land," Prior argues, "is *integrally linked* with the divine approval for the extermination of the indigenous people."[25] When two are "integrally linked," it means that one cannot stand without the other. Regina Schwartz pursues this point in her work, *The Curse of Cain*.[26] Here she argues that it is difficult to disentangle the rhetoric of liberation from the rhetoric of domination because they are "not simply opposites"; they are intertwined. Putting her argument in a retributive worldview and narrative, this is the logic: "[B]ecause we were (or will be) made homeless, we can seize another's home; because we were (or will be) conquered, we can conquer. Domination is the price exacted for having been dominated." Following such a retributive view, re-seizing the identical piece of land from the actual conquers is the logical move, but most often it is highly unlikely. So the once dominated finds a substitute, a weaker one. Schwartz is poignantly right: "Substitution is the soul of revenge."[27] This is what happened to the Palestinians.

Power-Differentials, the Rhetoric of Victimization, and Memory

In the opening section of this essay I shared a story about my experience in Cameroon and my recognition of my multiple social locations. I could always play the role of a victim, but I decided not to, for the reason that I am a real flesh-and-blood person whose location is multiple and shifting. We should not essentialize and eternalize social locations and power differentials. Traditional liberation hermeneutics falls into this trap when it essentializes and romanticizes the poor. While we can define the term "poor" abstractly, the face of the marginalized poor in history is always multiple and shifting. The danger of essentializing becomes concrete when certain groups—whose social reality has changed or whose social reality does not match with their current location in the power differentials—make use of the rhetoric of the essentialized poor/victims to pursue their hegemonic political agenda. One such case is the use of the memory of the victims by groups whose power location is already different from the victims whose memory it is seeking to exhume.

History is replete with cases of groups or nation-states using the memory of the victims to advance their political agenda. Memorialization of the victims of the Holocaust is an example. We must pay tribute to the victims of the Holocausts and to the victims of other heinous crimes, but we should act in ways that truly honor their memories. The memory of the victims is violated when their memory is used to victimize others or to perpetuate the cycle of violence. As Jewish theologian Marc Ellis puts it, "The use of suffering as a way of empowerment has, at least in the Jewish case, precipitated the Palestinian *diaspora* and the Jewish exile."[28] He continues, "The case of Jewish suffering in Europe has been told so often and memorialized so frequently, *as if Jews in the present are suffering*, that the charge against others of using suffering as a lever for advancement is mute."[29]

Still railing from anti-Semitic guilt, Christians in the West have constructed an essentialized and romanticized noble Jew, "as if Jews in the present are suffering" or, as if the Jews of the present State of Israel were still the dispersed and struggling biblical Israelites of old. They have constructed the noble Jew of the past (oppressed Jews of the biblical Egypt and, by extension, the victimized Jews of the Holocaust) as a way to restore (restoration myth) their lost innocence, by becoming oblivious of the social location of the present Jews. Since the myth of restoration gets stranded in the past, it retrieves the glorified powerless/victimized Jews and carries them to the present, which does not square with the current socio-political location of Jews and the power differentials that exist between Jews and Palestinians. With a hermeneutic lens of a mythic past that colonizes one's brain, the restorationist not only constructs the powerless Jew; the restorationist dwells in the past by projecting a powerful enemy (Canaanites) and anachronistically brings that enemy to the present (Arab world and Palestinians). Though this does not match the current socio-political picture, the notion of powerlessness and victimization has come out in Jewish and Christian Zionists' rhetoric, and it has been used against the Palestinians.

Ellis's comment, "as if Jews in the present are suffering," is a crucial reminder that power and social location can shift. Romanticizing the noble Jew resonates with essentializing and romanticizing of the poor in liberation hermeneutics, which can easily be manipulated to serve the interest of the power wielders. What liberation hermeneutics needs to do, I suggest, is to abandon the essentialization and romanticization of the poor and employ poststructuralist critique of power, such as the power-knowledge nexus, and thoroughly historicize the power dynamics so we can see the transformations, the shifting positions, and the power differentials diachronically and synchronically. When we do this, we not only de-mystify hegemonic power, we are also articulating a view of the power-knowledge nexus that will lead us to a new tomorrow, a view that must always remain critical of its own temptations and distortions.

How Shall We Proceed?

There is no way forward to a liberating hermeneutic that does not deal with the multiple and shifting/fluid locations in the web of social relations and its accompanying power-differentials. There is no escape from the power-knowledge nexus; any attempt is futile. Any claim to be outside of the power-knowledge nexus is a form of power-wielding masquerading as neutrality. The task requires not soaring beyond power-knowledge but, following Foucault, "detaching the power of truth from the powers of hegemony."[30] Counter-hegemonic hermeneutics does not escape from becoming a new hegemony by claiming that it is beyond the power-knowledge nexus, but only by exposing the power-knowledge nexus of all discourse, including its own. Counter-hegemonic movements of various stripes must constantly be vigilant and critical of their own regimes of truth if they are to maintain their liberating thrust.

Detaching the power of truth from the powers of hegemony is, however, only one crucial aspect. Beyond or along with the deconstruction, a liberating hermeneutic must make an imaginative-constructive move and must make normative claims. The work of detaching the power of truth from the powers of hegemony must be guided by a vision of a life-giving tomorrow. The idea of greater well-being in which all beings not only survive but also thrive provides the rationale and direction for the work of deconstruction and reconstruction. However, in the context of social inequality, in which others are wallowing in opulence while the majority of the people are dying before their time, the quest for greater well-being cannot continue as if it were impartial and neutral. Rather, it takes sides with the most vulnerable. Without losing sight of its larger commitment to greater well-being, liberationist reading judges all readings in terms of how they give life to those who are dying before their time.

How can we make sure that a certain reading promotes greater well-being in general and promotes the life of the most vulnerable in particular? How can we make certain that a reading continues to detach the power of truth from hegemony? It is not guaranteed by appeals to a liberating content, for a liberating content does not exist by itself, but only through a liberating method. What is critical is that the process of reading itself must be liberating. This, however, cannot be done apart from hermeneutic companions who are open to the journey of constructing the common, but without muting differences and uneven vulnerabilities and privileges. Hermeneutic companions are critical not only for undermining epistemic hegemonies but also for enlarging our world and realizing our vision.

Notes

1. Elisabeth Schüssler Fiorenza, "Transforming the Margin—Claiming Common Grounds: Charting a Different Paradigm of Biblical Studies," in *Still at the Margins: Biblical Scholarship Fifteen Years after the Voices from the Margins*, ed. R. S. Sugirtharajah (London: T&T Clark, 2008), 31.

2. Marcella María Althaus-Reid, "Gustavo Gutiérrez Goes to Disneyland: Theme Park Theologies and the Diaspora of the Discourse of the Popular Theologian in Liberation Theology,"

in *Interpreting Beyond Borders*, ed. Fernando F. Segovia (Sheffield: Sheffield Academic, 2000), 36–58.

3. R. S. Sugirtharajah, *Troublesome Texts: The Biblical in Colonial and Contemporary Culture* (Sheffield: Phoenix, 2008), 123.

4. Fernando F. Segovia, "Reading-Across: Intercultural Criticism and Textual Posture," in *Interpreting Beyond Borders* (Sheffield: Sheffield Academic, 2000), 64.

5. Ibid., 11–34.

6. R. S. Sugirtharajah, *The Bible and the Third World: Precolonial, Colonial, and Postcolonial Encounters* (London: Cambridge University Press, 2001), 57.

7. Ivan Petralla, ed., *Latin American Liberation Theology: The Next Generation* (Maryknoll: Orbis, 2005), 120.

8. Eleazar Fernandez, *Reimagining the Human: Theological Anthropology in Response to Systemic Evil* (Saint Louis: Chalice, 2004).

9. Michel Foucault and Paul Rabinow, eds., *The Foucault Reader* (New York: Pantheon).

10. Kyle Pasewark, *A Theology of Power: Being beyond Domination* (Minneapolis: Fortress Press, 1993), 9.

11. Elizabeth Schüssler Fiorenza, *The Power of the Word: Scripture and the Rhetoric of Empire* (Minneapolis: Fortress Press, 2007), 4.

12. Ibid.

13. Ibid., 6.

14. Ibid., 9.

15. Walter Wink, *The Powers That Be: Theology for a New Millennium* (New York: Doubleday, 1998), 39.

16. Ibid., 39–40.

17. Michael Hardt and Antonio Negri, *Empire* (Cambridge: Harvard University Press, 2000).

18. Michael Hardt and Antonio Negri, *Multitude: War and Democracy in the Age of Empires* (New York: Penguin Books, 2004), xiii.

19. R. S. Sugirtharajah, *Troublesome Texts: The Bible in Colonial and Contemporary Culture* (Sheffield: Sheffield Academic, 2008), 130.

20. Yan Celené Uregei, "The Kanak Struggle for Independence," in *Pacific People Sing Out Strong*, ed. William L. Coop (New York: Friendship, 1982), 66–69.

21. Michael Prior, *The Bible and Colonialism: A Moral Critique*, Biblical Seminar (Sheffield: Sheffield Academic, 1999), 201.

22. Regina Schwartz, *The Curse of Cain: The Violent Legacy of Monotheism* (Chicago: University of Chicago Press, 1997), 58.

23. Prior, *Bible and Colonialism*, 282; emphasis added.

24. Prior, *Bible and Colonialism*.

25. Ibid., 287.

26. Schwartz, *The Curse of Cain*.

27. Ibid., 56.

28. Marc Ellis, *Practicing Exile: The Religious Odyssey of an American Jew* (Minneapolis: Fortress Press, 2002).

29. Ibid., 31, emphasis supplied.

30. Foucault and Rabinow, eds., *The Foucault Reader*, 75.

11

Teaching the New Testament

Toward an Expanded Contextual Approach

Francisco Lozada Jr.

Introductions to the New Testament typically presume that to understand early Jewish and Christian literature, one must understand that literature within its originating context. Along with the general history of New Testament books (for example, author, date, provenance), introductions usually treat the literary, social, and historical features of the books of the New Testament as essential factors in clarifying context and meaning. Without a doubt the historical critical paradigm still characterizes the ethos and orientation of most introductions. The *ethos*[1] of introductions is one that values objectivity, positivism, and universality with regard to the role of the reader and how meaning is constructed. The *orientation* pertains to the reading strategy (methodological approach) one adopts to engage the text.

Very few introductions with a different ethos and orientation have appeared in mainstream and required classroom textbooks.[2] One reason for this is that, consciously or unconsciously, instructors prioritize a "scientific" or "Western/Northern" understanding of the New Testament that in turn gives rise to master narratives.[3] These types of narratives often omit or overlook differing or marginalized understandings of the New Testament.[4] In this essay, I shall argue that a shift toward a more expanded contextual approach to New Testament teaching is in order. In other words, by "contextual approach" I do not mean simply contextualizing the text and the reader, although this is a very important critical exercise, but also contextualizing our pedagogical discourses and practices. A "contextual approach" prepares for the future by way of new interpretations and new explanations.[5] It does not keep students in the past, but rather places the past in dialogue with the future. As such, teaching, like scholarship, is not simply a matter of rehearsing the master narrative, but also of challenging or destabilizing the master narrative by considering different outlooks and positions. I believe that if they are trained to be self-reflective, aware of the ethos and orientation of the materials that they are studying and introduced to diverse perspectives, students will be better equipped to engage the hidden underpinnings of other societal and ecclesial teachings, sacred scriptures, and political policies.[6]

The representative case that I will use to explore a thorough-going contextual approach to the New Testament touches on both my area of teaching (New Testament studies) and research (Johannine studies), and an area that Yak-Hwee Tan has already engaged in in this volume: reading the Johannine community. Since the latter third of the twentieth century, scholars of the Gospel of John have consistently employed an established master history/narrative to explain how the Fourth Gospel came to be. In essence, that narrative argues that that there was great tension between the Jesus followers (believers) and the larger Jewish society. This master narrative emanates from two foundational studies: J. Louis Martyn's *History and Theology in the Fourth Gospel* and Raymond E. Brown's *The Community of the Beloved Disciple*, and is often accepted as "canon."[7] Yet some scholars have challenged this account. For instance, Adele Reinhartz provides an alternative view that, rather than being expelled, the Jesus followers chose to leave the synagogue on their own accord.[8] In similar fashion, Warren Carter argues that no historically plausible evidence shows that an expulsion from the synagogue occurred, suggesting that those texts (John 9:22; 12:42; 16:2) that mention an expulsion are not objectively descriptive, but rather consequential texts (saying, this is what will happen as a result of an allegiance to Jesus).[9]

This essay extends this notion that the master narrative contains tacit yet powerful assumptions regarding culture, community and identity that may be limiting our perceptions of the formation of the Johannine community and perhaps of ourselves. One primary purpose of this chapter is to expose the pervasiveness of this master narrative about the development of the Johannine community in the pedagogical field of Johannine studies.[10] The secondary function of this chapter is to encourage a dialogue among Johannine scholars and others to reexamine the role of teaching the New Testament and its ethos and orientation relative to the construction of Johannine history (and other ancient histories for that matter).[11] Because this dialogue has not previously taken place, this master narrative is already considered the "official" history of the development of Johannine Christianity and, as a result, has shaped the historical consciousness of Christianity at the expense of "the Jews" and other non-believers. Therefore, to begin this challenge, I first examine Martyn's and Brown's theories of composition of the Johannine text to better understand what is being proposed and employed. Next, I examine how two widely-used introductory textbooks approach the Gospel of John. Specifically, I examine how these textbooks adopt and employ the Johannine master narrative. And finally, this work takes a brief look at the ethos and orientation of this master narrative in relation to ideological studies.

J. Louis Martyn and Raymond E. Brown: Establishing the Master Narratives

There is no question that both J. Louis Martyn and Raymond E. Brown are influential in the fields of Johannine studies.[12] Their theories about how the Gospel of John developed continue to be espoused in many studies.

1. Martyn's hypothesis begins with the claim that the Johannine community had been expelled from the Jewish synagogue. The clue that leads him to this premise is the Greek word *aposynagōgos* (expulsion), which appears in three places in the Gospel: 9:22; 12:42; and 16:2. The first text, 9:22, takes place in the story of the blind man (9:1-41), and is used to explain the consequences for anyone who confessed Jesus to be the Messiah—that he or she "would be put out of the synagogue" (*aposynagōgos*). The second text takes place in a narrative concerning the unbelief of the Jews (12:37-50). At 12:42, another statement is employed to explain that many, including some among the authorities, could not confess belief in Jesus as the Messiah because "they would be put out of the synagogue" (*aposynagōgoi).* Finally, the third main text used to explain the development of the Johannine community and the composition of the Gospel is 16:2. The word *aposynagōgos* is found in the Farewell Discourse during Jesus' discussion of the work of the Spirit (15:26–16:15). Once again the text explains the outcome for those who persist in their belief in Jesus as the Messiah: "they will be put out of the synagogues" (*aposynagōgous*). These three references "to being put out of the synagogue" led Martyn to surmise that perhaps the Gospel of John emerged among Jewish Christians who were once part of the synagogue, but who were expelled because of their faith in Jesus as the Messiah.

For Martyn, these three texts and more importantly, the word *aposynagōgos*, referred to a supposed expulsion of those Jewish believers of Jesus (Johannine Community) that occurred around 80 C.E. at the rabbinical council at Yavneh. According to Martyn, the leaders of the council wanted to consolidate Judaism under their authority. To do this they introduced a "blessing" called the *Birkat ha-Minim* (blessing of the heretics) to the Amidah or prayer of benediction used in the synagogue at Jamnia. This blessing read as follows:

> For the renegades let there be no hope, and may the arrogant kingdom soon be rooted out in our days, and the Nazarenes and the *minim* [heretic] perish as in a moment and be blotted out from the book of life, and with the righteous may they not be inscribed. Bessed art thou, O Lord, who humblest the arrogant.[13]

During the synagogue service, participants were required to bestow this "blessing" on heretics (followers of Jesus). Those who refused would be cast out of the synagogue. This would of course include those followers of Jesus (Christians) who attended the service and refused to say the prayer. According to Martyn experience of refusal and "expulsion" reflects the experience of the Johannine community that influenced the composition of the Gospel of John toward the end of the first century.

According to Martyn, the central conflict between the synagogue and the followers of Jesus is Christology and consisted of two primary questions. First, was Jesus the Messiah? This question was at the heart of 9:22, 12:42, and 16:2. Second, is Jesus equal to God? This question is reflected in 5:18, 8:58-59, and 10:33. Martyn argues that because of this conflict, the Gospel of John must be read on two levels. One level is the story about Jesus, situated in the early decades of the first century. The second level is the story about the expulsion of the Christians and the development of the Johannine community that occurred near the end of the first century. This two-drama approach has become the primary interpretive lens through which many Johannine scholars and students (and ministers) read and understand the Gospel. This interpretation has continued to be influential despite recent scholarship that has identified several problematic, historical data issues with this approach.[14]

2. Brown argues that the Gospel of John evolved in four phases. The first phase occurred prior to the writing of the Gospel around the mid-50s to the late 80s C.E. The second phase took place around 90 C.E. during the writing of the Gospel itself.

During the first phase, two main stages of development occurred. Stage 1 is reflected in John 1:35-41. This stage included an original group of Palestinian Jews, including followers of John the Baptist, who held some views found in the Dead Sea Scrolls (e.g., dualism of light/darkness). This group also had a traditional view of the Messiah (human or low Christology) as one descended from David and who worked miracles like Moses or Elijah. It is believed that this group collected synoptic-like sayings and miracles stories, the latter becoming the Signs Source, from which emerge the famous "seven signs" in John's Gospel. Some also believe that the Beloved Disciple, who was perhaps one of the former followers of the Baptist, was a member of this group.

Stage 2 is reflected in John 4:4-42, the story of the Samaritan woman. Jewish Christians who opposed the Temple, such as Stephen and the Hellenists (Acts 6-7), embarked on a mission to convert Samaritans. Interestingly, these Jewish Christians were influenced by Samaritan ideas, especially ideas that the Messiah was to be the new Moses—the "Savior of the World" (4:42). The incorporation of these Samaritan ideas by the Johannine community led to the more divine or high Christology that is reflected in the Gospel. According to Brown this higher Christology produced two significant outcomes. First, it led to a conflict with "the Jews" who believed the Johannine Christians were making Jesus a second God. Because of this the Christians were expelled from the synagogue. Second, the Johannine Christians moved away from a future-oriented, Judaism-based eschatology toward a present-oriented eschatology focused on the presence of Jesus.

The second phase (around 90 C.E.) also consists of two stages of development. Stage 1 is reflected in John 12:20-23, 37-42, which tells of the Greeks coming to Jesus. These gentiles were integrated into the Johannine community, thus sparking a more universalistic outlook. Perhaps at this time the Johannine Christians migrated from Palestine to the regions of Ephesus or some other city in Syria (7:35). Stage 2 occurs when the Gospel was written about 90 C.E. Brown identifies seven groups that were present and active during this stage: (a) three groups of outsiders (the world, "the Jews," and those continuing to follow John the Baptist) who encounter and conflict with the Johannine Christians, (b) three groups of sympathizers (Jews who secretly believe in Jesus, Christians whose faith is inadequate, and those believing Christians led by Peter), and the Johannine Christians themselves. All of these groups would be part of the Johannine community.

The third phase (around 100 C.E.) involves only one stage of development. This stage consists of the period involving the writing of the Johannine letters, to which may be added at least John 21 and 7:53-8:11. The letters stress that it is necessary both to believe that Jesus came "in the flesh" and to keep his commandments (adherents of the author of the epistles). Those who do not believe (secessionists; see 1 John 2:19-24) are said to be of the devil and the antichrist. Also, a debate emerges between those who stress a high Christology, paying less attention to the humanity of Jesus for purposes of salvation, and those who believe in maintaining Jesus' humanity (the Word became flesh).

Finally, the fourth phase (around the second century C.E.) takes place after the writing of the Johannine Epistles, when the Johannine community split into two groups. One group (Gnostics using the Gospel of John) believed that Jesus' humanity was not important for salvation. The other group (proto-orthodox Christianity) believed the Gnostics misused the Gospel's high Christology—an idea that paved the way for the acceptance of the Gospel into the canon in the late second century.

This brief sketch of the history and development of the Johannine text and community, complete with its assumptions and implications, is found in many introductions of the New Testament. Brown and Martyn's hypotheses are founded on the historical critical paradigm—meaning that both reconstructions are the products of an historical worldview constructed via the best scientific tools available at the time. Both positions are well articulated and initially seem quite convincing, and are thus often considered the seminal master narratives of the Fourth Gospel. Unfortunately, both perspectives are also problematic in their choice of which historical data to highlight.[15] Also, these positions suggest a monolithic or homogenous identity for both the Christian and the Jewish communities. Very little discussion emerges in Martyn and Brown (or in the textbooks that rely upon them) nuancing these identities in antiquity, let alone any nuancing of the identity of the scholars themselves. Yet precisely because their work is so influential, challenging the historical data that underlies their master narrative of both the Johannine community and the identities of the Christians and Jewish communities should remain an object of study. Otherwise, these narratives may become—if they are not already—universal and global. This lack of challenge and attention, particularly to identity as a construction, is also evident in the textbooks noted in the next section.

TEXTBOOKS

The two textbooks that I examine here are Bart Ehrman's *The New Testament* and Stephen Harris's *The New Testament*.[16] These two popular introductions to the New Testament, which employ one or both of the previously mentioned master narratives, are used in many public, private, Catholic, and Protestant settings.

BART D. EHRMAN, THE NEW TESTAMENT: A HISTORICAL INTRODUCTION TO THE EARLY CHRISTIAN WRITINGS

As the subtitle indicates, Ehrman's survey of the New Testament uses general historical information and research from modern biblical studies (for example, literary, social history, and rhetorical criticisms) to provide a detailed account of the history of the New Testament, its collection of books, and its ancient historical contexts. The chapter entitled "Jesus, the Man Sent from Heaven: The Gospel according to John" consists of seven major sections. I am here most concerned with the sixth one: "The Gospel of John from a Socio-Historical Perspective." That section is divided into two sub-sections: (1) Divergent Christologies in the Johannine Community, and (2) The History of the Johannine Community. It is this latter sub-section that is the focus of this discussion.

For Ehrman, the history of the Johannine community is divided into three stages of development. The first stage is framed within the time the Jesus followers were in the synagogue, the second stage when they were excluded from the synagogue, and the third stage when they were against the synagogue. In short, Ehrman is surely informed by Martyn's and Brown's positions on the socio-historical situation of the Johannine community and the historical development of the Gospel.[17]

During the first stage (in the synagogue), Ehrman identifies the Johnanine community as Jews who believed in Jesus as the messiah and who perhaps were from Palestine where they spoke Aramaic. Ehrman says he bases this on the oldest stories in the Gospel, but does not indicate specifically which stories he has in mind. However, he does state that his conclusions are based on those stories where Jesus' Jewishness and his identity as the messiah are emphasized. He also works under the assumption that these stories would have been told within Jewish communities where Aramaic was spoken and calls attention to Aramaic terms in the narrative: (a) rabbi (1:38), Christ (1:41); and Cephas (1:42). He suggests that the appearance of these terms may mean that they originated from an Aramaic-speaking Jewish community from Palestine. Consistent with Brown's position, Ehrman agrees that the Beloved Disciple was a leader among this originating community as suggested by the prominent positioning of the Beloved Disciple later in the Gospel (for example, John 13:23; 19:26-27; and 20:2-8). Finally, Ehrman also agrees with Brown's hypothesis that both the calling of the disciples in John 1 and the Signs Source served to proselytize members of the Jewish synagogue.

Ehrman's second stage (exclusion from the synagogue), is consistent with Martyn's position that some sort of traumatic event occurred in the synagogue that led to the Jesus followers' expulsion. Ehrman concedes that the event is difficult to pinpoint, but he does proceed to paint a "plausible" picture of what might have happened. For Ehrman, the issue centered on whether or not Jesus was the messiah. The majority of the first-century Jews did not view Jesus as the messiah, but as an itinerant preacher who would later be executed for treason against Rome.[18]

Ehrman suggests that the Jesus followers who were missionaries were rejected by the majority of Jews, mocked and marginalized, and thus forced to leave the synagogue. Ehrman supports this historical picture using Martyn's evidence, namely, the story of the blind man in John 9 whose parents, fearing expulsion from the synagogue, did not identify Jesus as the messiah. Ehrman's hypothesis is again dependent upon Brown's and Martyn's positions, and is contrary to Reinhartz's position that the Jesus followers could have left of their own accord rather than been forcibly evicted.

Ehrman's third stage (against the synagogue) draws upon modern sociology's conclusions regarding sects or religious groups that feel persecuted, including the duality between those who are "in the truth" and those who are not. Ehrman uses this sociological research to help readers understand that the developing Johannine community adopted this duality, which is reflected in the Gospel of John.

Informed by Martyn's and Brown's positions, Ehrman conforms to the traditional interpretation that the synagogue is the enemy who "took on a demonic hue in their eyes" (194). In other words, Ehrman holds to the traditional interpretation that the Jewish/Christian division was hostile and virulent. By adhering to this overall traditional framework, Ehrman reifies a history that supports a clearly divided community with two separate identities: Christian and Jewish. The implication of such clear-cut identities is that each functions as a mirror in which society sees itself.[19]

STEPHEN L. HARRIS, *THE NEW TESTAMENT: A STUDENT'S INTRODUCTION* (SEVENTH EDITION)

Another popular textbook used in many public and private academic settings is Stephen L. Harris's *The New Testament*. It differs slightly from the Ehrman approach in that Harris claims to allow the biblical authors to speak for themselves rather than allowing any interpretation from the modern reader to influence the process of reconstructing the New Testament. Whereas Erhman's approach draws upon the socio-historical context to integrate the stories behind the texts, Harris discounts any such approach. However, both Harris and Ehrman claim that they maintain an objectivist position in their reconstructions, informed by the historical critical paradigm. Both Ehrman and Harris adhere to the traditional master narrative of the development of the Johannine community's identity and the Gospel's composition.

Harris's chapter on John is titled, "John's Portrait of Jesus: Divine Wisdom Made Flesh." The chapter is divided into eight sections: (1) Key Themes, (2) Authorship, (3) Hymn to the Word (Logos), (4) The Book of Signs, (5) The Book of Glory, (6) John's Interpretation of the Passion, (7) Epilog, and (8) Summary. Interestingly, the identity of the Johannine community or the Gospel's compositional history is not in any of these sections. Rather, Harris places this information in a box (entitled "A Hypothetical Development of the Johannine Community"), separate from the main narration regarding the Gospel, thus highlighting the importance of the Gospel's historical development for understanding the identity of John's community. Again similar to Ehrman, Harris presents his history as plausible, needing no self-reflection. Further, Harris acknowledges that Brown's work on the evolution of the Johannine community is the most widely known reconstruction. Like Brown he also acknowledges that Christology was the central theological issue that gave rise to the development of the Johannine community. Finally and curiously, he does acknowledge other reconstructions, yet no reference to them is made available.

Harris reads Brown's reconstruction as a seven stage/phase process. In the first phase, similar to Brown's theory, the Johannine community began with Palestinian Jews identifying Jesus as the promised Davidic Messiah (John 1:35-41). This group had a low Christology and was perhaps associated with the Qumran community. He suggests that this group was also led by a disciple — perhaps a prototype of the Beloved Disciple. (Brown is more confident it was the Beloved Disciple.) Harris does note that recent scholarship in the field argues that the Qumran's dualistic and sectarian elements were perhaps added later after 68 C.E., and that the primitive Signs Gospel may have also been incorporated during this first phase. Thus, while staying close to Brown's position, Harris also incorporates recent scholarship.[20]

During the second phase, Harris discusses the arrival of the Samaritans to the Johannine community as reflected in John 4. Following Brown's thesis of the inclusion of the Samaritans into the Johannine community, Harris suggests that John 4 reflects the tradition of embracing an exalted Moses and may have contributed to Jesus' identity through an ascending and descending motif. It is also during this phase that Jesus may have been understood through the Wisdom tradition and identified with God. Harris supposes that both of these issues may have alienated the monotheistic Jews and led to a wider division between the Jews and the Christians.

The gentiles come to the Johannine community in the third phase, when the Johannine community adopts a more universalistic outlook, embracing Hellenistic and Gnostic perspectives. During this phase the Johannine community may have moved to Ephesus or Syria and may have identified Jesus as the eternal Logos and God's self-revelation. This high Christology antagonized the Jews and perhaps led to both the expulsion of the Jesus followers from the synagogue and the bitter rhetoric toward the Jews in the Fourth Gospel. These events would have taken place during the mid-80s C.E. Here Harris obviously draws on Martyn's position of expulsion but does not reference him. Harris maintains the traditional notion that there was an expulsion of the Jesus followers and that one must read the Gospel based on the two-level drama approach.

During the fourth phase, around the 90s C.E., this division between Jews and Jesus followers leads to a broader denouncement of all outsiders by the Johannine community, the presentation of Peter in the Gospel, as well as the redaction of major parts of the Gospel.

In Harris's fifth phase, the Johannine community refines its concept of Jesus's true divine nature, thus leading to a split within the community. The sixth phase, reflected in the anonymous writing of 1 John, involves criticism of those proto-Gnostic Christians who withdrew from the Johannine community because of their belief that Jesus was entirely divine. Also during this phase, John 21 was added to counter those proto-Gnostic Christians who could not believe that Jesus could have been human. Finally, during the seventh phase, the Johannine community was divided into two groups. The secessionists or Gnostics went their own way and the authors of 1,2, and 3 John merged with the international "mainstream" church, where Johannine ideas about Jesus became dominant. Harris's reconstruction is surely more detailed than Ehrman's. Yet he clearly keeps close to Brown's hypothesis, while subtly inserting ideas developed by Martyn.

Overall, Harris's reconstruction is not meant to be a competing history, but one that clearly fixes Brown's reconstruction in the minds of many students. Challenging this reconstruction, as Reinhartz and Carter have done, allows students to explore other options. That now-conventional history needs to be continuously reexamined and challenged—or at least compared to competing histories—allowing readers/students to make fresh evaluations. Comparing and analyzing competing histories is necessary to avoid the uncritical acceptance of a universal history or binary identity constructions. In other words, relying on only one perspective on Johannine history and highlighting two dominant communities/identities fails to describe adequately the complextity and difference between, for example, the Johannine Christians and the Jewish community and the otherness of others.

ETHOS AND ORIENTATION

Textbooks are not neutral, even if one allows for the socio-historical context or allows the author of a text to speak for him/herself. Thus the dominance of Martyn's and Brown's theories of composition and identity formation in many current surveys of the New Testament remains troubling. Such presence, as I have argued above, reifies the basic assumption that the Johannine community was expelled rather than possibly chose to leave. It also constructs a master narrative that influences how students see this history and how students, particularly Christian students, may relate to Jewish or other religious communities that hold beliefs that are different from their own. Textbooks do construct identities, and do create and make identities disappear. Such challenging of master narratives allows for these identities to reappear and pique the curiosities for another generation to challenge.[21] In this final section, I will explore what the ethos and orientation of teaching New Testament studies might look like from the perspective of ideological studies. In other words, I will consider the contributions of various areas of study—specifically ethnic/racial studies, postcolonial studies, and feminist studies — and their effect on the master narrative discussed above to imagine what other issues might arise and perhaps be beneficial for others to consider when reading introductions.

ETHNIC/RACIAL STUDIES

Looking at this master narrative from the field of ethnic/racial studies calls attention to the process of how groups or communities are formed along ethnic/racial lines. The history of the Johannine community proposed by Martyn and Brown and promulgated by textbooks strongly suggests that group identities are fixed rather than mutable. For instance, according to Brown and Martyn, Christology was a key reason that the Jesus believers were excluded from the Jewish synagogue. This division led to the construction of these groups into fixed identities: Christians versus "the Jews." According to the books discussed above, the religious discourse of John also contributes to the notion that these two groups have fixed identities. However, although ethnic/racial identity in antiquity was influenced by religious discourse it was also, as in the modern period, influenced by a host of other factors such as genealogies, language, and territory. My concern is that when such constructions of identities are not nuanced, students are left with the impression that ethnic/racial identity is only fixed. I would argue that ethnic/racial identities are both fluid and fixed.[22] From this perspective, the Jesus believers (and other groups) would eventually engage in negotiation with the larger Jewish community as well as the Roman world over their identity. The master narrative supported by Martyn and Brown creates fixed identities (Christians versus "the Jews"), rather than demonstrating that ethnic/racial identity in antiquity was also quite fluid (all communities could become Christian). This fluid position, however, was contingent upon one religious factor: belief in Jesus as Messiah, which ironically also participates in a fixed identity at the end; for instance, to be members of the Johannine Community one must believe in Jesus. The point here is that the history that we write and the positions that we construct from the text participate in the construction of ethnic/racial identity in antiquity as well as in the present.

POSTCOLONIAL STUDIES

From the perspective of postcolonial studies, claims about a master narrative raise a different set of questions. One of these questions concerns the relationship between constructed binaries such as the center and periphery, the majority and margins, the powerful and powerless, or the imperial and colonial. The Gospel of John presents a vision of conflict between similarly constructed binaries. For instance, there is the conflict between the world from above and the world from below, the world of God and the world of Satan, the worlds of darkness and light, the world of believers and the world of unbelievers. In the master narrative, this conflict unfolds between the Jesus believers (Christians) and "the Jews." Some may see this binary narrative as a tale of conversion (that is, the purpose of John is to make believers); however, the consequences for all those involved in this tale lead to outright hostility and rejection of those who do not believe (for example, the harsh rhetoric of John toward "the Jews") or the outright hostility and rejection upon those who believe (for example, the imperial center's [Rome] exercise of power over Jesus in the plot). Bringing a postcolonial optic to bear upon Martyn's and Brown's positions on the development of Johannine community and composition indeed presents a challenge to the master narrative, for master narratives formulate the cultural identities of communities. To uphold the Johannine master narrative, from a postcolonial perspective, is to refuse to challenge who we are, for master narratives simply keep us remaining in the past.[23]

FEMINIST STUDIES

Considering the perspectives of Martyn and Brown in light of feminist studies leads to different questions as well. One of those questions is the issue of inclusion/exclusion of women at the level of the world behind the text (as objects of study) as well as in the world in front of the text (as agents writing history). Is there a difference in meaning, students might consider asking, if historical data is considered differently or read differently from a feminist perspective? Would feminist scholars have different understandings? In other words, if the Jesus-followers were "expelled" or "chose" to leave the synagogue voluntarily, how would this affect both Jewish and Christian women? What would a feminist "Sitz-im-Leben" of John look like? What are the male "biases" in writing Johannine history? Is inclusion more of a concern for women than for men? Is community more of concern for women than for men? These questions raise other questions regarding epistemology, how knowledge is constructed, and how text and context may become blurred—which suggest other, hermeneutical questions regarding how one's social location affects the way one writes history.[24]

I believe one of the major challenges of teaching New Testament studies in the future is moving toward a more contextual approach to teaching. Part of this movement involves engaging the current ethos and orientation reflected in New Testament introductions. My challenge of the master narrative of the Johannine Community as presented here is also a broader call for other teachers/scholars/students to challenge other master narratives inherent in their own pedagogical discourses and practices. The master narrative clearly shuts down the role of readers and thus calls for one fixed identity for the reader and by extension, for only one way to read. Textbooks that continue to employ master narratives are simultaneously requiring readers to remain invisible during the reading of the narrative. By engaging and challenging the master narrative via perspectives from ethnic/racial studies, postcolonial studies, and feminist studies, and by proposing multiple perspectives and histories, we may allow the text to begin to reveal more about the people and communities of the Gospel—and perhaps even reveal something about ourselves. It is this push toward multiple perspectives and histories that will transform the ethos and orientation of New Testament studies and thus lead to a more inclusive contextual approach to understanding.

Notes

1. For an excellent discussion on ethos see Elisabeth Schüssler Fiorenza, "Transforming Graduate Biblical Education: Ethos and Discipline," in *Transforming Biblical Education: Ethos and Discipline*, ed. Elisabeth Schüssler Fiorenza and Kent Harold Richards, Global Perspectives on Biblical Scholarship 10 (Atlanta: Society of Biblical Literature, 2010), 1–16.

2. But see Marla J. Selvidge, *The New Testament: A Timeless Book for All Peoples* (Upper Saddle River: Prentice Hall, 1999) as an example of an introductory text with a different ethos (pluralism) and orientation (historical, social, and ideological).

3. Master narrative is defined here as universal histories with no place for otherness. See Jörn Rüsen, "Comparing Cultures in Intercultural Communications," in *Across Cultural Borders:*

Historiography in Global Perspective, ed. E. Fuchs and B. Stuchtey (Oxford: Rowman & Littlefield, 2002), 338–341.

4. See Joyce Appleby, Lynn Hunt, and Margaret Jacob, *Telling the Truth about History* (New York: Norton, 1994), and Gunnar Myrdal, *Objectivity in Social Research* (Middletown: Wesleyan University Press, 1969).

5. Appleby, *et al.*, *Telling the Truth About History*, 235.

6. See Cynthia Briggs Kittredge, "Biblical Studies for Ministry: Critical and Faithful Interpretation of Scripture in an Either/Or World," in *Transforming Graduate Biblical Education*, 293–306.

7. J. Louis Martyn, *History and Theology in the Fourth Gospel*, 3rd ed. (Nashville: Abingdon, 2003); Raymond E. Brown, *The Community of the Beloved Disciple: The Life, Loves, and Hates of an Individual Church in New Testament Times* (New York: Paulist, 1979).

8. See the very significant essay by Adele Reinhartz, "The Johannine Community and Its Jewish Neighbors: A Reappraisal," in *What is John?"* vol. 2, *Literary and Social Readings of the Fourth Gospel*, SBLSymS 7, ed. Fernando F. Segovia (Atlanta: Scholars, 1998), 111–38.

9. For an excellent overview of Martyn's work see Warren Carter, *John and Empire: Initial Explorations* (New York: T&T Clark, 2008), chap. 2.

10. My aim is not one of "demolition" of an argument or reading *per se*, but rather to engage my interlocutors' pedagogical discourse and practices. In fact, I have employed these studies in the classroom myself and have learned much from them.

11. Here I am indebted to my teacher, Fernando F. Segovia, who has continuously inspired and challenged me to reflect critically on how to teach texts in this day and age. Such questions are also addressed by Segovia in "Pedagogical Discourses and Practices in Cultural Studies: Toward a Contextual Biblical Pedagogy," in *Teaching the Bible: The Discourses and Politics of Biblical Pedagogy*, ed. Fernando F. Segovia and Mary A. Tolbert (New York: Orbis, 1998), 137–67.

12. See D. Moody Smith, "The Contributions of J. Louis Martyn to the Understanding of the Gospel of John," in Martyn, *History and Theology*, 1–19.

13. Quoted from Jo-Ann A. Brant, *John* (Paideia Commentaries on the New Testament; Grand Rapids: Baker, 2011), 166. Brant attributes the translation of the blessing from Hebrew into English to Jacób Jocz, *The Jewish People and Jesus Christ: A Study in the Controversy between Church and Synagogue* (London, SPCK, 1954), 53.

14. See Reinhartz, "The Johannine Community," and Carter, *John and Empire*.

15. See Reinhartz, "The Johannine Community."

16. Bart D. Ehrman, *The New Testament: A Historical Introduction to the Early Christian Writings*, 5th ed. (New York: Oxford University Press, 2012); Stephen L. Harris, *The New Testament: A Student's Introduction*, 7th ed. (New York: McGraw-Hill, 2012).

17. In Ehrman's "Suggestions for Further Reading," at the end of the chapter, both Brown and Martyn are listed, see p. 197.

18. Ehrman, *The New Testament*, 102.

19. Rüsen, "Comparing Cultures," 339.

20. In Harris's "recommended reading" list at the end of the chapter, both Brown and Martyn are cited. Scholars such as Reinhartz, Carter, and others who have contested the Martyn/Brown hypothesis are not mentioned, see 277–78.

21. Appleby, et. al., *Telling the Truth about History*, 294–95.

22. Here I am following the argument set forth by Denise Kimber Buell, *Why This New Race? Ethnic Reasoning in Early Christianity* (New York: Columbia University Press, 2005).

23. Rüsen, *Comparing Cultures*, 339.

24. See Angelika Epple and Angelika Schaser, "Multiple Histories? Changing Perspectives on Modern Historiography," in *Gendering Historiography Beyond National Canons*, ed. Angelika Epple and Angelika Schaser (Frankfurt: Campus, 2009), 7–23.

12

Geopolitical Hermeneutics

Kwok Pui-lan

The term *geopolitics* comes from Greek *Gē* (earth) and *Politiké* (politics) and refers to the causal relationships between geographical space and political power. In foreign policy analysis, it seeks to explain and predict international politics through geographical variables, such as the location and size of the country/ies involved, climate and natural resources, physical geography and topography, and levels of technological development. Geopolitical studies is interdisciplinary as it involves geography, history, political science, international law and relations, and other disciplines in the social sciences.[1]

The end of the Cold War and the disintegration of the former Soviet Bloc brought fundamental changes to the ways we look at geopolitics. The term "globalization" has been widely used since the 1990s to describe the interconnectedness brought about by the neo-liberal market, the mass media, and the information highway. The most significant shift in geopolitics in the last two decades has been the rapid economic expansion of China, India, and other emergent markets. China is the world's second largest economy and is poised to overtake that of United States in 2016, according to the International Monetary Fund.

Globalization brings fast movements of capital, labor, and resources across national boundaries. If colonialism in the past meant the control of foreign lands and peoples, today's Empire, as Michael Hardt and Antonio Negri argue, has no territorial center of power and no fixed boundaries.[2] Those who have been left out of economic globalization have become the disposable population. They live under war, violence, and economic upheaval, and for suvival they often have to travel from place to place. Geopolitical analyses must attend to migration, refugees, asylum-seeking, diaspora, displacement, and dispossession, issues that raise new questions about culture, identity, and power.

This chapter looks at the various ways biblical scholars and theologians have engaged the geopolitical. I discuss Marxist interpretation of the Bible and Empire Studies and the New Testament, before turning to postcolonial studies of the Bible. Fernando F. Segovia has used the term "geopolitical" frequently and made significant contributions to postcolonial biblical criticism. The last section of the chapter discusses the shift of geopolitics and describes how Chinese interpreters have responded to the rise and fall of China in the modern era.

Engaging the Geopolitical

The Bible lends itself to geopolitical hermeneutics because the Hebrew people lived under the Egyptian, Assyrian, Babylonian, Persian, Greek, and Roman empires. The Bible contains stories of exodus, exile, dispossesion, disapora, and return to the homeland. Latin American liberation theologians have used geopolitic hermeneutics to discuss their position in the world and to interpret the Bible. Often called America's backyard, resources from Latin America have been channeled to bolster the American economy. Using Marxist theory, which is international in its scope, Latin American theologians criticize the dependence theory of development and advocate social revolution.[3]

The exodus story provides a paradigmatic story for liberation theologians, for it reveals that God is a liberator. George V. Pixley and Clodovis Boff discuss the peasants' migration and uprising within Palestine during the time of the exodus. These peasant groups were joined around 1200 B.C. by the group led by Moses, who had risen up against the Pharoah and left Egypt to go to Palestine. In the course of the event, Yahweh is shown to have a preferential option for the Hebrew slaves and for the oppressed in the world.[4] The preferential option for the poor becomes a hermeneutical principle for liberation theologians.

In the New Testament, Jesus is seen as the liberator who challenges the exploitation of the poor and proclaims the Kingdom of God. Jon Sobrino criticizes both metaphysical and mystical interpretations of the cross, for they have covered up the liberating potentials of the gospel. For him, Jesus' death was the historical consequence of his life, for he dared to stand up against the religious and political authorities of his time. He suffered crucifixion, the punishement imposed upon political agitators by the Romans, instead of stoning, the punishement for religious blasphemers. Sobrino surmises that this shows clearly that Jesus had situated himself in the political situation of his day.[5]

If Latin Americans have read the Bible from the Global South, biblical scholars who have engaged in Empire Studies and the New Testament view it from the North, from the belly of the beast. In the past two decades, numerous books on the New Testament have been published with the term empire in their titles, such as *Jesus and Empire*; *God and Empire*; *Matthew and Empire*; *Paul and Empire*; *Paul and the Roman Imperial Order*; *In the Shadow of Empire*; and *Unveiling Empire: Reading Revelation Then and Now.*[6] These books were either written by Americans or published in North America, especially after the ascendency of American imperialism after September 11, 2001.

Richard A. Horsley stands out among these interpreters because of his voluminous output on the the subject. Influenced by materialist analysis, Horsley describes the rise and expansion of Rome through military and political domination, the patronage and tributory systems, the flow of resources to the imperial metropolis, the glorification of conquest, the maintenance of national security through terror and military force, and the use of client rulers and religious leaders.[7] But even as *Pax Romana* seemed to be all-pervasive, the empire was contested, as popular resistance and rebellions erupted in Judea and Galilee, as well as in Spain, Gaul, and North Africa. For Horsley, Jesus' movement was one such resistance movement, which could be compared to the kind of anti-imperial "nationalist" movements of our own time. If the anti-imperial nature of Jesus' movement is fully understood, it will provide a basis for theological critique of the Roman Empire in the past and the American Empire in the present.

Horsley contributes to the geopolitical reading of the New Testament by calling attention to the submerged cultures and local histories of Judea and Galilee, as well as cities outside Palestine such as Antioch, Philippi, Corinth, and Ephesus.[8] He shows that history is not running uncontested through Rome and the empire, and the Gospel of Mark presents a counter-narrative, beginning with the boundaries: "Mark has Jesus spreading the movement across the imperial boundaries of client rulers' territories, from the Galilee of Antipas to the 'villages' or 'regions' of Caesarea Philippi, Tyre, the cities of the Decapolis, and finally into the jurisdiction of the Jerusalem high priests under/and the Roman governor Pilate. . . . Not only were those peoples not all Judeans, they were not all Israelites."[9] Horsley has been influenced by postcolonial theory and is in conversations with postcolonial biblical scholars, to whose work I now turn.

THE GEOPOLITICAL IN POSTCOLONIAL BIBLICAL CRITICISM

Postcolonial biblical criticism has intimate connections to geopolitics. Stephen D. Moore lists the following concerns as falling within the purview of postcolonial criticism: "Imperialism, Orientalism, universalism, expansionism, exploration, invasion, slavery, settlement, resistance, revolt, terrorism, nationalism, nativism, negritude, assimilation, creolization, cosmopolitanism, colonial mimicry, hybridity, the subaltern, marginalization, migration, disapora, decolonization, neocolonialism, and globalization."[10] Even a cursory look at this list will identify many factors having to do with geography and politics.

Fernando F. Segovia has used the term "geopolitical" to describe his postcolonial project from the beginning. Born in Cuba, at the periphery of the United States, and marginalized as a Hispanic in the United States and as a racial and ethnic minority in the professional guild, the image of center and periphery was significant for him, as he wrote in 1999: "The proposed postcolonial optic in biblical studies is obviously a discourse of resistance and emancipation. It takes as its reading lens the geopolitical relationship between center and periphery, the imperial and the colonial, not only at the level of the text but also at the level of interpretation, of readings and readers of the text."[11] Later in his writings, he expands the center-periphery image to include more fluid and complex understandings of borders, places, flows of demographics, communities, and identities. In an important essay "Johannine Studies and the Geopolitical" published in 2007, Segovia no longer uses the image of center and periphery and says that postcolonial criticism has a "focus on geopolitics, and, more specifically, on the differential relations of power (domination and submission) at work within imperial-colonial frameworks."[12] In reviewing the deployment of the geopolitical in Johannine studies, he comes up with this long register: travel, space and spatial construction, movement, boundaries, borderland, border-crossing, crossroads, indigenized women and populations, ethnic formation, diasporic communities, rhizomic fragments, uprooting, displacing places, displacement, transplantation, internationl power relations, and globalization processes.[13]

Segovia has used the geopolitical to gauge the development of biblical criticism. He notes that the historical critical method was developed in Europe during the eighteenth and nineteenth centuries, with the rapid expansion of colonial powers. Biblical studies has been the perogative of male, clerical Europeans and Euro-Americans who have invented and inherited the legacy of colonization. Only with the infusion of a significant number of white women since the 1970s, as well as racial minorities in the West and scholars outside the West, has the discipline been broadened to include a diversity of methods, faces, and voices.[14] The different projects of liberation and decolonization vary according to specific contexts and concerns. Segovia argues that a dialogue between the global (cosmopolitics) and the local (micropolitics) is necessary to name both similarities and differences.[15]

Musa W. Dube from Botswana also focuses on geopolitics in her postcolonial feminist reading of the Bible. The struggles for liberation in Africa, often labeled the "dark continent," and the decolonization of the mind are important themes of her postcolonial criticism. Her reading of the stories of the Syro-Phoenician woman (Matt 15:21-28) and the Samaritan woman (John 4:1-42) highlights the imperial Roman setting, the sanction of travel to foreign lands, the competition of different ethnic groups, the representation of geography, and women as site of struggle in the contact zone.[16]

Dube suggests four questions to evaluate ancient texts in her postcolonial reading of the Bible:

> 1. Does this text have a clear stance against the political imperialism of its time?
> 2. Does this text encourage travel to distant and inhabited lands, and how does it justify itself?
> 3. How does this text construct difference: Is there dialogue and liberating interdependence or is there condemnation of all that is foreign?
> 4. Does this text employ gender and divine representations to construct relationships of subordination and domination?[17]

These four questions have strong connections to the geopolitical. Using these questions as her guide, Dube chastises the stories in Matthew 15 and John 4 as imperializing texts, since they authorize the colonizers to travel to and enter foreign lands and employ gender to construct difference and unequal power relations. Dube practices resistance by challenging imperializing texts and interpretations and by lifting up the voices of indigenous women (in her case, African women) as interpreters.

Segovia and Dube share similar concerns with liberation theology, because they emphasize domination and liberation in their methodology. Other postcolonial critics are more interested in the hybrid, in-between, "Third," and interstitial spaces that Homi Bhabha has identified.[18] These hybrid spaces result from the permeable and irregular boundaries that emerge in colonial contexts. For Stephen D. Moore, Bhabha's deconstructive move interrogates "any conceptual dichotomization of metropolis and periphery, empire and indigene, colonizer and colonized."[19] Moore, who grew up in Ireland and now teaches in the U.S., sees life under colonialism as ambivalent, involving an "unequal measure of loathing and admiration, resentment and envy, rejection and imitation, resistance and cooption, separation and surrender."[20] Moore is notable for bringing postcolonial interpretatin into conversation with poststructuralist theory, having written on the intersection between postcolonialism and postmodernism.[21]

In his reading of the Book of Revelation, which has long been recognized as anti-imperial, Moore does not gloss over the economic domination and political hegemony of *imperium Romanum.* Yet he adds to such a reading Bhabha's theory of colonial ambivalence and suggests that the book's anti-imperial potential is not as clear as many have assumed.[22] For example, Revelation implicitly claims that the Roman imperial court mimics the heavenly throne and heavenly liturgy. Christians are told to mimic Jesus, who in turn mimics his father, and who is depicted as mimicking the Roman Emperor. More troubling, Revelation re-inscribes the language and imagery of war, conquest, and empire. Just as the Roman Empire uses violence and military suppression, the messianic Empire is to be established through mass slaughter. Although Revelation repeatedly condemns collaboration with Rome, such as participation in the imperial cult, it also reveals that Christians have adopted a range of hybrid positions, ranging from assimilation to selective accommodation (since they lived physically under the empire), yet practiced forms of non-violent resistance. Thus, Moore finds the language of divine empire counteracting earthly empires ambivalent and problematic and urges his readers to imagine "the divine sphere as other than empire writ large."[23]

Tat-siong Benny Liew is another biblical critic inspired by Bhabha. An Asian American born in Hong Kong, Liew has written perceptively about the intersection between race and ethnicity and postcolonialism. While many racial and ethnic minority scholars in the U.S. focus on the American scene, Liew argues that postcolonialism expands our geopolitical horizon, because it provides "a theoretical framework to read race/ethnicity in a wider, international nexus of sociocultural and colonial politics."[24] The history of different waves of Asian immigrants to the United States tells us much about national ideology, citizenship, racial formation, legal discrimination, immigration quotas, global capitalism, and Asian-Pacific relations.[25]

In *What Is Asian American Biblical Hermeneutics?* Liew deftly uses Bhabha's theory to articulate the ambivalence of being an Asian American and the politics of racial/ethnic reading of the Bible. Bhabha has called attention to the "margins of the nation-space and . . . the boundaries of in-between nations and peoples."[26] Asian Americans are often situated in such in-between spaces. Though they may be born in the United States or have lived in the United States for a long time, Asian Americans are often asked, "Where do you come from?" Liew describes the ambiguous admittance of Asian Americans, even though they are hailed as the model minority, because they are "almost the same but not white," as Bhabha has so wittingly put it in another context.[27]

Asian American critics have used psychoanalytical theory to describe the melancholia of having to live in in-between spaces. This melancholia is not just the feeling of a loss, but is caused by living in colonized or racial and ethnic minoritized conditions.[28] Liew makes a unique contribution by employing psychoanalytical theory to read Asian America and the Bible, an approach often overlooked by postcolonial biblical critics.[29] Psychoanalysis has often been criticized as a universalized discourse, focusing primarily on the individual and based too narrowly on familial narratives, to the exclusion of social and political factors. Yet Liew's reading of Freud and Fanon, inflected through a racial/ethnic lens, enables him to read 1 Corinthians in new ways.[30] In this letter, Paul has to come to grips with the loss and death of Jesus the Savior and with melancholy as a colonized Jew. Just as Asian Americans face alterity as racial/ethnic minority, Liew says, Paul needs to negotiate with and survive "Roman imperialism and its abjection of Jewish bodies."[31]

The social and geographical locations of these biblical critics influence their ways of engaging the geopolitical, and so do their choices of method and reading strategies. The approaches taken by Segovia and Dube follow the imperial-colonial reading of Edward W. Said, while Moore and Liew's approaches are influenced by the poststructuralist theorists. Moore and Liew are more textual-oriented and attend to complex strategies in the biblical text, such as mimicry, parody, mockery, intertextuality, and translation. Yet Moore and Liew's readings are no less political and should not be lumped together with more playful, indeterminate postmodern readings, whose political import is highly suspect. As geopolitics operates on many fronts, geopolitical hermeneutics needs to pay attention to multiple ways of conceptualizing space and geography: physical space, imaginary space, narration of space, representation of geography, and the intersection of space and time. The reading of space is further inflected through race, class, gender, sexuality, and nation. Thus, geographical hermeneutics is a multiaxial and interdisciplinary project with many entry points and end results.

SHIFT OF GEOPOLITICS AND THE CHINESE INTERPRETERS

Bruce W. Jentleson describes the shift of geopolitics with the rise of China and other emergent markets as the transformation from a "Ptolemaic" to a "Copernican" world.[32] In the second century C.E., Ptolemy developed the view that the earth is at the center of the universe with other planets revolving around it. The United States was seen by many, and especially within the country itself, as the center of the Cold War world—the world's superpower and the champion of free-world ideology. But not anymore, as Jentleson says: "The twenty-first-century world is a Copernican one. The United States is not at the center. We have our own orbit. But other countries do too, and they all have their own interests, their own national identities, their own domestic politics."[33] While the U.S. still has some gravitational pull, it is not as strong as before such that others orbit around it.

One of the strong competitors of this multipolar world is China, which overtook Japan in 2010 to become the world's second-largest economy. The Chinese model of development has been called the Beijing Consensus, in contrast to the Washington Consenus of free-market promoted by the International Monetary Fund, the World Bank and the U.S. Treasury. With its newfound wealth and power, China has flexed its muscles and acted assertively in the East China Sea and South China Sea. But China has only recently enjoyed such economic power and stood among the poor nations for much of the twentieth century.

China was a semi-feudal and semi-colonial country since the mid-nineteenth century, with big foreign powers controlling "concessions" and "spheres of influence" in her land. In the 1930s, Japan invaded China and the two countries entered into a protracted war. During the dark hours when China's survival was at stake, Christian leader Wu Yaozong (also known as Y. T. Wu, 1893–1979) motivated Christians to embrace a revolutionary Christianity. Anticipating the liberation theology that emerged decades later, Wu said that Christianity should not only take care of humans' spiritual life but also care for their social life. He writes, "A true revival of the Church will come only when it has awakened to its social task and begins to tackle it fearlessly and sacrificially."[34] He argues that China could not go the way of capitalism, with its exploitation, oppression, and inequalities. Also, the imperialistic countries would not allow China to develop the capitalist way. China's only way out was a social revolution.[35]

Wu had to reinterpret Jesus' gospel of love and his pacifist ideal, especially his commandment to love our enemies. For Wu, Jesus was a pacifist and love was his central message. As a pacifist, Jesus was not sympathetic to the Jewish national struggles against the Roman Empire. He might have thought that the Jews were weak and there would be much bloodshed and sacrifice if they confronted the mighty Roman Empire.[36] Yet this did not mean that Jesus was a bystander. He was "*active* about exposing evils, only He overcame evil with good."[37] Although love is an ideal, said Wu, we live in an imperfect society and our ideal might never be realized. Therefore, the way of love is relative in its application to a particular situation, such as when China was under Japanese invasion. The use of violence was justified when it was used to serve the good.[38]

After the founding of the People's Republic in China, the Chinese churches began to sever their ties with foreign churches and missions and established the China Christian Three-Self Movement—self-governing, self-supporting, and self-propagating. During the Cultural Revolution (1966–1976), churches were closed down and religious activities suspended. Mao called upon the Red Guards to eradicate capitalist and traditional, cultural elements through violent class struggles. Familes were torn apart as children were asked to criticize their parents, and the movement significantly impacted China economically and socially. After the revolutionary furor was over, the Chinese Christians needed to hear a Gospel of reconciliation and forgiveness.

Bishop Ding Guangxun (also known as K. H. Ting, b.1915), leader of the Chinese Protestant church, emphasized Jesus' love and reconciliation in the aftermath of the Cultural Revolution. He wrote, "God is love—love made manifest in Christ."[39] He went on to describe how Jesus loved his friends, the rich young men, the Samaritan woman, the woman accused of adultery, the tax collector. He wept over Jerusalem and loved the disciples even when they fled during his passion. Ding used the overflowing love of God to oppose the destructiveness of class struggle. As the church came together to form a postdenominational church after the crucible of fire, Ding said that the church should build itself up in love, allowing for "diversity [that] does not aim at uniformity in matters of faith and worship."[40]

As China's economy has rapidly developed, the sleeping dragon of the East has finally awoken. Although commentators outside China have often spoken of China's imperialistic ambitions, Chinese leaders have repeatedly denied them and spoken of China's "peaceful rise." Chinese Christian leaders have not discussed the possibilities of China becoming an empire, but that does not mean that there is no self-critique. One of the problems of economic reform is discrimination against women in terms of education and job opportunities. Chinese female Christian leaders have drawn attention to the inequality between the sexes in the church and society. Wang Peng, an instructor of the New Testament at Nanjing Union Theological Seminary, argues that Paul's teaching that women should be silent in church (1 Cor. 14:34) should be understood in the particular situation of Corithinian church, in which some women disrupted prayers and worship.[41] His teachings of women's subordination and women covering their heads applied to "fixed conditions of the time, and are not an absolute and universal teaching for women regardless of time or place."[42]

Reform and liberalization and economic development bring new pressures on Chinese traditional understanding of marriage and family life. Meng Yanling, also from Nanjing Union Theological Seminary, writes about Pauline teachings on marriage and the relationship between the two sexes.[43] She challenges Paul's injunction that wives should be subject to their husbands in the Ephesian household code (Eph. 5: 22). The comparison that the husband as the head of the wife as Christ as the head of the church does not hold because the husband is far from being the savior of the wife. Meng says that Paul has also mentioned that in Christ, there is no longer male and female (Gal. 3:28). She writes, "We must not forget that Paul was situated in a maledominated social environment. Paul was attempting to bring the fellowship of the Christian ideal of male-female equality and the culture of the time into harmony."[44] Gender becomes a site of struggle for these Chinese female interpreters because women have often been caught in the tension between tradition and modernity.

Geopolitical hermeneutics is an interdisciplinary inquiry that can be found in many biblical critical methods—historical, Marxist, postcolonial, and feminist—and in the intersection of a number of these methods. As we face a post-American and multipolar world, our imagination of the world and its geography needs to be updated. This means that (1) we have to add the geographical to the social and political dimensions in biblical interpretation, paying attention to space and the construction of spatial relations, (2) we need to look at the ways communities and identities are reshaped in the changing geopolitics of the world, and (3) we must go beyond the orbit of Western biblical criticism to get to know how critics in other parts of the world are interpeting the Bible in order to become global citizens.

As I write this chapter, the Occupy Wall Street movement has spread to more than one thousand cities around the world. The Occupiers have built tent-cities, shared food, helped those in need, and formed alternative communities. The idea of "occupation" has something to do with space: Occupy Wall Street, Occupy London, Occupy Dewey Square, Occupy Harvard, and occupy everything. The movement points to the selfishness and coporate greed of big business and big banks and wants to take back what is due to the people. The movement has caught on so quickly because the results of the widening gap of wealth between the one percent and the 99% affect so many lives. I hope that the idea that the earth's resources belong to all people and should not be enjoyed by only a few will inspire us to seek a radical new ordering of the world.

Notes

1. "Geopolitics," Wikipedia, http://en.wikipedia.org/wiki/Geopolitics.

2. Michael Hardt and Antonio Negri, *Empire* (Cambridge: Harvard University Press, 2000).

3. Gustavo Gutiérrez, *A Theology of Liberation: History, Politics, and Salvation* (Maryknoll: Orbis, 1973), 21–42, 81–99; José Míguel Bonino, *Doing Theology in a Revolutionary Situation* (Philadelphia: Fortress Press, 1975).

4. George V. Pixley and Clodovis Boff, "A Latin American Perspective: The Option for the Poor in the Old Testament" in *Voices from the Margin: Interpreting the Bible in the Third World*, ed. R. S. Sugaratharjah (Maryknoll: Orbis, 1995), 215–27.

5. Jon Sobrino, *Christology at the Crossroads: A Latin American Approach*, trans. John Drury (London: SCM, 1978), 210–11.

6. Richard A. Horsley, *Jesus and Empire: The Kingdom of God and the New World Disorder* (Minneapolis: Fortress Press, 2002); John Dominic Crossan, *God and Empire: Jesus against Rome, Then and Now* (New York: HarperCollins, 2007); Warren Carter, *Matthew and Empire: Initial Explorations* (Harrisburg: Trinity International, 2001); Richard A. Horsley, ed., *Paul and Empire: Religion and Power in Roman Imperial Society* (Harrisburg: Trinity International, 1997); Horsley, ed., *Paul and the Roman Imperial Order* (Harrisburg: Trinity International, 2004); Horsley, ed., *In the Shadow of Empire: Reclaiming the Bible as a History of Faithful Resistance* (Louisville: Westminster John Knox, 2008); Wes Howard-Brook and Anthony Gwyther, *Unveiling Empire: Reading Revelation Then and Now*, Bible and Liberation (Maryknoll: Orbis, 1999).

7. Richard A. Horsley, *Jesus and Empire: The Kingdom of God and the New World Disorder* (Minneapolis: Fortress Press, 2003), 20–34.

8. Richard A. Horsley, "Feminist Scholarship and Postcolonial Criticism: Subverting Imperial Discourse and Reclaiming Submerged Histories," in *Walk in the Ways of Wisdom: Essays in Honor of Elisabeth Schüssler Fiorenza*, ed. Shelly Matthews, Cynthia Briggs Kittredge, and Melanie Johnson-Debaufre (Harrisburg: Trinity International, 2003), 297–317.

9. Richard A. Horsley, "Submerged Biblical Histories and Imperial Biblical Studies," in *The Postcolonial Bible*, ed. R. S. Sugirtharajah (Sheffield: Sheffield Academic, 1998), 160.

10. Stephen D. Moore, *Empire and Apocalypse: Postcolonialism and the New Testament* (Sheffield: Sheffield Phoenix, 2006), 9.

11. Fernando F. Segovia, "Notes toward Refining the Postcolonial Optic," *JSNT* 75 (1999): 111.

12. Fernando F. Segovia, "Johannine Studies and Geopolitical: Reflections upon Absence and Irruption," in *What We Have Heard from the Beginning: The Past, Present, and Future of Johannine Studies*, ed. Tom Thatcher (Waco: Baylor University Press, 2007), 284.

13. Ibid., 281–306.

14. Fernando F. Segovia, "Biblical Criticism and Postcolonial Studies: Toward a Postcolonial Optic," in *The Postcolonial Bible*, ed. R. S. Sugirtharajah (Sheffield: Sheffield Academic, 1998), 51–52, 58–63.

15. Segovia, "Notes toward Refining the Postcolonial Optic," 111.

16. Musa W. Dube, *Postcolonial Feminist Interpretation of the Bible* (Saint Louis: Chalice, 2000), 144-55; and Musa W. Dube, "Reading for Deconstruction (John 4:1–42)," *Semeia* 75 (1996): 37–59.

17. Dube, *Postcolonial Feminist Interpretation*, 201.

18. Homi K. Bhabha, *The Location of Culture* (London: Routlege, 1994).

19. Stephen D. Moore, *Empire and Apocalypse*, 109.

20. Ibid., x.

21. Stephen D. Moore, "Questions of Biblical Ambivalence and Authority under a Tree Outside Delhi; Or, the Postcolonial and the Postmodern," in *Postcolonial Biblical Criticism:*

Interdisciplinary Intersections, ed. Stephen D. Moore and Fernando F. Segovia (New York: T&T Clark, 2005), 79–96.

22. Stephen D. Moore, "'The World Empire Has Become the Empire of Our Lord and His Messiah': Representing Empire in Revelation," in *Empire and Apocalypse*, 97–121.

23. Ibid., 121.

24. Tat-Siong Benny Liew, "Margins and (Cutting-)Edges: On the (Il)legitimacy and Intersections of Race, Ethnicity, and (Post)colonialism," in *Postcolonial Biblical Criticism*, 125.

25. Lisa Lowe, "The International within the National: American Studies and Asian American Critique," *Cultural Critique* 40 (1998): 29–47.

26. Homi K. Bhabha, "Introduction: Narrating the Nation," in *Nation and Narration*, ed. Homi K. Bhabha (New York: Routledge, 1990), 4.

27. Bhabha, *The Location of Culture*, 89.

28. Anne Anlin Cheng, *The Melancholy of Race: Psychoanalysis, Assimilation, and Hidden Grief* (New York: Oxford University Press, 2001).

29. Liew, "Margins and (Cutting-)Edges," 143–44.

30. Tat-Siong Benny Liew, *What Is Asian American Biblical Hermeneutics? Reading the New Testament* (Honolulu: University of Hawaii Press, 2008), 98–114.

31. Ibid., 112.

32. Bruce W. Jentleson, "Accepting Limits: How to Adapt to a Copernican World," *Democracy: A Journal of Ideas* 23 (Winter 2012), http://www.democracyjournal.org/23/accepting-limits-how-to-adapt-to-a-copernican-world.php?page=1.

33. Ibid.

34. Y. T. Wu (Wu Yaozong), "China's Challenges to Christianity," *Chinese Recorder* 65 (1934): 10.

35. Y. T. Wu, "Christianity and China's Reconstruction," *Chinese Recorder* 67 (1936): 212.

36. Wu Yaozong, *Da shidai de zongjiao xinyang* (*Religious Belief in Crisis*) (Chengdu: Qingnian xiehui shuju, 1938), 24.

37. Wu, "Christianity and China's Reconstruction," 213–14. Emphasis his.

38. Ibid., 214.

39. K. H. Ting, "Love that Loves to the End," (1988) in *A Chinese Contribution to Ecumenical Theology*, ed. Janice and Philip Wickeri (Geneva: WCC, 2002), 88.

40. K. H. Ting, "Building Up the Body in Love," (1986) in ibid., 85.

41. Wang Peng, "On Paul's Prohibitions of Women in 1 Corinthians," *Chinese Theological Review* 15 (2001): 92–93.

42. Ibid., 91.

43. Meng Yanling, "Women, Faith, Marriage: A Feminist Look at the Challenges for Women," in *Hope Abundant: Third World and Indigenous Women's Theology*, ed. Kwok Pui-lan (Maryknoll: Orbis, 2010), 229–40.

44. Ibid., 235.

13

Colorful Readings

Racial/Ethnic Minority Readings of the New Testament in the United States

Tat-siong Benny Liew

For most people—at least those in the academy of biblical studies—racial/ethnic minority readings of the New Testament in the United States started in the 1970s.[1] Michael Joseph Brown's account of African American biblical scholarship, for instance, dates the rise of what he calls "blackening the Bible" to this same decade (2004:19). Brown helpfully accounted for the rise of this scholarship at least partly to the pioneering work of black theology in the 1960s (2004: 16-19). The sixties was, of course, a decade of popular or grassroots movement against racism and imperialism within the larger U.S. society. It was also a time when U.S. economic reorganization around global capital, and hence new patterns of migration and new laws of immigration, became even more clearly visible. For example, the 1965 Immigration Act allows more entries and with less concern over an immigrant's national origin. One can see here not only that scholarship (both theological and biblical) does not bypass material and social realities but also that racial/ethnic minority readings of the New Testament cannot be limited to the discipline of biblical studies.

New Testament readings became more colorful during this period as a result of James Cone's black theology (1969; 1970), Gustavo Gutiérrez's theology of liberation (1973), Choan-Seng Song's story theology (1979; 1984), and Ahn Byung Mu's minjung theology (1981). Osvaldo D. Vena, for example, mentions "Latin American Liberation Theology, Feminist Theology and Black Theology" as the first reading practices in his U.S. theological education that presented alternatives to the historical-critical ideal of searching for the authorial intentions of the biblical writers (2000: 86). This crossing between

177

theology and biblical studies, often a taboo among traditional biblical scholars who also believe in a clean separation between focusing on what a text meant in the past ("exegesis") and what that same text might mean today ("application"), is but a small clue to how racial/ethnic minority readings of the New Testament will blow things wide open not only between theology and biblical studies but also between biblical studies and disciplines outside of theological or religious studies (see Schüssler Fiorenza 2010: 381-82).

Kwok Pui-lan, with what she calls "parallel processing," suggests that one must transgress disciplinary boundaries to break new ground in biblical studies (1998: 80). Otherwise, one would be stuck and restricted within the disciplinary norms or regimes of truth already established within New Testament studies, the history of which is not devoid of race and racializing dynamics (Segovia 2000: 157–77; Kelley 2002). Kwok's suggestion is akin to an anthropologist's argument that going overseas and encountering another culture might open one's horizon to see that one's own cultural way of doing something is not necessarily the only way or best way. Rigid disciplinary boundaries are, in fact, built upon assumptions of origin and purity much like those used in national debates over immigration. Such assumptions idealize an "originator" or "owner" of a certain intellectual space that will only be sullied by trespasses or transplants.

The connection between interdisciplinary study and racial/ethnic minority New Testament readings should be evident by the "border-crossing" language I intentionally employ. Racial/ethnic minorities in this country, despite their nativity, are often racialized as perennial border-crossers who do not really belong. One can see in the recent controversy surrounding President Obama's birth certificate that, as this world becomes more and more global, African Americans are also not exempt from such racializing dynamics. Analogous assumptions and arguments are used to patrol not only racial/ethnic borders within a nation but also disciplinary borders within the academy. Racial/ethnic minority readings function, therefore, to resist a tyranny of purity in both academic *and* racial/ethnic terms. These readings are about much more than identity formation or cultural heritage; as important as these issues are, racial/ethnic minority readings confront and challenge the ideology of "purity"—and hence the politics, practices, and realities of exclusion and domination—in academy and society (Lowe 1998: 30, 39). Racial/ethnic minority readings are about not only different readers, but also different readings making a difference in how one sees a biblical text and even the entire discipline of New Testament studies.

Dynamics of Colors

Let me clarify, however, that it would be inaccurate—in fact, wrong—to blame racial/ethnic minorities for racializing the New Testament, or for making everything (including the New Testament) about race/ethnicity. I will give but a few examples. When the U.S. became a world power through its expansion into Asia in the late nineteenth century and Chinese, in (re)turn, started to come and seek entry into the nation from various shores, Greenberry G. Rupert helped popularize the threat of a "Yellow Peril" with his book of the same title. Most telling, however, is the book's subtitle: *Or, The Orient vs. the Occident as Viewed by Modern Statesmen and Ancient Prophets*. Rupert's phrase, "ancient prophets," was actually a reference to the Christian Bible. Understanding people from "China, India, Japan, and Korea" through the phrase "the kings of the east" in Revelation 16:12 (KJV), Rupert himself made a religious, racial, *and* political prophecy that Christ would stop these "kings" and their menace against the western world (1911: 9–22). Rupert also asked three questions that he thought "the world" would need to settle, because they would determine the ultimate question of "who shall rule the world" (1911: 6). His three questions are: (1) "the race question ... between the colored races of the world and the white race"; (2) "the religious question ... between the eastern nations, who are not professed Christians, and the western nations, who profess to be Christians"; and (3) "the financial question involv[ing] the wealth of the world" (1911: 6). In one short page and four succinct questions, Rupert demonstrated the intricate intersections among religion, race, capitalism, and imperialism against Asians, just as the Islamophobia after September 11 has once again shown.

Of course, the trans-Pacific advancement of the United States was predated by its involvement in the circum-Atlantic trading of black slaves. Given the Bible's role in the history of slavery of this country and the racial nature of U.S. slavery, it should not be a surprise that readings of the Bible by Whites—both popular and scholarly—have been key to not only the justification of slavery but also the racialization of persons within the United States' national borders (Harrill 2006: 165–92; Johnson 2010). In other words, racial/ethnic minority readings of the New Testament must be read within a wider context of "white supremacist" readings. Thornton Stringfellow, in an essay published in an 1860 volume, *Cotton Is King and Pro-Slavery Arguments*, read 1 Corinthians 7 and 1 Timothy 6 to affirm not only that the New Testament and slavery were compatible, but also that slavery was shown in the New Testament as a way of salvation for otherwise fallen persons or peoples—which, for Stringfellow, would include his contemporary Africans (John Byron 2008: 2–4). It was in response to these "white supremacist" readings that Frederick Douglass wrote:

"What do you do when you are told by the slaveholders of America that the Bible sanctions slavery? Do you go and throw your Bible into the fire? Do you sing out, 'No Union with the Bible!'? Do you declare that a thing is bad because it has been misused, abused, and made bad use of? Do you throw it away on that account? No! You press it to your bosom all the more closely; you read it all the more diligently; and prove from its pages that it is on the side of liberty—and not on the side of slavery" (cited in Harrill 2006: 177–78). For Douglass, reading race or racializing with the Bible did not begin with the enslaved but the slaveholders. Challenging such racialized interpretations, racial/ethnic minority readings of the New Testament—like the racial/ethnic minority bodies within the U.S.—end up functioning like a thorn in the flesh that cannot be excised or removed (2 Corinthians 12). Racial/ethnic minority readings refuse to let particular readings rule by default by continuing to reread the New Testament; they may also remind all readers that they are connected to one another through this common book no matter how differently they read.

Besides providing alternative readings, there is yet another reason why racial/ethnic minority readings are important. As racial/ethnic climates (including understandings of race/ethnicity) change over time, questions of race/ethnicity change and are not addressable in the same ways. For instance, overtly racist readings of the Bible might decrease, perhaps even disappear; yet, this does not necessarily mean that issues over race/ethnicity are over and done with. In a society or situation of "racism without racists" (Bonilla-Silva 2003; Ford 2008: 37–92), racial/ethnic *minority* readings have become one significant avenue to pursue and push conversations, education, and recognition about issues regarding race and ethnicity, boundary and community. This is especially so since New Testament texts are not only ambiguous and fluid in nature but also deal with feelings, anxieties, desires, dreams, memories, meanings, and values in terms of content or focus.

CHANGING COLORS

FIRST STAGE

When racial/ethnic minority readings of the Bible by scholars began in the 1970s, the main concern was twofold: first, to find minority subjects in the Bible; and second, taking a cue from feminist readings, to present positive or at least more complex pictures and images of minority subjects when they are "found" in the Bible.[2] Cain Hope Felder, like what Charles Copher does with the Hebrew Bible (1989; 1991), argues consistently that the New Testament presents Blacks as both recipients and mediators of God's salvation (Brown

2004: 24–53). Questioning the "mistaken notion that . . . the relation of Black people to the Bible is a post-biblical experience" (1989: xi), Felder goes on to argue not only that Mary and hence Jesus are more like "Yemenite, Trinidadian, or African American today" in appearance (1993: 192–94), but also that ancient writers of the Bible acknowledge and admire ancient Africans for having a great and glorious culture (1991). In fact, this question about "black presence" in the Bible constitutes one of the four sections of the first anthology on African American biblical interpretation, *Stony the Road We Trod* (Felder, ed. 1991).[3] The concern here involves recognition: African Americans are not only qualified interpreters of the Bible, but the Bible itself also contains black presence and appreciation of black culture.

Coming on the scene about a decade after their African American counterparts, the first generation of Asian American biblical scholars are also concerned about Asian presence in the Bible, but they go about arguing for that in a different way. Although Felder tends to refer to the ancient Hebrews as "Afro-Asiatics" (1991: 136), Asian American scholars of the Bible are reluctant to claim particular biblical characters as Asians. This reluctance has much to do with the fact that this "first" generation of Asian American Bible scholars are mainly of East Asian heritage and are thus distant geographically from West Asia and North Africa. Instead, they tend to identify racializing dynamics familiar to Asian Americans in a biblical text, and then identify with a particular biblical character in that text. Chan-Hie Kim, for instance, compares the Cornelius story in Acts 10–11 to his own experience as an Asian immigrant to the United States, since both Cornelius and Kim are outsiders interacting with and integrating into a community of another racial/ethnic group (1995).[4]

As racial/ethnic minority readings continue to develop, this attempt to find one's presence in the New Testament does not disappear (see, for example, Sadler 2007). For example, Russell G. Moy begins his reading of 1 Peter with an early twentieth-century quotation by Sui Sin Far that Chinese Americans could be comparable to both the Bible's composers and characters (2002). I will have more to say about Sui Sin Far, but will simply point here to Moy's movement to (1) parallel the Chinese Protestants in nineteenth-century San Francisco with the "resident aliens" or "diasporic exiles" of 1 Peter (1:1); and (2) argue that these Chinese Protestants actually lived out the vision and prescriptions of the letter. This Moy does, again, without ever suggesting that the "alien" or "diasporic" author and recipients of 1 Peter were Chinese. Instead, Moy presents them as a Jewish working-class in Asia Minor who did not have citizen status and hence were vulnerable to suspicion and discrimination, especially given their conversion to the small Christ cult. It is this double minority condition—in terms of both "race/ethnicity" and religion—that Moy focuses on to make the correspondence between 1 Peter and San Francisco's Chinese Protestants in the nineteenth century.

The move from specifying certain biblical characters as "Afro-Asiatic" to showing similar experiences being shared by those in the text and select racial/ethnic minority groups means that racial/ethic minority readings of the New Testament also begin to become less character-focused but more issue-oriented. Many—like Moy does regarding marginalization through both race and religion—are reading the New Testament in light of concerns that are relevant, prevalent, and important to their communities.

One can also see two underlying dynamics in this stage of racial/ethnic minority readings. First, these readings are all concerned with the power differential between majority Whites and minority persons of color. Second, they also seem to assume not only a stable and known identity but also a collective identity that all members of a particular racial/ethnic minority group should be ready to embrace.

This is perhaps best seen in an essay by Leticia Guardiola-Sáenz, a Latina New Testament scholar (1997). While the essay is titled "Borderless *Women* and Borderless Texts" (emphasis added), the "women question" is scarcely addressed. Guardiola-Sáenz's reading of the Canaanite woman (Matt 15:21-28) focuses on the social location of Mexican Americans in general. Everything she highlights—from Spanish colonization, U.S. imperialism, and the Treaty of Guadalupe-Hidalgo to bicultural and borderland experiences—seems to be applicable to both Mexican American men and women.

SECOND STAGE

At the same time, one can begin to detect another discreet yet discernible difference in the bibliographies of Guardiola-Sáenz's and Moy's on the one hand, and those of Felder's and Kim's on the other. Besides biblical and theological scholarship, Felder's and Kim's references are limited to works that have to do with the ancient world for Felder and one mention of the 1965 Immigration Act for Kim. In contrast, we find Guardiola-Sáenz and Moy citing respectively from what we would call today Latino/a studies and Asian American studies. In what I am calling the "second stage," racial/ethnic minority readings of the New Testament would be more thoroughly informed by scholarship in ethnic studies. While Guardiola-Sáenz's essay in 1997 has only one bibliographical entry from ethnic studies, David A. Sánchez's book on Revelation 12 (2008) actually contains a bibliography with four sections; two of those sections are typical in New Testament scholarship ("The Book of Revelation, Ancient Studies and Primary Sources" and "Theory and Methodology"), but an equal number of sections (two) fall under the broader umbrella of Latino/a studies ("Guadalupe and Mexican Colonial History" and "Chicana/o Studies and U.S. History").

In addition, in this second stage, racial/ethnic minority readings of the New Testament no longer begin with the New Testament and how it has been read (as even Guardiola-Sáenz and Moy still do), but start with a reader's own context and experience as a racial/ethnic minority person in the United States. We see this in another racial/ethnic minority reading of Revelation: the subtitle of Brian K. Blount's book is "Reading Revelation *through* African American Culture" (2005; emphasis added). This is consistent with Blount's earlier declaration that "a study of New Testament ethics in an African American context . . . should begin where African American theology, and, indeed, the African American church itself began: with the African American slave" (2001: 23).

The combination of these two changes signals for me a move from "reading Scripture reading race" to "reading race reading Scripture."[5] This simple turn of phrase refers to a change from the earlier emphasis on reading the New Testament to find and understand race to a new priority of reading and understanding race as a lens to read and make sense of the New Testament. The New Testament, in other words, is now explicitly *not* the first entry into an exploration. The concern is now less what the New Testament has to say about race/ethnicity, but more what a particular racial/ethnic minority group has to say about the New Testament. Inverting this process is important because New Testament studies as a discipline is not unaffected by the infection of racial/ethnic discriminations and colonial impulse. Inverting the process is, in effect, precisely the proposal submitted by Vincent Wimbush when he asks in the introduction to his encyclopedic project, *African Americans and the Bible*, "How might putting African Americans at the center of the study of the Bible affect the study of the Bible?" (2000: 2; see also Wimbush 2007; 2010).[6] Racial/ethnic minority scholarship of the New Testament at this stage moves beyond simple demographics to a shift of framework (see also Gay Byron 2009; Abraham Smith 2010: 91).

Another significant change as racial/ethnic minority readings of the New Testament enter what I call its second stage involves how the assumptions about struggle and identity we mentioned earlier also begin to change. In this stage, these readings begin to manifest a much greater diversity within each racial/ethnic minority group. As identity struggle involves internal differences, identity becomes multiple, contradictory, no longer singular, and less than stable. Intersections between race/ethnicity and other identity factors—like gender and sexuality—come increasingly into the picture. After presenting the challenges to Afrocentric readings by female readers like Renita Weems, Clarice Martin, Wilma Ann Bailey, and Cheryl Kirk-Duggan, Brown concludes his account of African American biblical scholarship with what he calls a "neo-womanist"—that is, queer—perspective to destabilize a binary understanding of gender (2004: 175–83; see also Brown 2011). One can also see this turn towards an intersectional emphasis in works of African American New Testament scholars like Raquel Annette Saint Clair (2008) and Demetrius Williams (2004; 2009).

The desire for recognition that we mentioned in the early stage, while still present, becomes perhaps less desirable once racial/ethnic minority scholars perceive that a recognized identity can become one dimensional and hence restrictive, with pressure to conform coming from one's own racial/ethnic minority community as well as from Whites. A good example that demonstrates this more complicated identity struggle within racial/ethnic minority New Testament interpretation is an essay by Sze-kar Wan, which highlights the methodological divergence, diversity, or fluidity of Asian American biblical interpretation by featuring a "hermeneutics of hyphenation" that can be somewhere or anywhere "betwixt and between"—for lack of better terms—a "historical" or an "ideological" emphasis (2006). This struggle to highlight and clarify the heterogeneity among Asian American readers of the New Testament can further be seen in Mary F. Foskett's reading—as an Asian adoptee in the United States—of adoption in Romans 8–9 (2002) and the scholarly search for early Christian origins (2006), as well as my reading of John's Jesus from not only a racial/ethnic but also a sexual minority perspective (2009).

Among Latino/a readers, Manuel Villalobos has recently performed a provocative reading of Acts 8:26-40 (2011), the story of the Ethiopian eunuch. Beginning with the feminist and queer work of Gloria Anzaldúa, Villalobos perceives the story as a site of transformation that brings hope to not only the Ethiopian eunuch's body but also Villalobos' own queer body that has often been denied and denounced by fellow Latinos. It is little wonder that Segovia emphasizes "the concept of Latin(o/a)ness" as a "construct" that "is neither self-evident nor determinate . . . [but] always subject to interpretation and debate . . . always evasive and fragile" (2009a: 199–200). In this second stage, racial/ethnic minority scholars of the New Testament are branching out beyond a homogenizing identity into "crossroads of ambiguity" (Anna Deavere Smith 2000: 24).

THIRD STAGE

As racial/ethnic minority readings of the New Testament move with this emphasis on intersectionality, internal diversity, or intra-communal negotiation into the twenty-first century, there are signs that we are inching toward a third stage that also works on inter-communal conversations across minority groups. Aside from an early attempt to establish contact between African American and Asian American Bible scholars (Liew and Wimbush 2002), the strongest indication of this inclination is the volume, *They Were All Together in One Place? Toward Minority Biblical Criticism* (Bailey, Liew, and Segovia 2009). While the individual essays within this volume do not necessarily demonstrate this crossing, the volume as a whole—by putting three racial/ethnic minority groups together in one volume even if they are not necessarily in one accord—does gesture a desire not only to seek recognition from each other as racial/ethnic minority communities but also to facilitate communication across color lines for association, affinity, and perhaps even—in Angela Davis's vocabulary—"unlikely coalitions" (1997: 322). Making scholars of other racial/ethnic minority groups rather than White scholars one's primary conversation partners signals a potential sea change. If racial/ethnic minority readings of the New Testament in the second stage show that racial/ethnic identity is not only constructed but also composite—that is, it involves and is made up of different and multiple elements—the crossings we begin to witness in this third stage hint that the underlying framework has changed from a bipolar ("majority/Whites" against "minority/persons of color") to a multipolar or multicentric one. Inter-communal crossings will help all racial/ethnic minority readers understand not only the New Testament's role in racialization (both helping and hurting racial/ethnic minorities) but also our role in other people's as well as our own oppression and liberation. This shift to inter-communal conversations across different racial/ethnic minority communities is hence not only a comparative but also a connective turn: instead of fortifying boundaries to allow for differences within but arrest invaders and interlopers from without, racial/ethnic minority readers from separate communities now seem to realize that "differences do not exist independently of each other . . . [but] converge and conflict and thus participate in each other" (Chuh 2003:148; see also Wimbush 2010: 359, 363).

COLORING THE FUTURE

If this is where racial/ethnic minority readings have been thus far, where might we go from here? Let me make just three suggestions. First, minority readings of the New Testament need to engage Native American readings. One of the most frequent feedbacks I have heard about *They Were All Together in One Place?* is the absence of Native American voices (see also Segovia 2009b: 297). The low number of Native American biblical scholars aside, I want to point out honestly that unfortunate tensions often exist between Native Americans and other racial/ethnic minorities. On the one hand, racial/ethnic minority analysis, perhaps out of an eagerness to "claim America," is often guilty of ignoring the genocide against indigenous peoples. On the other hand, Native activists *and* academics often argue for their sovereignty and land claims in terms of prior occupancy. This argument ("This land is 'ours,' not 'yours,' because we were here first!") can work against those who arrive late, including racial/ethnic minorities who came into the U.S. through immigration and migration. I have wondered elsewhere if the attempt by African American scholars to (re)claim the Bible by proclaiming black presence in the Bible would end up reinforcing the ideology of first rights (2002).

Given this concern about indigenous claims, let me go back to the origin story about racial/ethnic minority readings of the New Testament. Racial/ethnic minority scholars of the 1970s actually did not begin racial/ethnic minority readings of the New Testament. As much as scholars might like to take credit for being founders—or worse, "fathers"—of racial/ethnic minority readings, racial/ethnic minorities have been reading the New Testament for a long time. Slave narratives in and after the antebellum period, for instance, often include quotations from, comments on, and engagements with the Bible (Callahan 2006). While the publication of Elizabeth Cady Stanton's *Woman's Bible* at the end of the nineteenth century (2002) has become rather well known if not necessarily widely read, Virginia W. Broughton—a devout black Baptist missionary and advocate of women's rights—and her 1904 publication, *Women's Work, as Gleaned from the Women of the Bible and the Bible Women of Modern Times* (Carter 2010: 9–21), have remained unknown and unfamiliar to even most racial/ethnic minority scholars of the Bible.[7] Another example would be a contemporary of Broughton: Sui Sin Far, who has been called the "First Chinese-American Fictionist" (Solberg 1981), "the founder of the Chinese North American woman writer's tradition" (White-Parks, 1995: 6), as well as "the grand maternal figure of *all* Asian American letters" (David Shih 2005: 48). Despite these recent accolades, Sui Sin Far was not a famous writer in her own time and by no means a scholar. However, her writings are full of allusions to and quotations from the Bible. "[T]he stories in the Bible were more like Chinese than American stories," she writes, "[i]f you had not told me what you have about it, I should say that it was composed by the Chinese"

(Ling and White-Parks 1995: 78; see also Moy 2002: 52). One white literature professor—so not a minoritized Bible scholar—has even suggested provocatively that the Bible was "the single most important model" of Sui Sin Far's own writings, as it accounts for their "short," almost parable-like format and "didactic bent" (Ferens 2002: 95–96).

Second, racial/ethnic minorities in the United States started reading and writing about the New Testament a long time before racial/ethnic minority scholars did so in the 1970s. While I think tradition can change and thus be inventive, I also agree with R. S. Sugitharajah, a racial/ethnic minority New Testament scholar in the United Kingdom, that tracing a historical tradition through archival work can be inspiring in the sense of not only encouraging but also equipping us to further the work (2003: 93–94). Rather than reinventing the wheel, every generation can instead spend its time and energy to invent new elements and emphases to enlarge and enrich the tradition. Just as popular or grassroots anti-racist and anti-imperialist movements have facilitated academic developments, so-called popular readings of the New Testament by racial/ethnic minorities past *and* present will only contribute to future developments of such readings.

Ethnic studies scholar Lisa Lowe has argued that Enlightenment philosophy's emphasis on human freedom as a universal human right came into being only by robbing African slaves and Asian coolies of their freedom as a colonized labor force (2006). As racial/ethnic minority New Testament scholars, we must not forget what we affirm by dismissing racial/ethnic minority readers outside of the academy (see also Segovia 2009b: 281–82, 301–302). Doing so would effectually duplicate how the mainstream or "majority" group in society—whether national or academic—dismisses those whom it sees as "illiterate," "uneducated," or "not qualified." Among racial/ethnic minority New Testament scholars, Wimbush might have contributed most toward breaking this barrier, given his work on outlining an interpretive history of African Americans in general (1991) and on Olaudah Equiano (2009a) and Douglas (2009b) in particular (see also Abraham Smith 2003). As director of the Institute of Signifying Scripture, Wimbush is also branching out to do ethnographical work on how persons of color today read the Bible in faith communities that are not academic in focus (ed. forthcoming).

Finally, let me again return to my earlier reference to Latin America and Asia in linking theology with racial/ethnic minority New Testament scholarship. Brown actually also does something similar by way of Brazil and Nigeria in his more racial/ethnic specific account of black biblical scholarship (2004: 9–15). These references point to another potential crossing that racial/

ethnic minority New Testament scholars have not really developed since those incipient intervals of the 1970s. I am referring here to a transnational or transcontinental dimension of racial/ethnic minority scholarship (see also Segovia 2009b: 297, 302–3, 309).

While most people remember W. E. B. Du Bois' declaration, "the problem of the twentieth century is the problem of the color line," from *The Souls of Black Folk* (1903: xx), many have forgotten that Du Bois actually made that very statement first not only in France as part of the 1900 Pan-African Conference but also in a speech that he titled "To the Nations of the World" (1995). For Du Bois, the "Negro problem" or the question of race in the U.S. must be dealt with in terms of not only cultural nationalism but also "from the setting and in the name of a transnational gathering of men and women" (Edwards 2003: 2), as most cultures and societies do not operate in self-enclosed ways. Just as humanities scholars have highlighted the need to look at black slavery in a larger, trans-Atlantic frame (Curtin 1990; Roach 1996; Spillers 2003), racial/ethnic minority New Testament scholars need to develop a more frequent and serious crossing between "our" readings in the U.S. and readings in Africa, Asia, and Latin America, so we can—in Curtin's language—go beyond the "plantation complex" and redraw the boundaries to create a different type of transnational exploration and transcontinental comparison.

Fanon declared years ago that "comparison" should be "the first truth" of a colonized black person (1967: 210–22), because something dramatic happens when such a person moves from the metropole to the colony and vice versa (see also Shu-mei Shih 2008: 1349–52). The world might have come to the United States, but we cannot mistake the U.S. as the world. How do persons of the same race/ethnicity read over here and over there? The New Testament is already global; it is read by people around the globe, by people with doctorates and without. The question is whether our readings, including racial/ethnic minority readings in the United States, will catch up with that reality.

Notes

1. A different version of this essay that covers also scholarship on the Hebrew Bible is scheduled to appear in *The Future of the Biblical Past*, ed. Roland Boer and Fernando F. Segovia (Atlanta: Society of Biblical Literature, forthcoming).

2. My stage mapping here is more conceptual and less strictly temporal, though the temporal dimension is by no means absent. This temporal "flexibility" is necessary, since (1) the so-called first generation of New Testament scholars of different racial/ethnic minority groups came on the scene at different times; and (2) the duration of what is called a "stage" or "generation" also varies among various racial/ethnic minority groups. Given the more conceptual and heuristic nature of this mapping, readers should not (mis)take the beginning of a "new" stage as the end of a

previous stage; stages do overlap and run alongside each other. The same is true of an individual scholar; his or her work might develop and span over different stages.

3. The other three sections are devoted to (1) the authority of the Bible; (2) the method of and resources for biblical interpretation; and (3) the question of slavery.

4. Using Kim's article as well as others as examples, Amy-Jill Levine points out that racial/ethnic minority readings of the New Testament at times, perhaps even often, fall into a trap of "an anti-Judaism, wherein the oppressive system or the oppressor becomes 'the Jews.'" (2006: 180; see also 178, 181–82).

5. I am indebted to Kah-Jin Jeffrey Kuan for this turn of phrase.

6. The title of the volume is itself telling; it uses the conjunction "and" instead of the proposition "in" between African Americans and the Bible. In fact, Wimbush would go further to question if and how finding "black presence" could be "a desperate but ultimately unwise and self-defeating game" (2010: 357). I will have more to say about Wimbush's scholarship in relation to minoritized biblical criticism in general and African American readings in particular.

7. There are, of course, exceptions; see, for example, Williams 2004: 170–72.

Abbreviations

BibInt   *Biblical Interpretation*

BTB   *Biblical Theology Bulletin*

CBQ   *Catholic Biblical Quarterly*

ICC   International Critical Commentary

JBL   *Journal of Biblical Literature*

JECH   *Journal of Early Christian History*

JSJ   *Journal for the Study of Judaism*

JSNT   *Journal for the Study of the New Testament*

JSPSup   *Journal for the Study of the Pseudepigrapha* Supplement Series

SBLDS   Society of Biblical Literature Dissertation Series

SBLBSNA   Society of Biblical Literature Biblical Scholarship in North America

SBLSS   Society of Biblical Literature Semeia Studies

SBLSymS   Society of Biblical Literature Symposium Series

WW   *Word and World*

ZNTW   *Zeitschrift für die neutestamentliche Wissenschaft*

Bibliography

Ahn, Byung Mu. "Jesus and the Minjung in the Gospel of Mark." In *Minjung Theology: People as Subjects of History*, edited by Commission on Theological Concerns of the Christian Conferene of Asia, 138–52. Maryknoll: Orbis, 1981.

Allen, Willoughby C. *A Critical and Exegetical Commentary on the Gospel according to Saint Matthew.* ICC. Edinburgh: T&T Clark, 1907.

Althaus-Reid, Marcella María. "Gustavo Gutiérrez Goes to Disneyland: Theme Park Theologians and the Diaspora of the Discourse of the Popular Theologian in Liberation Theology." In *Interpreting Beyond Borders*, edited by Fernando F. Segovia, 36–58. The Bible and Postcolonialism. Sheffield: Sheffield Academic, 2000.

Anderson, Cheryl B. "Reflections in an Interethnic/racial Era on Interethnic/racial Marriage in Ezra." In *They Were All Together in One Place? Toward Minority Biblical Criticism*, edited by Randall C. Bailey, Tat-siong Benny Liew, and Fernando F. Segovia, 47–64. Society of Biblical Literature Semeia Series, 57. Atlanta: Society of Biblical Literature, 2009.

Anderson, Herbert, and Edward Foley, eds. *Mighty Stories, Dangerous Rituals: Weaving Together the Human and the Divine.* San Francisco: Jossey-Bass: 1998.

Anderson, Janice Capel and Stephen D. Moore, "Matthew and Masculinity." in *New Testament Masculinities*. Edited by Stephen D. Moore and Janice Capel Anderson. *Semeia* 45 (2003): 79–89.

_____. "Taking it Like a Man: Masculinity in 4 Maccabees." *Journal of Biblical Literature* 117 (1998): 249–73.

Andrade, Paulo Carneiro de. "Reading the Bible in the Ecclesial Base Communities of Latin America: The Meaning of Social Location." In *Reading from This Place,* volume 2, *Social Location and Biblical Interpretation in Global Perspective*, edited by Fernando Segovia and Mary Ann Tolbert, 237–49. Minneapolis: Fortress Press, 1995.

Appleby, Joyce, Lynn Hunt, and Margaret Jacob. *Telling the Truth about History.* New York: Norton, 1994.

Ashcroft, Bill, Gareth Griffiths and Helen Tiffin, eds. *Key Concepts in Post-Colonial Studies.* London: Routledge, 1998.

Assmann, Jan. "Collective Memory and Cultural Identity." *New German Critique* 65 (1995): 125–33.

______. "Cultural Memory: Script, Recollection, and Political Identity in Early Civilizations." *Historiography East and West* 1 (2003): 162–69.

______. *Religion and Cultural Memory: Ten Studies.* Translated by R. Livingstone. Stanford: Stanford University Press, 2006.

Bailey, Randall C., Tat-siong Benny Liew, and Fernando F. Segovia, eds., *They Were All Together in One Place? Toward Minority Biblical Criticism.* Society of Biblical Literature Semeia Studies 57. Atlanta: Society of Biblical Literature, 2009.

Baird, William. *History of New Testament Research.* Minneapolis: Fortress Press, 1992.

Baldwin, James. *Notes of a Native Son.* Boston: Beacon, 1984.

Balmer, Randall. "Casting Aside the Ballast of History and Tradition: White Protestants and the Bible in the Antebellum Period." In *African Americans and the Bible: Sacred Texts and Social Textures*, edited by Vincent L. Wimbush, 193–200. New York: Continuum, 2001.

Barclay, John M. G. "'Neither Jew nor Greek': Multiculturalism and the New Perspective on Paul." In *Ethnicity and the Bible*, edited by Mark G. Brett, 197–214. Boston: Brill, 2002.

Barker, Francis et al., eds. *Cannibalism and the Colonial World.* Cambridge: Cambridge University Press, 1998.

Barreto, Eric D. *Ethnic Negotiations: The Function of Race and Ethnicity in Acts 16.* Tübingen: Mohr Sieback, 2010.

______. "Negotiating Difference: Theology and Ethnicity in the Acts of the Apostles." *Word and World* 31 (2011): 129–37.

Bassler, Jouette M. *Navigating Paul: An Introduction to Key Theological Concepts.* Louisville: Westminster John Knox, 2007.

Bauckham, Richard. *Jesus and the Eyewitnesses: The Gospels as Eyewitness Testimony.* Grand Rapids: Eerdmans, 2006.

Bayer, Oswald. "Luther as an Interpreter of Holy Scripture." In *The Cambridge Companion to Martin Luther*, edited by Donald K. McKim, 73–85. New York: Cambridge University Press, 2003.

Beverly, John. *Subalternity and Representation: Arguments in Cultural Theory.* Durham: Duke University, 2004.

Bhabha, Homi K. *The Location of Culture.* London: Routledge, 1994.

______, ed. *Nation and Narration.* New York: Routledge, 1990.

The Bible and Culture Collective, "Ideological Criticism." In *The Postmodern Bible*, edited by the Bible and Culture Collective, 272–308. New Haven: Yale University Press, 1995.

Bielo, James S. "Introduction: Encountering Biblicism." In *The Social Life of Scriptures: Cross-Cultural Perspectives on Biblicism*, edited by James S. Bielo, 5–7. New Brunswick: Rutgers University Press, 2006.

Bird, Jennifer. *Abuse, Power, and Fearful Obedience: Reconsidering 1 Peter's Commands to Wives.* London: T&T Clark, 2011.

Blackmon, Douglas A. *Slavery by Another Name: The Re-Enslavement of Black Americans from the Civil War to World War II.* New York: Anchor, 2008.

Blount, Brian K. *Can I Get a Witness? Reading Revelation through African American Culture.* Louisville: John Knox Westminster, 2005.

______. *Then the Whisper Put on Flesh: New Testament Ethics in an African American Context.* Nashville: Abingdon, 2001.

______, ed. *True to Our Native Land: An African American New Testament Commentary.* Minneapolis: Fortress, 2007.

Boers, Hendrikus. *What Is New Testament Theology? The Rise of Criticism and the Problem of a Theology of the New Testament.* Philadelphia: Fortress Press, 1979.

Boff, Clodovis, and George V. Pixley. "A Latin American Perspective: The Option for the Poor in the Old Testament." In *Voices from the Margin: Interpreting the Bible in the Third World*, edited by R. S. Sugirtharajah, 215–27. Maryknoll: Orbis, 1991.

Bohache, Thomas. "Matthew." In *The Queer Bible Commentary*, edited by Deryn Gues, Robert Goss, Mona West, and Thomas Bohache. London: SCM, 2006.

Bonilla-Silva, Eduardo. *Racism without Racists: Color-Blind Racism and the Persistence of Racial Equality in the United States.* Lanham: Rowman and Littlefield, 2006.

Bonino, José Míguel. *Doing Theology in a Revolutionary Situation.* Philadelphia: Fortress Press, 1975.

Brant, Jo-Ann A. *John.* Paideia Commentaries on the New Testament. Grand Rapids: Baker, 2011.

Braxton, Brad R. *No Longer Slaves: Galatians and African American Experience.* Collegeville: Liturgical, 2002.

Brett, Mark G. *Decolonizing God: The Bible in the Tides of Empire.* Sheffield: Sheffield Phoenix, 2008.

______, ed. *Ethnicity and the Bible.* New York: Brill, 1996.

Brown, Michael Joseph. *Blackening of the Bible: The Aims of African American Biblical Scholarship*. Harrisburg: Trinity International, 2004.

______. "What Happens When Closets Open Up? A Response." In *Bible Trouble: Queer Reading at the Boundaries of Biblical Scholarship*, edited by Hornsby, Teresa J. and Ken Stone, 343–52. Atlanta: Society of Biblical Literature, 2011.

Brown, Raymond E. *The Community of the Beloved Disciple: The Life, Loves, and Hates of an Individual Church in New Testament Times*. New York: Paulist, 1979.

Buell, Denise Kimber. "God's Own People: Specters of Race, Ethnicity, and Gender in Early Christian Studies." In *Prejudice and Christian Beginnings: Investigating Race, Gender, and Ethnicity in Early Christian Studies*, edited by Laura Nasrallah and Elisabeth Schüssler Fiorenza, 159–90. Minneapolis: Fortress Press, 2009.

______. "Rethinking the Relevance of Race for Early Christian Self-Definition." *Harvard Theological Review* 94 (2001): 449–76.

______. *Why This New Race? Ethnic Reasoning in Early Christianity*. New York: Columbia University Press, 2005.

Buell, Denise Kimber, and Caroline Johnson Hodge. "The Politics of Interpretation: the Rhetoric and Race and Ethnicity in Paul." *Journal of Biblical Literature* 123 (2004): 235–41.

Burke, Trevor J. *Family Matters: A Socio-Historical Study of Kinship Metaphors in 1 Thessalonians*. London: T & T Clark, 2003.

Byron, Gay L. "Ancient Ethiopian and the New Testament: Ethnic (Con)texts and Racialized (Sub)texts." In *They Were All Together in One Place? Toward Minority Biblical Criticism*, edited by Randall C. Bailey, Tat-siong Benny Liew, and Fernando F. Segovia, 161–90. Society of Biblical Literature Semeia Studies 57. Atlanta: Society of Biblical Literature, 2009.

______. *Symbolic Blackness and Ethnic Difference in Early Christian Literature*. New York: Routledge, 2002.

Byron, John. *Recent Research on Paul and Slavery*. Sheffield: Sheffield Phoenix, 2008.

Cady Stanton, Elizabeth. *The Woman's Bible: A Classic Feminist Perspective*. Mineola: Dover, 2002.

Callahan, Allen Dwight. "'Brother Saul': An Ambivalent Witness to Freedom." *Semeia* 83/84 (1998): 235–50.

______. *The Talking Book: African Americans and the Bible*. New Haven: Yale University Press, 2006.

Cameron, Averil. *Christianity and the Rhetoric of Empire: The Development of Christian Discourse*. Sather Classical Lectures, 57. Berkeley: University of California Press, 1991.

Cannon, Katie Geneva. *Black Womanist Ethics*. AAR Academy Series 60. Atlanta: Scholars, 1988.

Carter, J. Kameron. *Race: A Theological Account*. New York: Oxford University Press, 2008.

Carter, Tomeiko Ashford, ed. *Virginia Broughton: The Life and Writings of a National Baptist Missionary*. Knoxville: University of Tennessee, 2010.

Carter, Warren. *John and Empire: Initial Explorations*. New York: T&T Clark, 2008.

______. *Matthew and Empire: Initial Explorations*. Harrisburg: Trinity International, 2001.

______. "Paul and the Roman Empire: Recent Perspectives," In *Paul Unbound: Other Perspectives on the Apostle*, edited by Mark D. Given, 7–26. Peabody: Hendrickson, 2010.

______. *The Roman Empire and the New Testament: An Essential Guide*. Nashville: Abingdon, 2006.

Castelli, Elizabeth A. *Imitating Paul: A Discourse of Power*. Louisville: Westminster John Knox, 1991.

Chaney, David. *The Cultural Turn: Scene-Setting Essays on Contemporary Cultural History*. London: Routledge, 1994.

Cheng, Anne Anlin. *The Melancholy of Race: Psychoanalysis, Assimilation, and Hidden Grief*. New York: Oxford University Press, 2001.

Chrulew, Matthew. "Feline Divinanimality: Derrida and the Discourse of Species in Genesis." *The Bible in Critical Theory* 2.2 (2008).

Chuh, Kandice. *Imagine Otherwise: On Asian American Critique*. Durham: Duke University Press, 2003.

Coble, Ann Louis. *Cotton Patch for the Kingdom: Clarence Jordan's Demonstration Plot at Koinonia Farm*. Scottdale: Herald, 2001.

Cohen, Shaye. *The Beginnings of Jewishness: Boundaries, Varieties, Uncertainties*. Berkeley: University of California Press, 2001.

Collins, Adela Yarbro, ed., *Feminist Perspectives on Biblical Scholarship*. Society of Biblical Literature Biblical Scholarship in North America 10. Chico: Society of Biblical Literature, 1985.

Collins, John J. *The Bible After Babel: Historical Criticism in a Postmodern Age*. Grand Rapids: Eerdmans, 2005.

______. *Daniel: A Commentary on the Book of Daniel*. Heremeneia. Minneapolis: Fortress, 1993.

Comaroff, Jean, and John Comaroff. *Of Revelation and Revolution*, vol. 2: *The Dialectics of Modernity on South African Frontier*. Chicago: University of Chicago Press, 1997.

______. "Through the Looking Glass: Colonial Encounters of the First Kind." *Journal of Historical Sociology* 1 (1988): 6–30.

Cone, James H. *Black Theology and Black Power*. New York: Seabury, 1969.

______. *A Black Theology of Liberation*. Philadelphia: Lippincott, 1970.

Connolly, Michele A. *Disorderly Women and the Order of God: An Australian Feminist Reading of the Gospel of Mark*. Ph.D. Dissertation, Graduate Theological Union, 2008.

Conrad, Joseph. *Heart of Darkness*. New York: Bantam, 1981.

Copher, Charles B. "The Black Presence in the Old Testament." In *Stony the Road We Trod: African American Biblical Interpretation*, edited by Cain Hope Felder, 146–64. Minneapolis: Fortress Press, 1991.

______. "Three Thousand Years of Biblical Interpretation with Reference to Black Peoples." In *African American Religious Studies: An Interdisciplinary Anthology*, edited by Gayraud Wilmore, 105–28. Durham: Duke University Press, 1989.

Cosgrove, Charles H. "Did Paul Value Ethnicity?" *CBQ* 68 (2006): 268–90.

Creed, Barbara, and Jeannette Hoorn, eds. *Body Trade: Captivity, Cannibalism and Colonialism in the Pacific*. New York: Routledge, 2001.

Crossan, John Dominic. *God and Empire: Jesus against Rome, Then and Now*. New York: HarperCollins, 2007.

Crowder, Stephanie Buckhanon. "The Pleasure Principle: Mark 1:9-15." *Huffington Post* (February 26, 2012).

Crowder, Stephanie Buckhanon. *Simon of Cyrene: A Case of Roman Conscription*. London: Peter Lang, 2002.

Culpepper, R. Alan. *Anatomy of the Fourth Gospel: A Study of Literary Design*. Philadelphia: Fortress Press. 1983.

Curtin, Philip D. *The Rise and Fall of the Plantation Complex: Essays in Atlantic History*. Cambridge: Cambridge University Press, 1990.

Dachs, A. J., ed. *Papers of John Mackenzie*. Johannesburg: Witwatersrand University Press, 1975.

Das, A. Andrew. "Paul and the Law: Pressure Points in the Debate." In *Paul Unbound: Other Perspectives on the Apostle*, edited by Mark D. Given, 99–116. Peabody: Hendrickson, 2010.

Davies, W. D. and Dale C. Allison. *A Critical and Exegetical Commentary on the Gospel According to Saint Matthew*, v.2. ICC. Edinburgh: T&T Clark, 1991.

Davis, Angela. "Reflections on Race, Gender, and Class in the U.S.A." In *The Politics of Culture in the Shadow of Capital*, edited by Lisa Lowe and David Lloyd, 303–23. Durham: Duke University Press, 1997.

Defoe, Daniel. *The Life and Strange Surprising Adventures of Robinson Crusoe, of York, Mariner*. London: Taylor, 1719.

Derrida, Jacques. *The Animal That Therefore I Am*. Translated by David Wills. Perspectives in Continental Philosophy. New York: Fordham University Press, 2008.

______. *The Beast and the Sovereign*, v. 1. Translated by Geoffrey Bennington. The Seminars of Jacqes Derrida, 1. Chicago: University of Chicago Press, 2009.

Donaldson, Laura E. "Gospel Hauntings: The Postcolonial Demons of New Testament Criticism." In *Postcolonial Biblical Criticism: Interdisciplinary Intersections*, edited by Stephen D. Moore and Fernando F. Segovia, 97–114. New York: T&T Clark, 2005.

Du Bois, W. E. B. *The Souls of Black Folk: Essays and Sketches*. Chicago: McClurg, 1903.

______. "To the Nations of the World." In *W. E. B. Du Bois: A Reader*, edited by David Levering Lewis, 639–41. New York: Henry Holt [1900], 1995.

Dube, Musa W. "Curriculum Transformation: Dreaming of Decolonization in Theological Studies." In *Border Crossings: Cross-Cultural Hermeneutics*, edited by Devadasan Nithya Premnath and R. S. Sugirtharajah. Maryknoll: Orbis, 2007.

______. "Post-Colonial Biblical Interpretations." In *Dictionary of Biblical Interpretation*, edited by John H. Hayes, 299–303. Nashville: Abingdon, 1999.

______. *Postcolonial Feminist Interpretation of the Bible*. Saint Louis: Chalice. 2000.

______. "Reading for Deconstruction (John 4:1-42)" *Semeia* 75 (1996): 37–59.

______. "Savior of the World but Not of This World: A Postcolonial Reading of Spatial Construction in John." In *The Post-Colonial Bible*, edited by R. S. Sugirtharajah, 118–35. Sheffield: Sheffield Academic, 1998.

Dube, Sauraby. *Stitches in Time: Colonial Textures and Postcolonial Tangles*. Durham: Duke University Press, 2003.

Duling, Dennis C. "Ethnicity, Ethnocentrism, and the Matthean Ethos." *Biblical Theological Bulletin* 35 (2005): 125–43.

Dunbar, Anthony P. *Against the Grain: Southern Radicals and Prophets, 1929–1959.* Charlottesville: University Press of Virginia, 1981.

Duncan, Christopher M. *Benjamin Morgan Palmer: Southern Presbyterian Divine.* Ph.D. dissertation, Auburn University, 2008.

Dunn, James D. G. "The New Perspective on Paul." *Bulletin of the John Rylands University Library of Manchester* 65 (1983): 95–122.

Dunning, Benjamin H. *Aliens and Sojourners: Self as Other in Early Christianity.* Philadelphia: University of Philadelphia Press, 2008.

Edwards, Brent Hayes. *The Practice of Diaspora: Literature, Translation, and the Rise of Black Internationalism.* Cambridge: Harvard University Press, 2003.

Ehrman, Bart D. *The New Testament: A Historical Introduction to the Early Christian Writings.* 5th edition. New York: Oxford University Press, 2012.

Eisenbaum, Paula. "Paul as the New Abraham." In *Paul and Politics: Ekklesia, Israel, Imperium, Interpretation,* edited by Richard Horsley, 130–45. Harrisburg: Trinity International, 2000.

Elliott, Neil. *The Arrogance of Nations: Reading Romans in the Shadow of Empire.* Minneapolis: Fortress Press, 2008.

Ellis, Marc. *Practicing Exile: The Religious Odyssey of an American Jew.* Minneapolis: Fortress Press, 2002.

Epple, Angelika, and Angelika Schaser. "Multiple Histories? Changing Perspectives on Modern Historiography." In *Gendering Historiography beyond National Canons,* edited by Angelika Epple and Angelika Schaser, 7–23. Frankfurt: Campus, 2009.

Fanon, Frantz. *Black Skin, White Masks.* Translated by Charles Lam Markmann. New York: Grove, 1967.

Fehribach, Adeline. *The Women in the Life of the Bridegroom: A Feminist Historical-Literary Analysis of the Female Characters in the Fourth Gospel.* Collegeville: Liturgical, 1998.

Felder, Cain Hope. "Cultural Ideology, Afrocentrism, and Biblical Interpretation." In *Black Theology: A Documentary History,* volume 2, *1980–1992,* edited by James H. Cone and Gayraud Wilmore, 184–95. 2 vols. Maryknoll: Orbis, 1993.

______, ed. *Edith and Winnifred Eaton: Chinatown Missions and Japanese Romances.* Urbana: University of Illinois Press, 2002.

______, ed. *Stony the Road We Trod: African American Biblical Interpretation.* Minneapolis: Fortress Press, 1991.

______. *Troubling Biblical Waters: Race, Class, and Family.* Maryknoll: Orbis, 1989.

Ferens, Dominika 2002. *Edith and Winnifred Eaton: Chinatown Missions and Japanese Romances*. Urbana: University of Illinois Press.

Fernandez, Eleazar S. *Reimagining the Human: Theological Anthropology in Response to Systemic Evil*. Saint Louis: Chalice, 2004.

Fernandez, Eleazar S., and Fernando F. Segovia, eds. *A Dream Unfinished: Theological Reflections on America from the Margins*. Maryknoll: Orbis, 2001.

Fiensy, David A. "The Roman Empire and Asia Minor." In *The Face of New Testament Studies: A Survey of Recent Research*, edited by Scot McKnight and Grant R. Osborne, 48–50. Grand Rapids: Baker Academic, 2004.

Ford, Richard Thompson. *The Race Card: How Bluffing about Bias Makes Race Relations Worse*. New York: Farrar, 2008.

Foskett, Mary F. "The Accidents of Being and the Politics of Identity: Biblical Images of Adoption and Asian Adoptees in America." *Semeia* 90/91 (2002): 135–44.

______. "Obscure Beginnings: Lessons from the Study of Christian Origins." In *Ways of Being, Ways of Reading: Asian American Biblical Interpretation*, edited by Mary Foskett and Jeffrey Kah-Jin Kuan eds., 178–91. Saint Louis: Chalice, 2006.

Foskett, Mary F. and Jeffrey Kah-Jin Kuan, eds. *Ways of Being, Ways of Reading: Asian American Biblical Interpretation*. Saint Louis: Chalice, 2006.

Foskett, Reginald, ed. *The Zambezi Journal and Letters of Dr. John Kirk, 1853–63*, vol. 1. Edinburgh: Oliver & Boyd, 1965.

Foucault, Michel. *Discipline and Punish: the Birth of Prison*. Translated by Alan Sheridan. New York: Random, 1977.

______. *Power/Knowledge: Selected Interviews and Other Writings 1972–1977*. Edited by Colin Gordon, Leo Marshall, John Mepham, and Kate Sopher. New York: Pantheon, 1980.

Foucault, Michel, and Paul Rabinow, eds. *The Foucault Reader*. New York: Pantheon, 1984.

Freeman, Elizabeth. *Time Binds: Queer Temporalities, Queer Histories*. Durham: Duke University Press, 2010.

Freud, Sigmund. *The Question of Lay Analysis (The Standard Edition)*. New York: Norton, 1926.

Freyne, Sean. "Vilifying the Other and Defining the Self: Matthew's and John's Anti-Jewish Polemic in Focus." In *"To See Ourselves as Others See Us": Christians, Jews, and "Others" in Late Antiquity*, edited by Jacob Neusner and Ernest S. Frerichs. Chico: Scholars, 1985.

Friedman, Susan Stanford. "Location Feminism: Gender, Cultural Geographies, and Geopolitical Literacy." In *Feminist Locations: Global and Local, Theory and Practice*, edited by Marianne Dekoven, 13–36. New Brunswick: Rutgers University Press, 2001.

Friesen, Steven J. "Paul and Economics: The Jerusalem Collection as an Alternative to Patronage." In *Paul Unbound: Other Perspectives on the Apostle*, edited by Mark D. Given, 27–54. Peabody: Hendrickson, 2010.

E. Fuchs and B. Stuchtey, ed. *Across Cultural Borders: Historiography in Global Perspective*. Oxford: Rowman & Littlefield, 2002.

Fulkerson, Mary McClintock. "Church Documents on Human Sexuality and the Authority of Scripture." *Interpretation* 49 (1995): 46–58.

Gilhus, Ingvild Saelid. *Animals, gods and Humans: Changing Attitudes to Animals in Greek, Roman and Early Christian Ideas*. London: Routledge, 2006.

Given, Mark D., ed. *Paul Unbound: Other Perspectives on the Apostle*. Peabody: Hendrickson, 2010.

González, Justo L. *Santa Biblia: The Bible through Hispanic Eyes*. Nashville: Abingdon, 1996.

Gruen, Erich S. *Rethinking the Other in Antiquity*. Princeton: Princeton University Press, 2011.

Guardiola-Sáenz, Leticia A. "Borderless Women and Borderless Texts: A Cultural Reading of Matthew 15:21-28." *Semeia* 78 (1997): 69–81.

Guijarro, Santiago. "Cultural Memory and Group Identity in Q." *Biblical Theology Bulletin* 37 (2007): 92.

Gutiérrez, Gustavo. *A Theology of Liberation: History, Politics, and Salvation*. Maryknoll: Orbis, 1973.

_____. *A Theology of Liberation: History, Politics, and Salvation*. Translated by Sister Caridad Inda and John Eagleson. Maryknoll: Orbis, 1997.

Hagedorn, Anselm C., Zeba A. Crook, and Eric Steward, eds. *In Other Words: Essays on Social Science Methods and the New Testament in Honor of Jerome H. Neyrey*. Sheffield: Sheffield Phoenix, 2007.

Halberstam, Judith. *In a Queer Time and Place: Transgender Bodies, Subcultural Lives*. New York: New York University Press, 2005.

Hall, Jonathan M. *Ethnic Identity in Greek Antiquity*. New York: Cambridge University Press, 1997.

Hall, Stuart, editor. *Representation: Cultural Representation and Signifying Practices*. London: Sage, 2011.

Halley, Janet and Andrew Parker. *After Sex? On Writing Since Queer Theory*. Durham: Duke University Press, 2010.

Hardt, Michael and Antonio Negri. *Empire*. Cambridge: Harvard University Press, 2000.

______. *Multitude: War and Democracy in the Age of Empires*. New York: Penguin, 2004.

Harrill, J. Albert. *Slaves in the New Testament: Literary, Social, and Moral Dimensions*. Minneapolis: Fortress Press, 2006.

Harris, Stephen L. *The New Testament: A Student's Introduction*. 7th edition. New York: McGraw-Hill, 2012.

Hayes, John H., and Carl R. Holladay. *Biblical Exegesis: A Beginner's Handbook*, rev. ed. Atlanta: John Knox, 1987.

Haynes, Stephen R. *Noah's Curse: The Biblical Justification of American Slavery*. New York: Oxford University Press, 2002.

Hegel, G. W. F. *The Philosopher of History*. Translated by J. Jibree. New York: Dover, 1956.

Heschel, Susannah. *The Aryan Jesus: Christian Theologians and the Bible in Nazi Germany*. Princeton: Princeton University Press, 2008.

Hess, Mary E. "The Bible and Popular Culture: Engaging Sacred Text in a World of Others." In *New Paradigms for Bible Study: the Bible in the Third Millenium*, edited by Robert M. Fowler, Edith V. Blumhofer, and Fernando F. Segovia, 209–26. New York: T&T Clark, 2004.

Hiebert, Theodore. "The Tower of the Babel and the Origin of the World's Cultures." *JBL* 126 (2007): 29–58.

Hodge, Carolyn Johnson. *If Sons, Then Heirs: A Study of Kinship and Ethnicity in the Letters of Paul*. New York: Oxford University, 2007.

Hornsby, Teresa J. and Ken Stone, eds. *Bible Trouble: Queer Reading at the Boundaries of Biblical Scholarship*. Atlanta: Society of Biblical Literature, 2011.

Horsley, Richard A. "Feminist Scholarship and Postcolonial Criticism: Subverting Imperial Discourse and Reclaiming Submerged Histories." In *Walk in the Ways of Wisdom: Essays in Honor of Elisabeth Schüssler Fiorenza*, edited by Shelly Matthews, Cynthia Briggs Kittredge, and Melanie Johnson-Debaufre, 297–317. Harrisburg: Trinity International, 2003.

______, ed. *In the Shadow of Empire: Reclaiming the Bible as a History of Faithful Resistance*. Louisville: Westminster John Knox, 2008.

______. *Jesus and Empire: The Kingdom of God and the New World Disorder*. Minneapolis: Fortress Press, 2002.

______, ed. *Paul and Empire: Religion and Power in Roman Imperial Society*. Harrisburg: Trinity International, 1997.

_____, ed. *Paul and Politics: Ekklesia, Israel, Imperium, Interpretation.* Harrisburg: Trinity International, 2000.

_____, ed. *Paul and the Roman Imperial Order.* Harrisburg: Trinity International, 2004.

_____. "Submerged Biblical Histories and Imperial Biblical Studies." In *The Postcolonial Bible*, edited by R. S. Sugirtharajah. Sheffield: Sheffield Academic, 1998.

Howard-Brook, Wes, and Anthony Gwyther. *Unveiling Empire: Reading Revelation Then and Now.* Bible and Liberation. Maryknoll: Orbis, 1999.

Huggan, Graham, and Helen Tiffin. *Postcolonialism Ecocriticism: Literature, Animals, and Environment.* New York: Routledge, 2010.

Humphries-Brooks, Stephenson. "The Canaanite Woman in Matthew." In *The Feminist Companion to Matthew*, edited by Amy-Jill Levine with Marianne Blickenstaff. Sheffield: Sheffield Academic, 2001.

Isasi-Díaz, Ada María, and Fernando F. Segovia, editors. *Hispanic/Latino Theology: Challenge and Promise.* Minneapolis: Fortress Press, 1996.

Jennings, Willie James. *The Christian Imagination: Theology and the Origins of Race.* New Haven: Yale University Press, 2010.

Jentleson, Bruce W. "Accepting Limits: How to Adapt to a Copernican World." *Democracy: A Journal of Ideas* 23 (Winter 2003).

Jocz, Jacób. *The Jewish People and Jesus Christ: A Study in the Controversy between Church and Synagogue.* London: SPCK, 1954.

Johnson, Elizabeth A. *She Who Is: The Mystery of God in Feminist Theological Discourse.* New York: Crossroad, 1998.

Johnson, Sylverster A. *"The Bible, Slavery, and the Problem of Slavery."* In *Beyond Slavery: Overcoming Its Religious and Sexual Legacies*, edited by Bernadette Brooten, 231–48. New York: Palgrave, 2010.

Johnson-DeBaufre, Melanie, and Laura S. Nasrallah. "Beyond the Heroic Paul: Toward a Feminist and Decolonizing Approach to the Letters of Paul." In *The Colonized Apostle: Paul through Postcolonial Eyes*, edited by Christopher D. Stanley, 161–67. Minneapolis: Fortress Press, 2011.

Jones, Amos, Jr. *Paul's Message of Freedom: What Does It Mean to the Black Church?* Valley Forge: Judson, 1984.

Jordan, Clarence. *The Cotton Patch Version of Hebrews and the General Epistles.* New York: Association, 1973.

_____. *The Cotton Patch Version of Luke and Acts: Jesus' Doings and the Happenings.* New York: Association, 1969.

______. *The Cotton Patch Version of Matthew and John.* New York: Association, 1970.

______. *The Cotton Patch Version of Paul's Epistles.* New York: Association, 1968.

Jordan, Mark D. *The Ethics of Sex.* Oxford: Blackwell, 2002.

Kelley, Shawn. *Racializing Jesus: Race, Ideology, and the Formation of Modern Biblical Scholarship.* London: Routledge, 2006.

Key, Tom, Russell Treyz, and Harry Chapin. *Cotton Patch Gospel: A Toe-Tapping Full-Length Musical.* Woodstock: Dramatic, 1983.

Kim, Chan-Hie. "Reading the Cornelius Story from an Asian Immigrant Perspective." In *Reading from This Place*, vol. 1, *Social Location and Biblical Interpretation in the United States*, edited by Fernando F. Segovia and Mary Ann Tolbert, 165–74. Minneapolis: Fortress Press, 1995.

Kirk, Alan. "Social and Cultural Memory." In *Memory, Tradition, and Text: Uses of the Past in Early Christianity*, edited by Alan Kirk and Tom Thatcher, 1–24. Semeia Studies 52. Atlanta: Society of Biblical Literature, 2005.

Kittredge, Cynthia Briggs. "Biblical Studies for Ministry: Critical and Faithful Interpretation of Scripture in an Either/Or World." In *Transforming Graduate Biblical Education: Ethos and Discipline*, edited by Elisabeth Schüssler Fiorenza and Kent Harold Richards, 293–306. Atlanta: Society of Biblical Literature, 2010.

Koosed, Jennifer. *The Bible and the Posthuman.* Semeia. Atlanta: Society of Biblical Literature, forthcoming.

Krause, Deborah. "Paul and Women: Telling Women to Shut Up Is More Complicated Than You Might Think." In *Paul Unbound: Other Perspectives on the Apostle*, edited by Mark D. Given, 161–74. Peabody: Hendrickson, 2010.

Kwok, Pui-lan. *Discovering the Bible in the Non-Biblical World.* Maryknoll: Orbis, 1995.

______. "Jesus/the Native: Biblical Studies from a Postcolonial Perspective." In *Teaching the Bible: The Discourses and Politics of Biblical Pedagogy*, edited by Fernando F. Segovia and Mary Ann Tolbert, 69–85. Maryknoll: Orbis, 1998.

Lategan, Bernard C. "History and Reality in the Interpretation of Biblical Texts." In *Konstruktion von Wirklichkeit: Beiträge aus geschichtstheoretischer, philosophischer und theologischer Perspektive*, edited by J. Schröter and A. Eddelbüttel. Berlin: de Gruyter, 2004.

Lawrence, Louise J. "Crumb Trails and Puppy-Dog Tales: Reading Afterlives of a Canaanite Woman." In *From the Margins 2: Women of the New Testament and Their Afterlives*, edited by Christine E. Joynes and Christopher C. Rowland, 262–78. The Bible in the Modern World 27. Sheffield: Sheffield Phoenix, 2009.

Leander, Hans. *Discourses of Empire: The Gospel of Mark from a Postcolonial Perspective*. Göteburg: University of Gothenburg, 2011.

Leonard, Bill J. "Biblicists, but not Always Biblical? Revisiting Baptist Hermeneutics." In *The Challenge of Being Baptist: Owning a Scandalous Past and an Uncertain Future*, 53–74. Waco: Baylor University Press, 2010.

Leonardo, Zeus. "The Souls of White Folk: Critical Pedagogy, Whiteness Studies, and Globalization Discourse." *Race Ethnicity and Education* 5 (2002): 29–50.

Levine, Amy-Jill. *The Misunderstood Jew: The Church and the Scandal of the Jewish Jesus*. San Francisco: HarperSanFrancisco, 2006.

Lieu, Judith M. *Christian Identity in the Jewish and Graeco-roman World*. Oxford: Oxford University Press, 2004.

Liew, Tat-Siong Benny. "Acts," In *Global Bible Commentary*, edited by Daniel Patte, 419–28. Nashville: Abingdon, 2004.

______. "Margins and (Cutting-)Edges: On the (Il)legitimacy and Intersections of Race, Ethnicity, and (Post)colonialism." In *Postcolonial Biblical Criticism: Interdisciplinary Intersections*, edited by Stephen D. Moore and Fernando F. Segovia, 114–65. New York: T&T Clark, 2005.

______. "More Than Personal Encounters: Identity, Community, and Interpretation." *Union Seminary Quarterly Review* 56 (2002): 41–44.

______. "Queering Closets and Perverting Desires: Cross-Examining John's Engendering and Transgendering Word Across Different Worlds." In *They Were All Together in One Place? Toward Minority Biblical Criticism*, edited by Bailey, Liew, and Segovia, 251–88. Society of Biblical Literature Semeia Studies 57. Atlanta: Society of Biblical Literature, 2009.

______. *What Is Asian American Biblical Hermeneutics? Reading the New Testament*. Honolulu: University of Hawaii Press, 2008.

Liew, Tat-siong Benny and Vincent L. Wimbush. "Contact Zones and Zoning Contexts: From the Los Angeles 'Riot' to a New York Symposium." *Union Seminary Quarterly Review* 56 (2002): 21–40.

Ling, Amy and Annette White-Parks, eds. *Mrs. Spring Fragrance and Other Writings*. Urbana: University of Illinois Press, 1995.

Lopez, Davina C. *Apostle to the Conquered: Reimagining Paul's Mission*. Minneapolis: Fortress, 2008.

______. "Visualizing Significant Otherness: Reimagining Paul(ine Studies) through Hybrid Lenses." In *The Colonized Apostle: Paul through Postcolonial Eyes*, edited by C. D. Stanley, 74–94. Paul in Critical Contexts. Minneapolis: Fortress Press, 2011.

Lowe, Lisa. "The International within the National: American Studies and Asian American Critique." *Cultural Critique* 40 (1998): 29–47.

______. "The Intimacies of Four Continents." In *Haunted by Empire: Geographies of Intimacy in North American History*, edited by Ann Laura Stoler, 191–212. Durham: Duke University Press, 2006.

Lowery, Rick. *Sabbath and Jubilee.* Saint Louis: Chalice, 2000.

Lozada, Francisco, Jr. "Social Location and Johannine Scholarship: Looking Ahead." In *New Currents through John: A Global Perspective*, edited by Francisco Lozada Jr. and Tom Thatcher, 183–97. Atlanta: Society of Biblical Literature, 2006.

Lozada, Francisco, Jr., and Tom Thatcher, eds. *New Currents through John: A Global Perspective.* Atlanta: Society of Biblical Literature, 2006.

Luz, Ulrich. *Matthew 8–20.* Hermeneia. Minneapolis: Fortress Press, 2001.

Malina, Bruce J., and Jerome H. Neyrey. *Portraits of Paul: An Archaeology of Ancient Personality.* Louisville: Westminster John Knox, 1996.

Marchal, Joseph A. "Military Images in Philippians 1–2: A Feminist Analysis of the Rhetorics of Scholarship, Philippians, and Current Contexts," In *Her Master's Tools? Feminist and Postcolonial Engagements of Historical-Critical Discourse*, edited by Todd Penner and Caroline Vander Stichele, 265–86. Atlanta: Society of Biblical Literature, 2005.

______. *The Politics of Heaven: Women, Gender, and Empire in the Study of Paul.* Minneapolis: Fortress Press, 2008.

Martin, Clarice J. "A Chamberlain's Journey and the Challenges of Interpretation for Liberation." *Semeia* 47 (1989): 105–35.

______. "The Haustafeln (Household Codes) in African American Biblical Interpretation: "Free Slaves and Subordinate Women."" In *Stony the Road We Trod: African American Biblical Interpretation*, edited by Cain Hope Felder, 206–31. Minneapolis: Fortress Press, 1991.

______. "'Somebody Done Hoodoo'd the Hoodoo Man': Language, Power, Resistance, and the Effective History of Pauline Texts in American Slavery." *Semeia* 83/84 (1998): 203–33.

Martyn, J. Louis. "Glimpses into the History of the Johannine Community" In *The Gospel of John in Christian History*, 90–121. Essays for Interpretation. New York: Paulist, 1978.

______. *History and Theology in the Fourth Gospel.* 3rd edition. Louisville: Westminster John Knox, 2003.

Mason, Steve. "Jews, Judeans, Judaizing, Judaism: Problems of Categorization in Ancient History." *Journal for the Study of Judaism* 38 (2007): 457–512.

Matlock, Barry. "Almost Cultural Studies: Reflection on the 'New Perspective' on Paul." In *Biblical Studies/Cultural Studies*, edited by J. Cheryl Exum and Stephen D. Moore, 433–59. Sheffield: Sheffield Academic, 1998.

McIntyre, Alice. *Making Meaning of Whiteness: Exploring Racial Identity with White Teachers.* Albany: SUNY Press, 1997.

Meeks, Wayne A. *The First Urban Christians: The Social World of the Apostle Paul.* New Haven: Yale University Press, 1983.

______. "The Man from Heaven in Johannine Sectarianism." *Journal of Biblical Literature* 19 (1972): 44–72.

______. *The Writings of Saint Paul.* Norton Critical Edition. New York: Norton, 1972.

Mendels, Doron. *Identity, Religion, and Historiography: Studies in Hellenistic History.* Journal for the Study of the Pseudoepigraphica Supplement Series 24. Sheffield: Sheffield Academic, 1998.

______. *Memory in Jewish, Pagan, and Christian Societies of the Graeco-Roman World.* Library of the Second Temple Studies 45. New York: T&T Clark, 2004.

Mgadla, Part Themba, and Stephen C. Volz, eds. *Words of Batswana: Letters to Mahoka a Becwana 1883–1896.* Translated by P. Mgadla and S. C. Volz. Vlaeburg: van Riebeeck Society, 2006.

Mickelson, A. Berkeley. *Interpreting the Bible.* Grand Rapids: Eerdmans, 1963.

Moffat, Robert. "Africa, or the Gospel of Light Shining in the Midst of Heathen Darkness." London: John Snox, 1840.

Moore, Stephen D. *Empire and Apocalypse: Postcolonialism and the New Testament.* Sheffield: Sheffield Phoenix, 2006.

______. *God's Beauy Parlor and Other Queer Spaces in and around the Bible.* Contraversions: Jews and other Differences. Stanford: Stanford University Press, 2001.

______. "Questions of Biblical Ambivalence and Authority under a Tree Outside Delhi; Or, the Postcolonial and the Postmodern." In *Postcolonial Biblical Criticism: Interdisciplinary Intersections*, edited by Stephen D. Moore and Fernando F. Segovia, 79–96. New York: T&T Clark, 2005.

______. "'The World Empire Has Become the Empire of Our Lord and His Messiah': Representing Empire in Revelation." In *Empire and Apocalypse:*

Postcolonialism and the New Testament, edited by Stephen D. Moore, 97–121. Sheffield: Sheffield Phoenix, 2006.

______. "Why There Are No Humans or Animals in the Gospel of Mark." In *Mark as Story: Retrospect and Prospect*, edited by Kelly R. Iverson and Christopher W. Skinner, 71–94. Atlanta: Society of Biblical Literature, 2011.

Moore, Stephen D., and Fernando F. Segovia, eds. *Postcolonial Biblical Criticism: Interdisciplinary Intersections*. The Bible and Postcolonialism. New York: T&T Clark, 2007.

Moore, Stephen D., and Yvonne Sherwood. "Biblical Studies 'after' Theory: Onward Toward the Past," in three parts: "Part One: After 'after Theory', and Other Apocalyptic Conceits," *BibInt* 18 (2010): 1–27; "Part Two: The Secret Vices of the Biblical God," *BibInt* 18 (2010): 87–113; and "Part Three: Theory in the First and Second Waves," *BibInt* 18 (2010): 191–225.

______. *The Invention of the Biblical Scholar: A Critical Manifesto*. Minneapolis: Fortress Press, 2011.

Morrison, Toni. *Playing in the Dark: Whiteness and the Literary Imagination*. New York: Vintage, 1993.

Moxnes, Halvor, ed. *Constructing Early Christian Families: Family as Social Reality and Metaphor*. New York: Routledge, 1997.

Moy, Russell G. "Resident Aliens of the Diaspora: 1 Peter and Chinese Protestants in San Francisco." *Semeia* 90/91 (2002): 52–68.

Mudimbe, V. Y. *The Invention of Africa: Gnosis, Philosophy and the Order of Knowledge*. Bloomington: Indiana University Press, 1988.

Myers, Ched. *Say to This Mountain: Mark's Story of Discipleship*. Maryknoll: Orbis, 1996.

Myrdal, Gunnar. *Objectivity in Social Research*. Middleton: Wesleyan University Press, 1969.

Nanos, Mark D. "The Inter- and Intra-Jewish Contexts of Paul and Galatians." In *Paul and Politics: Ekklesia, Israel, Imperium, and Interpretation*, edited by Richard Horsley, 146–59. Harrisburg: Trinity International, 2000.

Nasrallah, Laura, and Elisabeth Schüssler Fiorenza, eds. *Prejudice and Christian Beginnings: Investigating Race, Gender, and Ethnicity in Early Christian Studies*. Minneapolis: Fortress Press, 2009.

Nelavala, Surekha. *Liberation beyond Borders: Dalit Feminist Hermeneutics and Four Gospel Women*. Saarbrücken: Lambert Academic, 2009.

Neufeld, Deitmar, and Richard E. DeMaris, eds. *Understanding the Social World of the New Testament*. London: Routledge, 2010.

Newsom, Carol A., and Sharon H. Ringe, eds. *Women's Bible Commentary*. Expanded edition. Louisville: Westminster John Knox, 1998.

O'Day, Gail. R. "John." In *Women's Bible Commentary. Expanded Edition with Apocrypha*, edited by Carol A. Newsom and Sharon H. Ringe, 381–93. Louisville: Westminster John Knox, 1998.

Page, Hugh, ed. *The Africana Bible: Reading Israel's Scriptures*. Minneapolis: Fortress Press, 2010.

Pasewark, Kyle. *A Theology of Power: Being beyond Domination*. Minneapolis: Fortress Press, 1993.

Peng, Wang. "On Paul's Prohibitions of Women in 1 Corinthians." *Chinese Theological Review* 15 (2001): 92–93.

Perkins, Judith. *Roman Imperial Identities in the Early Christian Era*. Routledge Monographs in Classical Studies. London: Routledge, 2008.

Perkinson, Jim. "A Canaanite Word in the Logos of Christ; or the Difference the Syro-Phoenician Woman Makes to Jesus." *Semeia* 75 (1996): 61–86.

Pervo, Richard. *Acts: A Commentary*. Hermeneia. Minneapolis: Fortress, 2009.

______. *Profit with Delight: The Literary Genre of the Acts of the Apostles*. Philadelphia: Fortress Press, 1987.

Petralla, Ivan, ed. *Latin American Liberation Theology: The Next Generation*. Maryknoll: Orbis, 2005.

Phillips, Thomas E. *Paul, His Letters, and Acts*. Peabody: Hendrickson, 2009.

Pippin, Tina, ed. *Ideological Criticism of Biblical Texts*. Semeia 59. Atlanta: Society of Biblical Literature, 1992

______. "Ideology, Ideological Criticism and the Bible." *Currents in Research: Biblical Studies*, vol. 4. (1996): 60.

Polaski, Sandra Hack. *A Feminist Companion to Paul*. Saint Louis: Chalice. 2005.

Powery, Emerson. "The Gospel of Mark." In *True to Our Native Land: An African American New Testament Commentary*, edited by Brian Blount, Clarice Martin, and Emerson Power, 121–57. Minneapolis: Fortress Press, 2007.

Pratt, Mary Louise. *Imperial Eyes: Travel Writing and Transculturation*. London: Routledge, 1992.

Prior, Michael. *The Bible and Colonialism: A Moral Critique*. Biblical Seminar. Sheffield: Sheffield Academic, 1999.

Punt, Jeremy. "Identity, Memory and Scriptural Warrant: Arguing Paul's Case." *Journal of Early Christian History* (forthcoming).

Raboteau, Albert. *A Fire in the Bones: Reflections on African-American Religious History*. Boston: Beacon, 1995.

Reinhartz, Adele. "The Johannine Community and Its Jewish Neighbors: A Reappraisal." In *What Is John?*, vol. 2, *Literary and Social Readings of the Fourth Gospel*. Society of Biblical Literature Symposium Series 7, edited by R. Alan Culpepper and Fernando F. Segovia, 111–38. Atlanta: Scholars.

Richardson, Marilyn, ed. *Maria Stewart: America's First Black Woman Political Writer*. Bloomington: Indiana University, 1987.

Roach, Joseph. *Cities of the Dead: Circum-Atlantic Performance*. New York: Columbia University Press, 1996.

Roetzel, Calvin J. *Paul: The Man and the Myth*. Minneapolis: Fortress Press, 1999.

Romanow, Rebecca Fine. *The Postcolonial Body in Queer Space and Time*. Newcastle upon Tyne: Cambridge Scholars, 2008.

Rothschild, Clare. *Luke-Acts and the Rhetoric of History: An Investigation of Early Christian Historiography*. Tübingen: Mohr Siebeck, 2004.

Rupert, Greenberry G. *The Yellow Peril: Or, The Orient Vs. the Occident as Viewed by Modern Statesmen and Ancient Prophets*. Britton: Union, 1911.

Rüsen, Jörn. "Comparing Cultures in Intercultural Communications." In *Across Cultural Borders: Historiography in Global Perspective*, edited by E. Fuchs and B. Stuchtey, 338–41. Oxford: Rowman & Littlefield, 2002.

Sadler, Rodney. "The Place and Role of Africa and African Imagery in the Bible." In *True to Our Native Land: An African American Commentary on the New Testament*, edited by Brian Blount, Clarice Martin, Cain Felder, and Emery Powery, 23–30. Minneapolis: Fortress Press 2007.

Sadler, Rodney, and Emerson Powery. "Reading against Jesus: Nineteenth-Century African Americans' View of Sabbath Law," http://www.sblsite.org/publications/article.aspx?articleId=403, June 2005.

Said, Edward W. *Orientalism*. New York: Vintage, 1979.

Saillant, John. "Origins of African American Biblical Hermeneutics in Eighteenth-Century Black Opposition to the Slave Trade and Slavery." In *African Americans and the Bible: Sacred Texts and Social Textures*, edited by Vincent L. Wimbush, 236–50. New York: Continuum, 2001.

Sampley, J. Paul. *Walking between the Times: Paul's Moral Reasoning*. Minneapolis: Fortress Press, 1991.

Sánchez, David A. *From Patmos to the Barrio: Subverting Imperial Myths*. Minneapolis: Fortress Press, 2008.

Sanders, E. P. *Paul and Palestinian Judaism: A Comparison of Patterns of Religion*. Minneapolis: Fortress Press, 1977.

Scott, James C. *Domination and the Arts of Resistance: Hidden Transcripts*. New Haven: Yale University, 1990.

Schüssler Fiorenza, Elisabeth. "1 Peter." In *A Postcolonial Commentary on the New Testament Writings*, edited by Fernando F. Segovia and R. S. Sugirtharajah, 380–403. New York: Continuum, 2007.

______. *Bread Not Stone: The Challenge of Feminist Biblical Interpretation*. Boston: Beacon, 1984.

______. *The Power of the Word: Scripture and the Rhetoric of Empire*. Minneapolis: Fortress Press, 2007.

______. "Remembering the Past in Creating the Future: Historical-Critical Scholarship and Feminist Interpretation," In *Feminist Perspectives on Biblical Scholarship*, edited by Adela Yarbro Collins, 46–63. SBL Biblical Scholarship in America 10. Chico: Scholars, 1985.

______. "Rethinking the Educational Practics of Biblical Doctoral Studies." In *Transforming Graduate Biblical Education: Ethos and Discipline*, edited by Elizabeth Schüssler Fiorenza and Kent Richards, 373–93. Atlanta: Society of Biblical Literature, 2010.

______. *Rhetoric and Ethic: The Politics of Biblical Studies*. Minneapolis: Fortress Press, 1999.

______, ed. *Searching the Scriptures*, vol. 1, *A Feminist Introduction*. New York: Crossroad, 1993.

______, ed. *Searching the Scriptures*, vol. 2, *A Feminist Commentary*. New York: Crossroad, 1994.

______. "Transforming Graduate Biblical Education: Ethos and Discipline." In *Transforming Graduate Biblical Education: Ethos and Discipline*, edited by Elisabeth Schüssler Fiorenza and Kent Harold Richards, 1–16. Atlanta: Society of Biblical Literature, 2010.

______. "Transforming the Margin—Claiming Common Grounds: Charting a Different Paradigm of Biblical Studies." In *Still at the Margins: Biblical Scholarship Fifteen Years after Voices from the Margins*, edited by R. S. Sugarthirajah, 22–39. London: Continuum, 2008.

Schüssler Fiorenza, Elisabeth and Kent Harold Richards, eds. *Transforming Graduate Biblical Education: Ethos and Discipline*. Atlanta: Society of Biblical Literature, 2010.

Schwartz, Barry. *Abraham Lincoln and the Forge of National Memory*. Chicago: University of Chicago, 2000.

Schwartz, Regina. *The Curse of Cain: The Violent Legacy of Monotheism*. Chicago: University of Chicago Press, 1997.

Schweitzer, Albert. *The Quest of the Historical Jesus*, edited by John Bowden. Fortress Classics in Biblical Studies. Minneapolis: Fortress Press, 2001.

Sechrest, Love L. *A Former Jew: Paul and the Dialectics of Race.* New York: T&T Clark, 2009.

Sedgwick, Kosofsky. *Tendencies.* Durham: Duke University Press, 1993.

Segovia, Fernando F. "The Bible as Text in Cultures: An Introduction." In *The People's Bible*, edited by Curtiss P. DeYoung, Leticia Guardiola-Sáenz, Wilda Gafney, George Tinker, and Frank Yamada, 25–29. Minneapolis: Fortress Press, 2008.

______. "Biblical Criticism and Postcolonial Studies: Toward a Postcolonial Optic." In *The Postcolonial Bible*, edited by R. S. Sugirtharajah, 51–63. Sheffield: Sheffield Academic, 1998.

______. "Cultural Studies and Contemporary Biblical Criticism: Ideological Criticism as Mode of Discourse." In *Reading from This Place*, vol. 2, *Social Location and Biblical Interpretation in Global Perspective*, edited by Fernando Segovia and Mary Ann Tolbert 1–17. Minneapolis: Fortress Press, 1995.

______. *Decolonizing Biblical Studies: A View from the Margins.* Maryknoll: Orbis, 2000.

______, ed. *Discipleship in the New Testament.* Philadelphia: Fortress Press, 1985.

______. *The Farewell of the Word: The Johannine Call to Abide.* Minneapolis: Fortress Press, 1991.

______. "Inclusion and Exclusion in John 17: An Intercultural Reading." In *What Is John?*, vol. 2, *Literary and Social Readings of the Fourth Gospel.* Society of Biblical Literature Symposium Series 7, edited by R. Alan Culpepper and Fernando F. Segovia, 183–209. Atlanta: Scholars.

______, ed. *Interpreting beyond Borders.* Bible and Postcolonialism. Sheffield: Sheffield Academic, 2000.

______. "Johannine Studies and the Geopolitical: Reflections upon Absence and Irruption." In *What We Have Heard from the Beginning: The Past, Present, and Future of Johannine Studies*, edited by Tom Thatcher, 284. Waco: Baylor University Press, 2007.

______. "John 1:1–18 as Entrée into Johannine Reality: Representation and Ramifications." In *Word, Theology, and Community in John*, edited by John Painter, R. Alan Culpepper, and Fernando F. Segovia, 33–64. Saint Louis: Chalice, 2002.

______. "The Journey(s) of the Word: A Reading of the Plot of the Fourth Gospel," *Semeia* 53 (1991): 23–54.

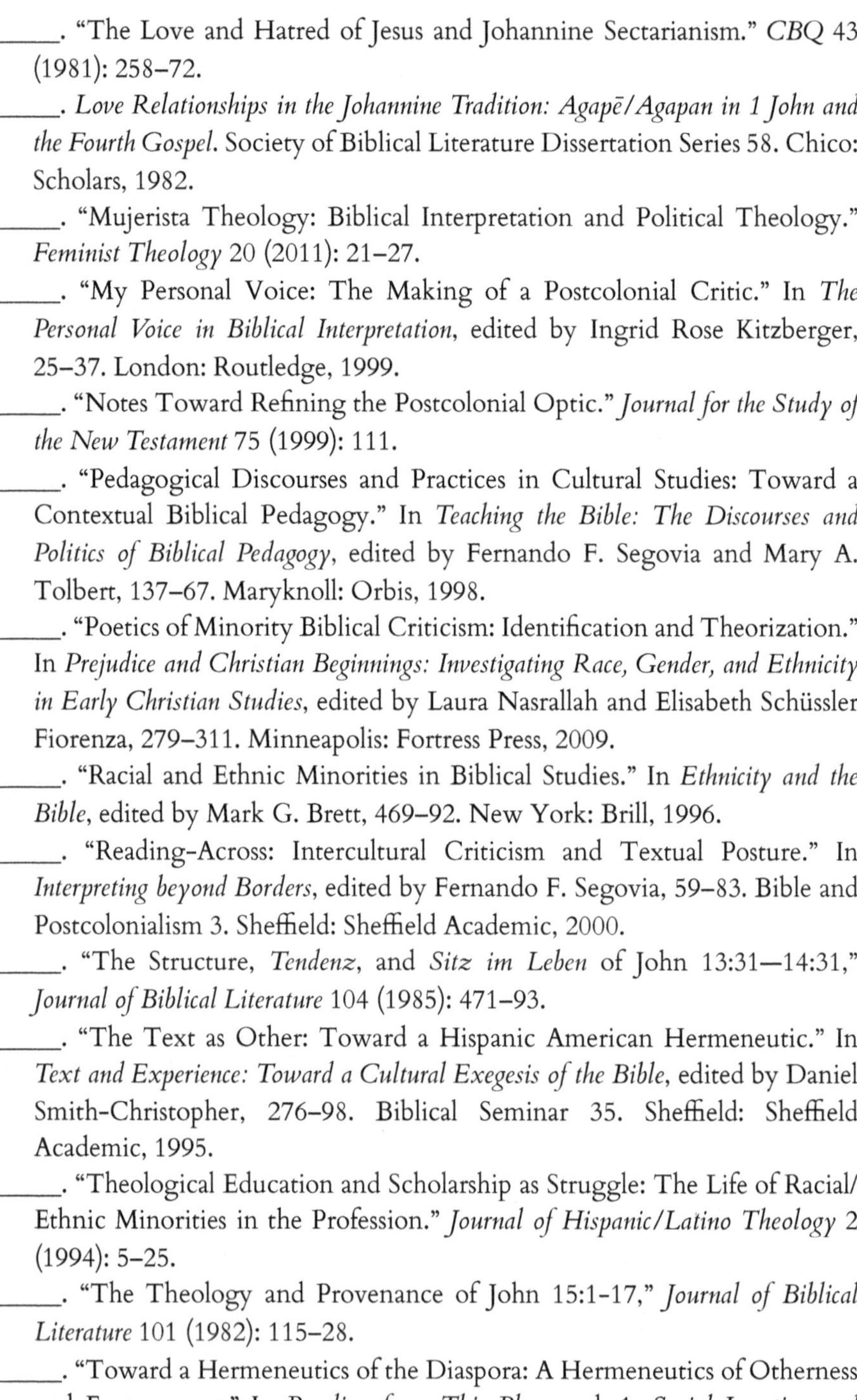

______. "The Love and Hatred of Jesus and Johannine Sectarianism." *CBQ* 43 (1981): 258–72.

______. *Love Relationships in the Johannine Tradition: Agapē/Agapan in 1 John and the Fourth Gospel.* Society of Biblical Literature Dissertation Series 58. Chico: Scholars, 1982.

______. "Mujerista Theology: Biblical Interpretation and Political Theology." *Feminist Theology* 20 (2011): 21–27.

______. "My Personal Voice: The Making of a Postcolonial Critic." In *The Personal Voice in Biblical Interpretation*, edited by Ingrid Rose Kitzberger, 25–37. London: Routledge, 1999.

______. "Notes Toward Refining the Postcolonial Optic." *Journal for the Study of the New Testament* 75 (1999): 111.

______. "Pedagogical Discourses and Practices in Cultural Studies: Toward a Contextual Biblical Pedagogy." In *Teaching the Bible: The Discourses and Politics of Biblical Pedagogy*, edited by Fernando F. Segovia and Mary A. Tolbert, 137–67. Maryknoll: Orbis, 1998.

______. "Poetics of Minority Biblical Criticism: Identification and Theorization." In *Prejudice and Christian Beginnings: Investigating Race, Gender, and Ethnicity in Early Christian Studies*, edited by Laura Nasrallah and Elisabeth Schüssler Fiorenza, 279–311. Minneapolis: Fortress Press, 2009.

______. "Racial and Ethnic Minorities in Biblical Studies." In *Ethnicity and the Bible*, edited by Mark G. Brett, 469–92. New York: Brill, 1996.

______. "Reading-Across: Intercultural Criticism and Textual Posture." In *Interpreting beyond Borders*, edited by Fernando F. Segovia, 59–83. Bible and Postcolonialism 3. Sheffield: Sheffield Academic, 2000.

______. "The Structure, *Tendenz*, and *Sitz im Leben* of John 13:31—14:31," *Journal of Biblical Literature* 104 (1985): 471–93.

______. "The Text as Other: Toward a Hispanic American Hermeneutic." In *Text and Experience: Toward a Cultural Exegesis of the Bible*, edited by Daniel Smith-Christopher, 276–98. Biblical Seminar 35. Sheffield: Sheffield Academic, 1995.

______. "Theological Education and Scholarship as Struggle: The Life of Racial/Ethnic Minorities in the Profession." *Journal of Hispanic/Latino Theology* 2 (1994): 5–25.

______. "The Theology and Provenance of John 15:1-17," *Journal of Biblical Literature* 101 (1982): 115–28.

______. "Toward a Hermeneutics of the Diaspora: A Hermeneutics of Otherness and Engagement." In *Reading from This Place*, vol. 1, *Social Location and*

Biblical Interpretation in the United States, edited by Fernando F. Segovia and Mary Ann Tolbert, 57–74. Minneapolis: Fortress Press, 1995.

______. "Toward Intercultural Criticism: A Reading Strategy from the Diaspora." In *Reading from This Place*, vol. 2, *Social Location and Biblical Interpretation in Global Perspective*, edited by Fernando Segovia and Mary Ann Tolbert, 303–30. Minneapolis: Fortress Press, 1995.

______, ed. *Toward a New Heaven and a New Earth: Essays in Honor of Elisabeth Schüssler Fiorenza*. Markyknoll: Orbis, 2003.

______. "The Tradition History of the Fourth Gospel," In *Exploring the Gospel of John: Essays in Honor of D. Moody Smith*, edited by R. Alan Culpepper and Clifton Black, 179–89. Louisville: Westminster John Knox, 1996.

Segovia, Fernando F., and R. S. Sugirtharajah, eds. *A Postcolonial Commentary on the New Testament Writings*. Bible and Postcolonialism 13. London: T&T Clark, 2009.

Segovia, Fernando F., and Mary Ann Tolbert, eds. *Reading from This Place*, vol. 1, *Social Location and Biblical Interpretation in the United States*. Minneapolis: Fortress Press, 1995.

______. *Reading from This Place*, vol. 2, *Social Location and Biblical Interpretation in Global Perspective*. Minneapolis: Fortress Press, 1995.

______. *Teaching the Bible: The Discourses and Politics of Biblical Pedagogy*. Minneapolis: Fortress Press, 2009 (1998).

Selvidge, Marla J. *The New Testament: A Timeless Book for All Peoples*. New Jersey: Prentice Hall, 1999.

Sernett, Milton, ed. *Afro-American Religious History*. Durham: Duke University, 1985.

Shih, David. "The Seduction of Origins: Sui Sin Far and the Race for Tradition." In *Form and Transformation in Asian American Literature*, edited by Zhou Xiaojing and Samina Najmi, 48–76. Seattle: University of Seattle Press, 2005.

Shih, Shu-mei. "Comparative Racialization: An Introduction." *Publications of the Modern Language Association of America* 123 (2008): 1347–62.

Siker, Jeffrey S. "Historicizing a Racialized Jesus: Case Studies in the 'Black Christ,' the 'Mestizo Christ,' and White Critique." *BibInt* 15:1 (2007): 26–53.

Smith, Abraham. "Paul and African American Biblical Interpretation." In *True to Our Native Land: An African American Commentary on the New Testament*, edited by Brian Blount, Clarice Martin, Cain Felder and Emery Powery, 31–42. Minneapolis: Fortress Press, 2007.

______. "A Prodigal Sings the Blues: The Characterization of Harriett Williams in Langston Hughes's *Not without Laughter*." In *Yet with a Steady Beat: Contemporary U.S. Afrocentric Biblical Interpretation*, edited by Randall C. Bailey, 145–58. Atlanta: Society of Biblical Literature, 2003.

______. "Putting 'Paul' Back together Again: William Wells Brown's *Clotel* and Black Abolitionist Approaches to Paul." *Semeia* 83/84 (1998): 251–62.

______. "Taking Space Seriously: The Politics of Space and the Future of Western Biblical Studies." In *Transforming Graduate Biblical Education: Ethos and Discipline*, edited by Elisabeth Schüssler Fiorenza and Kent Harold Richards, 59–92. Atlanta: Society of Biblical Literature, 2010.

______. "Unmasking the Powers: Toward a Postcolonial Analysis of 1 Thessalonians." *In Paul and the Roman Imperial Order*, edited by Richard A. Horsley. Harrisburg: Trinity International, 2004.

Smith, Alexander McCall. *The No. 1 Lady Detective Agency*. New York: Anchor, 2002.

Smith, Anna Deavere. *Talk to Me: Listening between the Lines*. New York: Random, 2000.

Smith, D. Moody. "The Contributions of J. Louis Martyn to the Understanding of the Gospel of John." In *History and Theology in the Fourth Gospel*. 3rd edition. Edited by J. Louis Martyn, 1–19. Louisville: Westminster John Knox, 2003.

Smith, Jonathan Z. "What a Difference a Difference Makes." In *"To See Ourselves as Others See Us": Christians, Jews, "Others," in Late Antiquity*, edited by J. Neusner and E. S. Frerichs, 3–48. Chico: Scholars, 1985.

Sobrino, Jon. *Christology at the Crossroads: A Latin American Approach*. Translated by John Drury. London: SCM, 1978.

Söderström, Ola. "Representation." In *Cultural Geography: A Critical Dictionary of Key Concepts*, edited by David Atkinson, Peter Jackson, David Sibley, and Neil Washbourne, 11–15. London: Tauris, 2005.

Solberg, S. E. "Sui Sin Far/Edith Eaton: First Chinese-American FictioniSaint" *MELUS* 8 (1981): 27–39.

Song, Choan-Seng. *Tell Us Our Names: Story Theology from an Asian Perspective*. Maryknoll: Orbis, 1984.

______. *Third-Eye Theology: Theology in Formation in Asian Settings*. Maryknoll: Orbis, 1979.

Spillers, Hortense J. *Black, White, and in Color: Essays on American Literature and Culture*. Chicago: University of Chicago Press, 2003.

Spivak, Gayatri Chakravorty. "Can the Subaltern Speak?" In *Marxism and the Interpretation of Culture*, edited by Cary Nelson and Larry Grossberg, 271–313. Urbana: University of Illinois Press, 1988.

Saint Clair, Raquel Annette. *Call and Consequences: A Womanist Reading of Mark*. Minneapolis: Fortress Press, 2008.

Stanley, H. M. *In Darkest Africa: Quest, Rescue, and Retreat of Emin Governor of Equitima.* Toronto: Scribner, 1890.

______. *Through the Dark Continent.* vol. 1. New York: Dove, 1975 [1877].

Steiner, Gary. "Descartes, Christianity, and Contemporary Speciesism." In *A Communion of Subjects: Animals in Religion, Science, and Ethics*, edited by Paul Waldau and Kimberly Patton, 117–31. New York: Columbia University Press, 2006.

Stendahl, Krister. "The Apostle Paul and the Introspective Conscience of the WeSaint" *Harvard Theological Review* 56 (1976): 199–215.

Stimpson, Catherine R. "Feminist Criticism." In *Redrawing the Boundaries: The Transformation of English and American Literary Studies*, edited by Stephen J. Greenblatt and Giles B. Gunn, 252. New York: Modern Language Association of America, 1992.

Stratton, Beverly J. "Ideology." In *Handbook of Postmodern Biblical Interpretation*, edited by A. K. M. Adam, 120–27. Saint Louis: Chalice, 2000.

Stuckey, Sterling. "'My Burden Lightened': Frederick Douglass, the Bible, and Slave Culture." In *African Americans and the Bible: Sacred Texts and Social Textures*, edited by Vincent L. Wimbush, 251–65. New York: Continuum, 2001.

Sugirtharajah, R. S. *The Bible and the Third World: Precolonial, Colonial, and Postcolonial Encounters.* Cambridge: Cambridge University Press, 2001.

______. "Introduction: The Margin as a Site of Creative Re-visioning." In *Voices from the Margin: Interpreting the Bible in the Third World*, edited by R. S. Sugirtharajah, 1–8. Maryknoll: Orbis, 1991.

______. *Postcolonial Reconfigurations: An Alternative Way of Reading the Bible and Doing Theology.* Saint Louis: Chalice, 2003.

______. *Troublesome Texts: The Bible in Colonial and Contemporary Culture.* Sheffield: Sheffield Academic, 2008.

______, ed. *Voices from the Margin: Interpreting the Bible in the Third World.* 2nd Edition. Maryknoll: Orbis, 1995.

Sullivan, Nikki. *A Critical Introduction to Queer Theory.* New York: New York University Press, 2003.

Sumney, Jerry L. "Paul and His Opponents: The Search." In *Paul Unbound: Other Perspectives on the Apostle*, edited by Mark D. Given, 55–70. Peabody: Hendrickson, 2010.

Tajfel, Henri. "Introduction." In *Social Identity and Intergroup Relations*, edited by Henri Tajfel. European Studies in Social Psychology. New York: Cambridge University Press, 1982.

Tan, Yak-Hwee. "The Johannine Community: Caught in 'Two Worlds.'" In *New Currents Through John: A Global Perspective*, edited by Francisco Lozada Jr. and Tom Thatcher, 167–79. Atlanta: Society of Biblical Literature, 2006.

______. *Re-presenting the Johannine Community: A Postcolonial Perspective*. New York: Peter Lang, 2008.

Tate, W. Randolph. *Biblical Interpretation: An Integrated Approach*. Revised Edition. Peabody: Hendrickson, 1997.

Thatcher, Adrian. *The Savage Text: The Use and Abuse of the Bible*. Malden: Blackwell, 2008.

Ting, K. H. "Building Up the Body in Love." In *A Chinese Contribution to Ecumenical Theology*, edited by Janice and Philip Wickeri. Geneva: WCC, 2002.

______. "Love That Loves to the End." In *A Chinese Contribution to Ecumenical Theology*, edited by Janice and Philip Wickeri. Geneva: WCC, 2002.

______. *Sowing the Gospel: Mark's World in Literary-Historical Perspective*. Minneapolis: Fortress Press, 1996.

Trible, Phyllis. *Texts of Terror: Literary-Feminist Readings of Biblical Narratives*. Overtures to Biblical Theology. Philadelphia: Fortress, 1984.

Turner, John C. "Toward a Cognitive Redefinition of the Social Group." In *Social Identity and Intergroup Relations*, edited by Henri Tajfel, 15–40. European Studies in Social Psychology. New York: Cambridge University Press, 1982.

Uregei, Yan Celené. "The Kanak Struggle for Independence." In *Pacific People Sing Out Strong*, edited by William L. Coop, 66–69. New York: Friendship, 1982.

Vena, Osvaldo D. "My Hermeneutical Journey and Daily Journey into Hermeneutics: Meaning-Making and Biblical Interpretation in the North American Diaspora." In *Interpreting Beyond Borders*, edited by Fernando F. Segovia, 84–106. Sheffield: Sheffield Academic. 2000.

Villalobos, Manuel. "Bodies *Del Otro Lado* Finding Life and Hope in the Borderland: Gloria Anzaldúa, the Ethiopian Eunuch of Acts 8:26-40, *y Yo*." In *Bible Trouble: Queer Reading at the Boundaries of Biblical Scholarship*, edited by Teresa Hornsby and Ken Stone, 191–221. Atlanta: Society of Biblical Litererature, 2011.

Wainwright, Elaine M. "Not without my Daughter: Gender and Demon Possession in Matthew 15:21-28." In *A Feminist Companion to Matthew*, edited by Amy-Jill Levine with Marianne Blickenstaff, 126–37. Sheffield: Sheffield Academic, 2001.

Walker, Alice. *In Search of Our Mothers' Gardens.* San Diego: HBJ, 1983.

Wan, Sze-kar. "Betwixt and Between: Toward a Hermeneutics of Hyphenation." In *Ways of Being, Ways of Reading: Asian American Biblical Interpretation*, edited by Mary F. Foskett and Jeffrey Kah-Jin Kuan, 137–51. Saint Louis: Chalice, 2006.

______. "The Letter to the Galatians." In *A Postcolonial Commentary on the New Testament Writings*, edited by Fernando F. Segovia and R. S. Sugirtharajah, 246–47. London: T&T Clark, 2009.

White, L. Michael, and O. Larry Yarbrough, eds. *The Social World of the First Christians: Essays in Honor of Wayne A. Meeks.* Minneapolis: Fortress Press, 1995.

White-Parks, Annette. *Sui Sin Far/Edith Maude Eaton: A Literary Biography.* Urbana: University of Illinois Press, 1995.

Williams, Delores. "Hagar in African American Biblical Appropriation." In *Hagar, Sarah, and Their Children*, edited by Phyllis Trible and Letty M. Russell, 171–84. Louisville: Westminster John Knox, 2006.

Williams, Demetrius K. *An End to This Strife: The Politics of Gender in African American Churches.* Minneapolis: Fortress Press, 2004.

______. "'Upon All Flesh': Acts 2, African Americans, and Intersectional Realities." In *They Were All Together in One Place? Toward Minority Biblical Criticism*, edited by Randall Bailey, Tat-siong Liew, and Fernando Segovia, 289–310. Atlanta: Society of Biblical Literature, 2009.

Willink, Kate. *Bringing Desegregation Home: Memories of the Struggle toward School Integration in Rural North Carolina.* Palgrave Studies in Oral History. New York: Macmillan, 2009.

Wills, Lawrence M. *Not God's People: Insiders and Outsiders in the Biblical World.* Lanham: Rowman & Littlefield, 2008.

Wimbush, Vincent L., ed. *African Americans and the Bible: Sacred Texts and Social Textures.* New York: Continuum, 2001.

______. *The Bible and African Americans.* Facets. Minneapolis: Fortress Press, 2003.

______. "Interpreters—Enslaving/Enslaved/Runagate." *Journal of Biblical Literature* 130, no.1 (2011): 5–24.

______. "'Naturally Veiled and Half Articulate': Scriptures, Modernity and the Formation of African America." In *Still at the Margins: Biblical Scholarship Fifteen Years after Voices from the Margins*, edited by R. S. Sugarthirajah, 56–68. London: Continuum, 2008.

______. "'No Modern Joshua': Nationalization, Scriptures, and Race." In *Prejudice and Christian Beginnings: Investigating Race, Gender, and Ethnicity in Early Christian Studies*, edited by Laura Nasrallah and Elisabeth Schüssler Fiorenza, 259–78. Minneapolis: Fortress Press, 2009.

______. "Scriptures for Strangers: The Making of an Africanized Bible." In *Postcolonial Interventions: Essays in Honor of R. S. Sugirtharajah*, edited by Tat-siong Benny Liew, 162–77. Sheffield: Sheffield Phoenix, 2009.

______. "We Will Make Our own Future Text: An Alternate Orientation to Interpretation." In *True to Our Native Land: An African American New Testament Commentary*, edited by Blount, 43–53. Minneapolis: Fortress Press, 2007.

______. "The Work We Make Scriptures Do for Us: An Argument for Signifying (on) Scriptures as Intellectual Project." In *Transforming Graduate Biblical Education: Ethos and Discipline*, edited by Elisabeth Schüssler Fiorenza and Kent Harold Richards, 355–66. Atlanta: Society of Biblical Literature, 2010.

Wink, Walter. *The Powers That Be: Theology for a New Millenium*. New York: Doubleday, 1998.

Wolfe, Cary. "Human, All Too Human: 'Animal Studies' and the Humanities." *Publications of the Modern Language Association of America* 124 (2009): 564–75.

Wu, Y. T. "China's Challenges to Christianity." *Chinese Recorder* 65 (1934): 10.

______. "Christianity and China's Reconstruction." *Chinese Recorder* 67 (1936): 212–14

Yanling, Meng. "Women, Faith, Marriage: A Feminist Look at the Challenges for Women." In *Hope Abundant: Third World and Indigenous Women's Theology*, edited by Know Pui-lan, 229–40. Maryknoll: Orbis, 2010.

Yinger, Kent L. *The New Perspective on Paul: An Introduction*. Eugene: Cascade, 2011.

Zetterholm, Magnus. *Approaches to Paul: A Student's Guide to Recent Scholarship*. Minneapolis: Fortress Press, 2009.

Author Index

Biblical and Ancient Texts Index